D0407885

Lesbian and Gay Psychology

PSYCHOLOGICAL PERSPECTIVES ON LESBIAN AND GAY ISSUES

▼ 1. Lesbian and Gay Psychology: Theory, Research, and Clinical Applications

Edited by Beverly Greene and Gregory M. Herek

▼ 2. AIDS and the Lesbian and Gay Community

Edited by Gregory M. Herek and Beverly Greene

▼ 3. Ethnic and Cultural Diversity in the Lesbian and Gay Community

Edited by Beverly Greene and Gregory M. Herek

Lesbian and Gay Psychology

Theory, Research, and Clinical Applications

editors

Beverly Greene
Gregory M. Herek

Psychological Perspectives on Lesbian and Gay Issues

Volume 1

Sponsored by the Society for the Psychological Study of Lesbian and Gay Issues, Division 44 of the American Psychological Association

SAGE Publications
International Educational and Professional Publisher
Thousand Oaks London New Delhi

For information address:

SAGE Publications, Inc.
2455 Teller Road
Thousand Oaks, California 91320

SAGE Publications Ltd.
6 Bonhill Street
London EC2A 4PU
United Kingdom

SAGE Publications India Pvt. Ltd.
M-32 Market
Greater Kailash I
New Delhi 110 048 India

Printed in the United States of America

Library of Congress Cataloging-in-Publication Data

ISBN 0-8039-5311-9 (cloth) ISBN 0-8039-5312-7 (paper)
ISSN 1072-7841

94 95 96 97 10 9 8 7 6 5 4 3 2

Sage Production Editor: Yvonne Könneker

When citing a volume from **Psychological Perspectives on Lesbian and Gay Issues,** please use the following reference style:

Greene, B., & Herek, G. M. (Eds.). (1994). *Psychological perspectives on lesbian and gay issues: Vol. 1. Lesbian and gay psychology: Theory, research, and clinical applications.* Thousand Oaks, CA: Sage.

Contents

Foreword

I am honored to introduce the first annual *Psychological Perspectives on Lesbian and Gay Issues* volume, an idea that I had some role in developing but that was translated into reality by Beverly Greene and Greg Herek. When a number of people in Division 44—the Society for the Psychological Study of Lesbian and Gay Issues—began discussing this idea, the hope was to provide a uniquely psychological voice among affirmative perspectives about lesbian and gay people.

A number of similar publications exist, but none is specifically psychological. Many are multidisciplinary, and those that are mental health oriented are clinically focused and multidisciplinary within mental health. The decision to publish this as an annual reflects a caution both on the part of Division 44 leadership and Sage Publications about the extent of a market for this publication. Those of us involved in the planning had an intuitive sense that a specifically psychological voice was needed, but it was hard to be certain.

In January 1993 I provided court testimony for the coalition of civil rights organizations seeking an injunction to stop Colorado's Amendment 2, which would have prohibited antidiscrimination ordinances for lesbian and gay citizens. That experience convinced me that our intuitions were correct. In the course of preparing and giving testimony about the psychosocial realities lesbian and gay citizens' experience and why this amendment would be destructive, it became apparent to me that psychology—a peculiar and at times uneasy, but ultimately vibrant, hybrid of science and practice—indeed offers contributions that no other discipline duplicates.

Psychology has much to say about current public policy debates on sexual orientation; what it has to say is empirically robust, theoretically rich, diverse in its perspectives, and consistently relevant. As psychologists, we have much to offer.

The current political and public policy debates offer significant challenges to affirmative perspectives in lesbian and gay psychology. The challenges from the Right are obvious. In an environment in which the stakes are very high, we are called on to rethink and hone our arguments carefully, to look honestly at areas in which we do and do not have empirical support for our positions, and to present our opinions—no matter how deeply held—as psychological scientists first and foremost. A silver lining in these ominous challenges from the right wing may exist. We are required to reformulate and clarify our positions in a more intellectually rigorous and precise manner under the harsh scrutiny of public debate and the courts, more so than is likely in the more accepting embrace of our colleagues.

I suggest there is another set of challenges, often overlooked, that is at least as troublesome, perhaps more so. A significant challenge from the "politically correct" left also exists when dogma is substituted for critical thinking. I believe that lesbian and gay affirmative perspectives in psychology are imperiled to the extent they partake of this fad. Now, more than ever, we need diversity of perspectives and ideas (not only of people), and critical thinking.

Lesbian and gay affirmative perspectives in psychology have come of age. We successfully challenged the illness model of homosexuality and defeated it, primarily by critical thinking and arguments based on empirical information, and have developed the beginnings of a rich theoretical structure with which to understand the lives of lesbian women and gay men without recourse to illness mythologies. That this development is currently more theoretical than empirical is as it can only be; but the time has come for us to take our ideas, submit them to empirical validation, and have the flexibility and courage to revise our theories as data demand. Politically correct thought, with its insistence that no other perspectives are viable, offers only a blind alley and myopic vision for lesbian and gay affirmative psychologies.

For some years I have observed the lack of inclusiveness of biological and psychological perspectives in most gay and lesbian studies programs in North America. Literature, history, sociology, and the arts are well represented. Psychology, if it is included at all, is relegated to its least empirical, debiologized forms; biology is virtually banned. Often, such programs seem inward looking and self-absorbed with arcane academic debates and, in the process, increasingly become intellectually rigid and irrelevant both to the lives of gay and lesbian citizens and to honest intellectual inquiry.

I have come to a conclusion that there is not a lot of intellectual meat on academia's politically correct bones. Its intellectual intolerance and smugness contain assumptions that are ultimately corrosive to civil rights and intellectual activity, especially one as demanding as lesbian and gay affirmative psychologies. Thus our task is to repsychologize gay and lesbian affirmative psychologies: to put our theories to empirical test; to engage in theoretical revision as necessary; and most important, to reconnect our theories and data to the main body of psychological theory, research, and practice. If gay and lesbian affirmative perspectives end up being merely interesting anomalies or curiosities of late-20th-century North American psychology, we will have failed. The current politically correct foolishness offers such a fast lane into obscurity and irrelevance.

It is my deep hope that this annual publication provides a vehicle for our uniquely psychological voices to understand and affirm the lives of lesbian and gay individuals and to do so within the highest standards of scholarship and intellectual integrity.

JOHN C. GONSIOREK

Preface

This is the first of a series of planned annual publications sponsored by the Society for the Psychological Study of Lesbian and Gay Issues of the American Psychological Association. Its aim is to provide a forum for the dissemination of contemporary lesbian and gay affirmative perspectives that are distinctively psychological. The hope is that this series will evolve into an official division journal.

Lesbian and gay psychology has matured beyond its role as merely lesbian and gay affirmative. It is not sufficient simply to acknowledge that gay and lesbian sexual orientations are within the realm of psychological normalcy. We are challenged to use the tools of this and other mental health disciplines to explore the many complexities and subtleties of lesbian and gay sexual orientations; the unique developmental tasks and stressors among lesbians and gay men; the special nuances and dynamics of same-gender relationships; and the treatment of lesbian and gay clients from diverse racial, ethnic, and class backgrounds as well as to design programs of research and to include material relevant to these issues in the training of psychologists in the broadest sense.

Contributors to this volume draw from a wide range of experiences in diverse areas of psychology. Contents include innovative empirical studies on the children of lesbians, internalized homophobia, lesbian and gay male development, and aspects of relationship quality in cohabiting couples. Theoretical analyses of the relationship between the feminist political movement and choice in sexual orientation, sexual pride and shame in lesbians, and lesbians and physical appearance are also included. The role of individual differences in reactions to lesbians and gay men and empirical research with the Attitudes Toward Lesbians and Gay Men

(ATLG) Scale are reviewed as well as a discussion of appropriate therapeutic boundaries when lesbian therapists treat clients within the lesbian community. The contents of this volume address a variety of general concerns. Future volumes will be organized around specific themes, including AIDS, ethnic and cultural diversity in the gay and lesbian community, and others.

It is fitting that my coeditor and I acknowledge the contributions of the people who were responsible for taking this series from its early stages as an intriguing idea to practical reality. In August 1988 Charles (Terry) Hendrix, the editor of this series at Sage Publications, suggested that Division 44 might want to consider sponsoring a regular publication. The executive committee of Division 44 directed John Gonsiorek to begin discussions with Sage and to lay the important groundwork for this series. While other commitments precluded John's continued direct involvement with the series, we recognize his efforts as critical to its development and are deeply indebted to him. Of course, Terry, his able assistant Dale Mary Grenfell, and the executive committee of Division 44 have been of invaluable assistance in bringing this project to fruition.

Finally, my coeditor and I dedicate this first volume to our departed friend and colleague Adrienne J. Smith. Adrienne was a member of the first executive committee of Division 44, in 1984, and served as our president in 1989 and 1990. Her public coming out as a lesbian on the David Suskind show in 1973; her early leadership as an open lesbian feminist therapist when it was not popular to be open; her persistent encouragement and mentoring of anyone in her path to take a more active role in the division's work; and her commitment to bring antiracist, multicultural perspectives to this work provided many of the present generation with a powerful professional role model when there were few. In the last of several conversations with Adrienne, and within weeks of her expected death, I had the pleasure of informing her of the decision to dedicate this volume to her in appreciation for her work. She was pleased and excited that there was a desire to recognize tangibly her significant contributions to Division 44 and to lesbian and gay affirmative psychology and political activism. Her infectious spirit and enthusiasm, her openness and personal warmth will be missed but will always be remembered.

BEVERLY GREENE

1

Lesbian and Gay Sexual Orientations

Implications for Clinical Training, Practice, and Research

BEVERLY GREENE

An Overview

A special issue of the *Family Therapy Networker* (1991) posed the following question: "Gays and lesbians are out of the closet . . . are therapists still in the dark?" (Markowitz, 1991, p. 27). In 1975 the American Psychological Association adopted the official policy that homosexuality per se implies no impairment in judgment, stability, reliability, or general social and vocational capabilities and urged all mental health professionals to take the lead in removing the stigma of mental illness that has been long associated with gay and lesbian sexual orientations (Committee on Lesbian & Gay Concerns [CLGC], 1986; Morin & Rothblum, 1991). Before this policy statement, reproductive sexuality was presumed to represent psychological normalcy. Lesbian and gay sexual orientations were presumed to represent the outcome of a disturbance or pathological arrest in development. These long-overdue changes in the diagnostic nomenclature did not develop in a vacuum.

An intense period of political activism and advocacy for gay and lesbian civil rights and the lobbying efforts of gay and lesbian mental health

---

AUTHOR'S NOTE: This chapter is the extended version of the following article: Greene, B. (1993). Human diversity in clinical psychology: Lesbian and gay sexual orientations. *The Clinical Psychologist, 46*(2), 74-82.

professionals led to the removal of homosexuality from the American Psychiatric Association's *Diagnostic and Statistical Manual of Mental Disorders* (*DSM*) in 1973 (Haldeman, 1991). The Association of Gay Psychologists (AGP) was formed in August 1973, the first organized lobbying effort by gay and lesbian psychologists within the American Psychological Association (Giusti & Katz, 1992). It developed, with the support of the Society for the Psychological Study of Social Issues, Psychologists for Social Action, and the Association for Women in Psychology, a set of objectives that was adopted by the APA Board of Social and Ethical Responsibility in Psychology (BSERP) in October 1975.

BSERP recommended the establishment of a task force on the status of lesbian and gay male psychologists within APA of which half of its membership would consist of AGP members. The task force became the first officially sanctioned and funded gay and lesbian group within a major professional organization (Giusti & Katz, 1992).

The task force also recommended that a continuing committee be established within BSERP as an official part of APA governance. The function of this committee would be to continue as an advocacy group for gay and lesbian issues within APA and to continue the work begun by the task force. Approved in 1980, the Committee on Lesbian and Gay Concerns (CLGC) has been instrumental in developing policy statements on gay and lesbian issues for the association and in establishing standards for eliminating heterosexist bias in psychological research and practice with gay and lesbian persons. Since 1990 the committee has functioned under the aegis of the Board for Psychology in the Public Interest. In 1984 the council of representatives voted to approve the establishment of a formal division, Division 44, within APA to be dedicated to the psychological study of lesbian and gay issues, called the Society for the Psychological Study of Lesbian and Gay Issues (SPSLGI).

Now, 19 years after the introduction of APA policy changes regarding gay and lesbian sexual orientations, gay men and lesbians, once an invisible and silent minority, have assumed a higher level of visibility among those who seek professional psychological services. Although major changes have been made in the diagnostic nomenclature in the interest of depathologizing gay and lesbian sexual orientations, clinical practice, research, and training continue to operate out of both negative bias and misinformation about lesbians and gay men, their respective lifestyles and concerns, and their clinical needs (Garnets & Kimmel, 1991; Markowitz, 1991).

In 1986 a task force of the CLGC conducted an investigation of bias in psychotherapy with lesbians and gay men. The task force surveyed 2,544 psychologists, using open-ended questions, in an attempt to discern major themes of both biased and sensitive practice. Survey results suggest that there is a wide range of variance in the degree to which psychologists adhere to unbiased practice standards with lesbian and gay male clients (Garnets, Hancock, Cochran, Goodchilds, & Peplau, 1991). Data from this study suggest that practice does not conform to APA policy standards, leaving much to be done with respect to educating psychologists about sexual orientation (Garnets et al., 1991). With the introduction of this volume, SPSLGI hopes to advance this slow process another step.

Demographics

It is difficult to determine the exact population of gay men and lesbians in the United States. Estimates range from 4% to 17% (Gonsiorek & Weinrich, 1991), depending on the sampling methods and sources used. Unlike racial or ethnic minorities or members of other groups with physical characteristics that identify them, gay men and lesbians are usually identified by self-report. That is, such people are considered gay or lesbian if they define themselves as gay or lesbian. Few objective measures exist to make such determinations reliably (Gonsiorek & Weinrich, 1991). Golden (Chapter 3 in this volume) discussed the problematic aspects of viewing sexual orientation as a discrete and static rather than a continuous and dynamic phenomenon with multiple components.

For the purposes of this discussion, individuals are presumed to be *lesbians* or *gay men* if their primary affectional/erotic attractions are to people of the same gender (Garnets & Kimmel, 1991; Gonsiorek & Weinrich, 1991). *Bisexuals* are defined as people whose affectional/erotic attractions are to both men and women. *Heterosexuals* are those individuals whose affectional/erotic attractions are to members of the other gender. Although distinctions are made between members of these groups for the sake of clarity, human sexuality exists along a continuum in most persons as an interaction of biological, cultural, historical, and psychosocial influences (Garnets & Kimmel, 1991).

Lesbians and gay men are often presumed to be a part of a monolithic community. This obscures the wide range of diversity within a group that cuts across all cultural, racial, economic, social, age, and other lines.

Brown (1989) suggested that there is no unitary lesbian or gay reality, rather there are multiple realities.

Because lesbians and gay men are not readily identifiable on the basis of physical characteristics, they are often presumed to be and treated as if they were heterosexual. Such treatment forces gay men and lesbians to make conscious decisions about whether to reveal their sexual orientation routinely. A corollary of this, however, is that men and women who do not closely adhere to the traditional gender stereotypes of roles, physical appearance, and mannerisms are often presumed to be gay or lesbian when they are not. Hence there is a tendency among many people to presume that conformity with gender role stereotypes is consistent with a heterosexual orientation. Conversely, the failure to conform to such stereotypes is interpreted as evidence of a gay or lesbian sexual orientation. Although many gay men and lesbians do not adhere rigidly to such stereotypes, many do. The same is true for heterosexuals. This presumption may also reflect the disparaging and distorted view of gay men and lesbians as defective, less attractive, and not "real" men or women or as individuals who do not wish to be members of their own gender. Rothblum (Chapter 5 in this volume) reviewed some of the negative appearance stereotypes that many heterosexuals hold of lesbians. Included in these assumptions is the belief that lesbians are unattractive women. Similarly Kite (Chapter 2 in this volume) discussed the perception that adherence to gender role stereotypes is linked to sexual orientation and to perceptions of gay men and lesbians.

The relative invisibility of gay men and lesbians allows them to "pass" as heterosexual. Both passing and "being out" have their own distinct variations of negative and positive consequences. Rothblum discussed the implications of passing for lesbians who require some way of identifying one another. Both passing and being out are accompanied by varying types and degrees of psychological demands and the stress that is a result of those demands. Gay men and lesbians pass when they do not challenge the assumption that they are heterosexual or when they actively conceal their sexual orientation. Concealing a lesbian or gay sexual orientation is referred to as being closeted.

Passing can be an adaptive coping strategy when used strategically. It has been used historically by racial minorities in threatening situations and can be an adaptive survival tool. It was often effective in helping its users avoid or escape imminent harm or to obtain goods, services, or jobs that would be otherwise inaccessible to them because of discrimination

(Greene, 1992). When used as a long-term survival tool, however, it deprives its user of the spontaneity required for authenticity in interpersonal relationships. There is a consistent pressure to conceal parts of one's self and live with the constant dread of being discovered (Greene, 1992). When passing is accompanied by the belief that being gay or lesbian is a sign of inferiority or pathology, it represents an expression of internalized homophobia. Lesbians and gay men who pass, particularly when it is dangerous not to do so, are confronted with stressors that can leave them at risk for negative psychological outcomes.

Not only does legislation leave lesbians and gay men unprotected by laws that prohibit discrimination based on group membership, but some legislation exists that actually requires discrimination against them, for example, military regulations. Bisexual persons are frequently the objects of hostility from gay men, lesbians, and heterosexuals as well. They may be perceived by members of the gay and lesbian community as individuals who are really gay or lesbian but who conceal or deny their true identity to avoid the stigma (Garnets & Kimmel, 1991). Conversely, they may be viewed by heterosexuals as less normal than or inferior to heterosexuals (Garnets & Kimmel, 1991). Golden (Chapter 3 in this volume) analyzed many of the historical tensions within the feminist community regarding sexual orientation and the frequent demand to declare loyalty by choosing one exclusive identification.

Although there is always great interest in the "cause" of gay and lesbian sexual orientations, the origins of any sexual orientation are not well understood. It is likely, however, that there are multiple determinants (Garnets & Kimmel, 1991). Sexual orientation is likely established by adolescence, usually before sexual activity begins, preceded by a subjective awareness of same-gender attraction (Bell, Weinberg, & Hammersmith, 1981; Garnets & Kimmel, 1991; Gonsiorek & Weinrich, 1991). Sexual orientation appears to be a stable characteristic over the life span for some individuals; for others, one orientation may be adopted after lengthy experience with the other as an adult. Money (1988) referred to the latter as sequential bisexuality (Garnets & Kimmel, 1991).

Before changes in the diagnostic nomenclature, most psychotherapy with lesbian and gay clients was directed at changing their sexual orientation with the assumptions that heterosexuality was the psychological norm and that it was more desirable. Even after homosexuality was removed from the *DSM* in 1973, it was replaced with the diagnosis of ego dystonic homosexuality. Homosexuality remains a part of the International Classification of Diseases (ICD) diagnostic classification system. The diagnosis of ego dystonic homosexuality was finally dropped from the *DSM* in 1988 (Haldeman, 1991). Despite these changes, efforts to change the sexual orientation of gay and lesbian clients have persisted and are referred to as conversion therapies (Haldeman, 1991). There is no credible empirical evidence to warrant the assumption that therapies aimed at altering sexual orientation are successful. There are serious questions about whether it is even possible to do so without directly reinforcing and acting out heterosexist bias. Hence there are serious ethical questions about these practices. Studies and reports of such undertakings are often plagued by methodological problems. APA commentary on conversion therapies states, "These findings suggest that efforts to repair homosexuals are nothing more than social prejudice garbed in psychological accoutrements" (Welch quoted in Haldeman, 1991, p. 160).

Treatment Issues

Coming Out as a Developmental Task and Stressor

Coming out has been defined at its simplest as the realization of one's gay or lesbian sexual orientation and the subsequent disclosure of that orientation to others (Dworkin & Gutierrez, 1992; Garnets & Kimmel, 1991). Although this definition describes the salient features of coming out, the phenomenological aspects of this process are complex and incorporate the process by which an individual constructs a sense of self as a gay man or lesbian, across the life span, in a culture that has legitimized—often religiously sanctioned—intense, negative reactions to such persons (Garnets & Kimmel, 1991). This should not suggest that religious scripture clearly denounces gay and lesbian sexual orientations or that the consensus of theological opinions in this matter are uniform. Religious arguments, however, are frequently and selectively used to justify punitive and rejecting behaviors, which are a function of negative social attitudes toward gay men and lesbians. Because coming out is a contextual process, it will be experienced and understood in ways that are consistent with gender differences in socialization, ethnicity, and other aspects of an individual's identity. Golden (Chapter 3 in this volume) and D'Augelli (Chapter 7 in this volume) each discussed the complexity of sexual orientation and its development throughout the life span. Gonsiorek (1988) suggested that this process may be more abrupt for males who come out during the adolescent period than for females and that men tend to act on their sexual feelings at an earlier stage than women. He cited differences in identity development caused by gender socialization differences as one determinant. Women may engage in a broader range of emotional and behavioral interactions with other women without the assumption that they are lesbian. Male counterparts interacting similarly have a greater likelihood of being presumed gay.

There are numerous theories of sequential stages in identity development in gay men and lesbians (Cass, 1984; Coleman, 1981-1982; Weinberg, 1983). A smooth transition through the stages of any model is complicated by the ubiquitous presence of negative cultural attitudes toward gay men and lesbians as well as the presence of pervasive negative stereotypes about them.

Unlike most ethnic minorities, gay men and lesbians learn a range of negative stereotypes and attitudes about gay and lesbian persons, not simply from the dominant culture but also from their own cultures and their families as well (Greene, 1994a). This takes place long before they know that they are gay or lesbian themselves. The subsequent internalization of such attitudes complicates the process of self-acceptance. Such complications occur when an individual harbors beliefs that he or she has learned to accept uncritically or even enthusiastically. Long after such an individual internalizes heterosexist attitudes, those very attitudes may be consciously and unconsciously directed at the recently discovered dimension of his or her self. Shidlo (Chapter 10 in this volume) viewed the elimination of internalized homophobia as an important therapeutic goal and discussed difficulties in conceptualizing and measuring this variable.

Successfully moving through the different stages of any model may take years to accomplish. The precise length of time required, however, will also vary from person to person. There is frequently a delay in time between the discovery of a gay or lesbian sexual orientation and its acceptance as a healthy and acceptable part of one's own identity (Garnets & Kimmel, 1991). D'Augelli (Chapter 7 in this volume) suggested that development in gay men and lesbians should be approached from the perspective of exceptionality, given the superior coping strategies required for them to successfully negotiate developmental tasks in an antagonistic environment. Such an approach, he suggested, will be more likely to yield important information about adaptive and perhaps exceptional coping strategies that might otherwise be obscured.

The process of coming out is further complicated by the frequent absence of routinely available and explicit role models that socially affirm gay and lesbian identities. Media images of lesbians and gay men routinely depict them as reflections of their negative stereotypes or as seriously flawed and tragic characters. Such depictions leave many persons struggling with their newfound identity, reluctant to identify with a group that is perceived to have no redeeming features. As a result, many individuals must develop their own personal framework for identity and for maintaining self-esteem (Garnets & Kimmel, 1991).

Different stages of the coming out process may be extremely anxiety provoking. The discovery or confirmation of a lesbian or gay sexual orientation may be experienced as frightening, ego alien and/or a source of great subjective distress (Gonsiorek, 1982). It may often be the reason for seeking psychological services. As such, it may lead to the expression of behaviors or feelings that resemble symptoms of severe psychopathology. However, the presence of such behavior under these circumstances should not automatically lead to the assumption that an underlying psychiatric disorder is present (Gonsiorek, 1982). For many clients, the clinician is observing the individual's difficult struggle to confront the real nature of his or her sexual orientation, perhaps for the first time. For other clients, however, the intense stress inherent in this process may act as a precipitant for those who do have serious underlying psychiatric disorders. In the latter case, a person with limited psychological resources must manage a realistically stressful life event. Another diagnostic possibility is observed in the client who is consumed with great anxiety or fears of delusional proportions that he or she may be gay or lesbian, despite the absence of any rational foundation for such beliefs. It is important to attend to diagnostic distinctions in these situations. A comprehensive discussion of differential diagnostic factors is beyond the scope of this chapter, but Gonsiorek (1982) has provided a more detailed examination.

Morin (1977) defined heterosexual (also referred to as heterosexist or homophobic) bias as the belief system that values heterosexuality as superior to and/or more natural or normal than gay and lesbian sexual orientations. Heterosexism and its concomitant stigmatizing stereotypes of gay men and lesbians have been so much a part of the definition of psychological normalcy that they predispose practitioners to make a range of erroneous assumptions about gay and lesbian clients that they have not been sensitized to recognize (Glassgold, 1992; Markowitz, 1991).

One example of such an error is the presumption of the heterosexuality of clients until proven otherwise. This can be particularly problematic for individuals who are in the early stages of coming out, who lack a sense of clarity about their sexual orientation, who are uncomfortable with it, or who have internalized the dominant culture's heterosexist bias. The client may not necessarily disclose a gay or lesbian sexual orientation at all, or they may do so at any point in treatment (Garnets & Kimmel, 1991; Markowitz, 1991; Youngstrom, 1991). Like other factors that vary from person to person, it may be centrally or distantly related to the presenting problem. Many individuals, however, may depend on the therapy process and the therapist's acceptance to help them navigate this uncharted and frequently anxiety-ridden course. A former therapy client recounted:

> My experience as a therapy client was valuable; I had the privilege of working with clinicians who I still greatly respect. . . . But not one of them was prepared or brave enough to ask me the one question that might have saved me—and two ex-wives—a lot of pain. . . . Do you think you might be gay? (Woolley, 1991, p. 30)

Errors in treatment can occur at either of two extremes and, of course, at any point along the continuum between those extremes. Broadly, on one end of the spectrum, the therapist may minimize the importance of the client's sexual orientation and the negative impact of heterosexism on the client's life (Garnets et al., 1991; Youngstrom, 1991). At the other end, the therapist may tend to focus on the client's lesbian or gay sexual orientation as pathological and the source of all of the client's problems (Garnets et al., 1991; Markowitz, 1991). Similarly, therapists may focus on the client's sexual orientation in a voyeuristic manner, wishing to hear unnecessary details about the client's sexual relationships, neglecting other areas of inquiry important to the client's treatment (Dworkin & Gutierrez, 1992; Garnets & Kimmel, 1991; Gonsiorek & Weinrich, 1991; Markowitz, 1991).

Many clients report finding that when they themselves raise questions about their sexual orientation in therapy, they are often confronted with the therapist's anxiety about the topic and subsequent avoidance of inquiries into it or the therapist's outright denial that the client could be gay. This may be accompanied by the therapist's actively discouraging the client from having or adopting a gay or lesbian sexual orientation (Garnets et al., 1991; Youngstrom, 1991). On these occasions, many clients simply drop the issue. Others move on to another therapist. Still others leave therapy altogether, the worse for the experience.

Generally, therapists who work with lesbians and gay men must appreciate the individual client's dilemma in the context of real and not fantasied prejudice and discrimination of intense and increasingly violent proportions (Herek & Berrill, 1992). Gay men and lesbians face the routine tasks of assessing realistic dangers associated with divulging the nature of their sexual orientation, the requirement to make decisions about when and where to be closeted, when and where to be out, and to whom. Many endure painful isolation from their families of origin who do not accept their identity as well as the painful process of rejection that often precedes it. They face internalized homophobia in themselves, which can negatively affect their psychological adjustment. Data on bias crimes suggest that 92% of lesbians and gay men report being targets of antigay verbal abuse or threats, and that 24% report physical attacks, of which some result in death (Herek, 1989). Both lesbians and gay men face the realistic potential for physical abuse and violent attack (gay bashing) that can be life-threatening.

Those who are out face the formidable task of negotiating nontraditional relationships and family structures with few models and little support for doing so in a ubiquitously hostile environment. In such a climate, many people who would consider expressions of racism or ethnic bigotry wholly inappropriate are quite comfortable expressing heterosexist bigotry and find support for doing so. These issues are further complicated for gay men and lesbians who are members of ethnic minority or other marginalized groups (Greene, 1990b, 1994b, in press).

Therapists must begin to assess the impact of a legacy of negative stereotypes about gay men and lesbians on their own thinking, and they must do so before a gay or lesbian client ever appears before them. Markowitz (1991) warned that therapists must acknowledge and understand the extent to which they have internalized society's negative depictions of gay men and lesbians. It is not sufficient simply not to believe the stereotypes without an inquiry into their personal effects on deeper levels (Markowitz, 1991).

Unexamined fears in the therapist may be triggered by a client's accusation that the therapist is homophobic or, if the therapist is supportive, that they must be gay or lesbian as well. The therapist may then respond in a defensive manner, needing to confirm or deny the client's assumptions. The therapist may respond to the client's accusation that the therapist is homophobic by failing to set or maintain appropriate limits, as if this disproves the client's assumptions. Such behavior on the therapist's part is not done with the client's interests in mind, rather it is often the therapist's response to his or her own feelings of guilt or unease.

This does not mean that a client's perception of homophobia in the therapist is never accurate. In this example, it is the therapist's responsibility to be familiar with his or her own personal feelings and attitudes toward lesbian and gay persons and the ways they may be manifested in the therapy process. The therapist must then assess the client's complaint in this context while simultaneously exploring the range of conscious and unconscious purposes that may be served by the client's beliefs about the therapist.

The issue of therapist neutrality must be handled with care. Because gay men and lesbians are frequently the objects of intense disapproval, a client may misunderstand the therapist's neutrality as disapproval. The therapist in such encounters must also be careful not to press his or her own agenda, no matter how well intentioned, or to push the client toward acknowledging a gay or lesbian sexual orientation before the client is psychologically prepared to manage it. Rather, the therapist must be affirming and supportive of the client, helping the client see heterosexist bias for what it is and not as the client's flaw or defect (Dahlheimer & Feigal, 1991).

Just as the authentic inclusion of ethnic minorities in a group forces the group to transform itself into a realistic reflection of its members, the visible presence of gay men and lesbians who seek psychological services forces us to rethink our traditional notions about personality development; developmental tasks and stressors; and what kinds of constellations of persons constitute a couple, a marriage, and a family.

Family Issues

Lesbians and gay men need the same strong connections with family members as everyone else. It may be said that strong family ties are even more crucial to lesbians and gay men given the hostility and rejection they face in the outside world. They may not, however, presume the support that heterosexual family members facing a crisis might take for granted. Therapists should be attuned to the possibility that the absence of such support has more negative consequences for gay and lesbian family members than for their heterosexual counterparts.

Many lesbian and gay clients struggle at some point in their lives with crises related to maintaining secrecy about their sexual orientation and the ongoing problems that are a consequence of that decision and to coming out to family members and the consequences of that decision as well. Many clients will express great confusion in making this decision and may even feel guilty about their disclosure if it upsets family members. The therapist in these situations must be careful not to reinforce the client's guilt by discouraging disclosure when it is appropriate or by suggesting that the family's rejection is justified.

Although it may be expected that a family member's disclosure may upset some family members or disrupt family functioning, there is no uniform way in which families respond. Each client's family is different and the range and intensity of the responses will vary from acceptance or perhaps disappointment to outrage and outright rejection. Over time, some families will come to accept the lesbian or gay member's sexual orientation to varying degrees and others will not. Responses of families will be as diverse as the racial, ethnic, and class groups they represent. It may be helpful to remind clients of the sometimes lengthy and difficult process of coming out that they have previously negotiated. This process required that they reevaluate their previously accepted attitudes about gay and lesbian persons and come to accept and embrace their identity. Just as they required time and understanding to do so, as painful or infuriating as the process may be for them personally, their family members will require time as well. Strommen (1989) and Brown (1988) have provided a more detailed discussion of the psychological adjustment of gay and lesbian family members and their relatives.

Gay and Lesbian Couples

Gay men and lesbians form and attempt to sustain relationships in a context in which there is little support for them. Most lesbians and gay men grew up in families in which their parents were heterosexual and in which they had few useful role models for understanding what normal transitions and developmental periods in gay and lesbian relationships would be like (Garnets & Kimmel, 1991). For some couples, there may be a tendency to idealize relationships with members of the same gender. This belief may have some of its origins in the assumptions that their gender similarity makes them the same and that the sameness presumes an ease in relating. Gender similarity does not preclude conflicts and disagreement, and in some cases may even intensify it. Hence, many gay and lesbian couples are alarmed and disappointed when they encounter problems or conflicts within their relationships, even when they are within the normal range of problems between couples. They may harbor the notion that they are the negative exception to their idealized image of lesbian or gay relationships.

One example is the belief among many women that battering could not occur in lesbian relationships because it is inaccurately presumed that women are not physically abusive. Hence, lesbians in battering relationships may be confused and unable to appropriately label such behavior, despite the fact that it is happening to them. Renzetti (1992) documented the problem of partner abuse in lesbian relationships and offered a helpful analysis. Kanuha (1990) provided a discussion of this problem as it occurs in lesbian women of color.

If lesbian and gay couples are out, their relationship may be constantly minimized and challenged. If they are not out, the invisibility of their relationship will become a problem as well. The invisible relationship goes unnoticed. Although this is, in part, the idea, it means that the status accorded the relationship and the special pressures and responsibilities that accompany it remain unacknowledged as well. Family members who perceive a relative to be single or without the responsibility of a family of his or her own may be more demanding of a relative's time or resources. They may fail to understand the responsibility to a partner or relationship that they do not see or one that they choose not to recognize. On this informal level, when the couple has problems or when a relationship is terminated, responses from heterosexual peers and family members may be inconsistent with the realistic magnitude and significance of the loss or with the attentiveness that would be given to a marital partner in a heterosexual relationship. Thus members of couples may not derive appropriate support during critical times from resources commonly available to heterosexual couples. Lack of legal status for gay and lesbian relationships in all but about 20 cities in the United States has direct economic consequences, because they may not accrue the benefits of joint tax returns, insurance coverage, and so on.

Therapists who are unfamiliar with gay and lesbian couples, and some couples themselves, may attempt to impose male-female models on them, as there are no similar models for same-sex couples (Markowitz, 1991). Appropriate models would need to take into account differences between male and female socialization and its effects on relationships in which both persons received the same gender socialization (Markowitz, 1991). Rose (Chapter 4 in this volume) provided an analysis of sexual pride and shame in lesbian relationships from a self-psychology perspective. She raised important questions about the origins of these variables and their respective roles and effects in sexual activity within lesbian couples.

Peplau (1991) discussed a range of commonly believed stereotypes about gay and lesbian couples. Among them are the assumptions that gay men and lesbians do not want and are not capable of enduring relationships, that they grow old unhappy and alone, that their relationships are inferior imitations of heterosexual relationships, and that traditional husband and wife and other traditional gender roles are reversed. Such stereotypes are tenaciously held by many therapists despite the absence of any credible evidence to support them and in the presence of a growing body of social science literature that disputes such contentions. Clunis and Green (1988) provided a detailed review of issues facing lesbian couples that may be particularly helpful to the therapist with no experience or training in this area. Kurdek (Chapter 8 in this volume) discussed the results of his extensive study of cohabiting gay, lesbian, and heterosexual couples.

Gay and Lesbian Parents

It has been traditionally and incorrectly presumed that gay men and lesbians do not wish to have children and that they do not make appropriate parents (Greene, 1990a). Nonetheless, gay men and lesbians become parents in many different ways, as do heterosexual parents; however, they do so amid the pervasive assumption that their sexual orientation makes them inappropriate parenting figures. This assumption is often based on the false belief that they will increase the likelihood that their child will be gay, lesbian, or psychologically defective.

There is a pervasive belief that gay men and lesbians do not make appropriate parents or that they will adversely affect their child's development. To the contrary, Patterson's (Chapter 9 in this volume) exhaustive study provided important data that dispute such contentions. She furnished us with a rare, systematic study of the behavioral adjustment, self-concepts, and sex role identity of children of the lesbian baby boom.

Many gay men and lesbians choose to limit their social world to other gay men and lesbians whenever possible. Those who have children, however, are forced to interact with and negotiate systems (e.g., schools) that they might otherwise avoid. They find themselves presented with the dilemma of how to present their unique family constellation in ways that maintain its integrity, protect its privacy, and are sensitive to the child's needs as well. Those who are involved in shared custody arrangements with a former heterosexual spouse often face the realistic danger of having the courts remove their children from their custody if the true nature of their relationship is exposed. The problem of maintaining secrecy in families in which a gay or lesbian parent is not out is complex. Care must be taken to determine how to create the privacy or secrecy the family needs without leaving children feeling so fearful or burdened that it interferes with their own emotional needs and development.

Disclosure of lesbian or gay sexual orientation to children is an anxiety-laden process for the parent and child. Many of the dynamics discussed in Strommen (1989) and Brown (1988) can be applied to an understanding of problems that may arise in such disclosures to children. Bigner and Bozett (1987), Crawford (1987), Falk (1989), and Green and Bozett (1991) provided detailed reviews of the issues faced by gay and lesbian parents relevant to disclosure, family dynamics, clinical strategies, and pertinent research.

Gay and Lesbian Youth

Gay and lesbian youth force us to take a second look at traditional assumptions about developmental tasks and tensions during the adolescent period. Despite the highly sexualized nature of pop culture in the United States, most adolescents have little accurate information about sexuality, at a time when they may be in greatest need of it. They have even less knowledge about gay and lesbian sexual orientation that is not pejorative.

Gonsiorek (1988), Savin-Williams (1989), and Herdt (1989) described a range of intense social and personal pressures facing gay and lesbian adolescents. All are complicated by the normative rigidity and intolerance of differences adolescents maintain toward themselves and others.

Adolescents who disclose their concerns about their sexual orientation are almost sure to find themselves in the midst of conflict with other family members as well as peers. The negative stereotypes associated with gay and lesbian sexual orientations and the dominant culture's denial of sexuality during this developmental period intensify this conflict. This denial is manifested in a conspicuous absence of institutional support for these youngsters. Coping strategies may include withdrawal from social activities, denial, overcompensation, emotional constriction, and self-destructive behavior (Gonsiorek, 1988; Savin-Williams, 1989).

Most adolescents do not reveal their concerns about their sexual orientation to their families or other people who are close to them out of realistic fears of rejection and punishment (Hersch, 1991). Instead, they often withdraw at a time when they are in critical need of support. The high rate of suicide among adolescents believed to be gay and lesbian underscores the dire implications of this problem and warrants the serious attention of mental health practitioners. Support groups; accessible health and social services; the availability of healthy role models, advocacy, and education; and information about sexually transmitted diseases, particularly AIDS, are suggested as needed services for gay and lesbian adolescents, a vulnerable population (Gonsiorek, 1988; Hersch, 1991).

Summary

Today's practitioners may find themselves confronted by the family in crisis, after an adolescent member has disclosed that they are lesbian or gay, or by the adolescent who is in the throes of deciding whether or not or who to tell. Similarly, they may be consulted by the wife or husband who has chosen or struggles with the decision about whether or not to leave a heterosexual marriage to come out. They may also be consulted by the confused and angry heterosexual spouse.

This may raise the issue of blended families with unfamiliar complications. Aside from issues of custody and marital conflict in parents, it is not uncommon to be asked to treat a child or children, in both the public and private sectors, who must in these arrangements acknowledge this previously feared or unknown aspect of their parent's life in conjunction with the sudden upheaval and breakup of their family unit. As gay men and lesbians actively embrace their lifestyles and choose to form their own families, therapists are frequently consulted to assist them in addressing difficulties in their own relationships as well as making decisions to have children in nontraditional ways. It is incumbent on therapists in these scenarios to be aware of the unwarranted but realistic level of prejudice and discrimination, particularly in custody hearings and court proceedings, against gay and lesbian parents.

Training

Educational institutions are not exempt from the pervasive heterosexist bias in Western culture. In fact, they are often the instruments of communicating this bias and the tools for lending legitimacy to it. Institutions responsible for training psychologists are no exception. Hence, psychologists are not immune to the effects of the pervasive themes of heterosexist bias in the dominant culture. Such bias has often served as an integral part of the underpinnings of theoretical and research paradigms. Hence this bias insidiously pervades research and practice despite the intentions of many well-meaning research scientists and practitioners. For example, psychoanalytic theories evolved out of traditional culturally bound views of gender roles. Its theory of etiology of sexual orientation has its origins in views that privilege reproductive sexuality as the only healthy outcome of psychosexual development. Despite the work of Hooker (1957); Kinsey, Pomeroy, and Martin (1948); Kinsey, Pomeroy, Martin, and Gebhard (1953); and others that established that lesbian and gay sexual orientations were not synonymous with poor psychological adjustment, ignorance and heterosexist bias, which formal training rarely addresses, continue to influence significantly the delivery of psychological services to gay and lesbian clients as well as research in areas relevant to developing a better understanding of this group.

Buhrke's (1989a) findings suggest that students receive little exposure to information relevant to the delivery of services to gay and lesbian clients during the course of their formal training. Youngstrom (1991); Garnets et al. (1991); and Graham, Rawlings, Halpern, and Hermes (1984) recommend that current research and findings on lesbians and gay men be discussed in graduate programs, continuing education, and inservice training as well as in undergraduate courses.

Within the past decade, a significant body of psychological literature has grown that appropriately addresses the aforementioned concerns. It has not, however, found its way into the mainstream of clinical psychology training programs and curriculums. Buhrke (1989b) and King (1988) review a range of resources (see Dworkin & Gutierrez, 1989; Stone, 1991) that may be useful in supplementing traditional graduate and undergraduate psychology courses, rendering them more sensitive and relevant to gay, lesbian, and bisexual persons. Herek (Chapter 11 in this volume) reviewed empirical research with a scale used to assess attitudes toward lesbians and gay men. Gay and lesbian sexual orientations are topics that most persons socialized in the United States have intense feelings about. Hence, it is important that psychologists learn to explore and understand these issues appropriately in both their clients and themselves. Few topics, however, are more scrupulously avoided in the formal training of psychologists. Just as members of ethnic minority groups have been harmed by a legacy of racially stigmatizing psychological folklore, gay and lesbian clients also are harmed by negative heterosexist bias and the misinformation that pervades psychotherapy practice and has similarly pervaded psychological research. Just as ethnic minority clients can be harmed by the unexamined racism in the therapist or inherent in a research design, gay and lesbian clients can be similarly harmed by unexamined heterosexist bias.

As greater numbers of gay and lesbian individuals and families seek counseling and psychotherapy, many therapists find themselves ill-equipped to provide services sensitive to what may be seen as a distinct cultural group. It is important that therapists be aware of the ways in which routine life stressors may be intensified for individuals who are actively discriminated against by the dominant culture and who, unlike members of oppressed ethnic groups, may not find a similar point of identification with family members. Such identification and sense of shared struggle with family members has been an important coping mechanism in the adaptive banding together against the outside oppressor for many members of oppressed racial groups. Although family members of ethnic minority group members often teach their children to actively challenge the dominant culture's views of them, they are more likely to embrace heterosexist attitudes and join in the dominant culture's rejection of gay and lesbian persons.

The ethnic minority gay man or lesbian depends on the protective armoring of their family and ethnic community more than their white counterparts but may find themselves on the outskirts of that protective buffer against racism. In addition to the dominant culture's racism, gay men and lesbians of color face the additional stress of coping with the gay and lesbian community's racism, the dominant culture's heterosexism, and the heterosexist bias of their own ethnic group. This results in a complex interrelationship of loyalties and estrangements (Greene, 1990b, 1994a, 1994b, in press).

Clinicians in these encounters are confronted with the difficult and challenging task of disentangling characterological and personal distress from lifestyle pressures, societal inequities, and their effects on mental health. This cannot be accomplished without a realistic portrayal of the institutional barriers that regularly confront lesbians and gay men. This includes an understanding of the role of heterosexist bias in many psychological treatment and research paradigms. Despite the extreme hostility and discrimination that gay men and lesbians routinely encounter, they are not inevitable psychological cripples. The resilience and unique skills that many out gay men and lesbians develop, despite the hostility and barriers they face, must be more fully explored along with the negative outcomes. D'Augelli (Chapter 7 in this volume) proposed an analysis that does this from an affirmative perspective. Although the realistic need for secrecy and often justifiable suspicion the gay and lesbian community holds for mental health practitioners and research scientists complicate research endeavors, they are not impossible to negotiate.

In the research arena, Garnets et al. (1991) suggested the continued use of survey research as a means of reducing sampling bias found in many studies on lesbians and gay men. Caution must exercised when making generalizations from samples that are nonrepresentative, and replication of results is important (Gonsiorek & Weinrich, 1991).

Although the APA has charged psychologists with the task of challenging heterosexist bias in both research and practice, it has provided little in their formal training to assist them in making the necessary shifts in practice as well as attitude. Just as clients are presumed to be heterosexual, so are psychologists in training. Heterosexist bias in training programs may make it unsafe for lesbian and gay students to divulge their sexual orientation before their formal training is completed. To do so they risk a form of discrimination that may be subtle but nonetheless can adversely affect their training status within their programs. The requirement to manage the heterosexism of faculty members, supervisors, and fellow students can leave gay and lesbian students with an additional burden that is neither appropriate nor shared by their heterosexual counterparts. It also deprives them of the opportunity to explore authentically their own feelings, ideas, and appropriate use of self as a clinical instrument in their work with clients. Hence there is a failure to explore appropriately countertransference problems as well as issues that may arise when the therapist and client are both gay or lesbian. Gartrell (Chapter 6 in this volume) provided us with valuable insights into the dilemma of establishing appropriate therapeutic boundaries when lesbian therapists treat lesbian clients.

Dahlheimer and Feigal (1991) suggest that therapists may use a variety of techniques in conjunction with didactic training to develop greater sensitivities toward gay and lesbian clients. They suggest the use of role-playing and the review of case material for insensitive approaches. I use case material in which supervisees are asked to review data or client histories and determine how they might view the case if the heterosexual client were lesbian or gay and vice versa.

Another suggestion directs therapists as a part of their training to purchase a gay or lesbian magazine (that is clearly labeled as such), to carry it visibly throughout the course of their day, to monitor their feelings about doing so as well as their internal and overt responses to the inquiries and responses of others, and to discuss these experiences in supervision. It is suggested that these exercises be used to develop a subjective sense of the level of self-consciousness, shame, fear, vulnerability, or anger that many of their clients must manage routinely (Dahlheimer & Feigal, 1991). Participation in such exercises does not mean that doing so will give heterosexual therapists a complete understanding of what life is like for their gay or lesbian clients. Rather it is intended to provide therapists with some realistic, albeit minimal, understanding of what their clients experience every day, without the luxury of terminating the exercise when they are uncomfortable or in danger.

Practitioners who lack formal training in or experience working with lesbian and gay clients and their families are advised to use cogroup and cofamily therapist arrangements; others may use peer and/or other forms of supervision with practitioners who have this professional experience and training.

Scasta, editor of the *Journal of Gay and Lesbian Psychotherapy* (Markowitz, 1991), writes that the treatment of gay men and lesbians is a specialized field that requires a heightened level of self-awareness in the clinician and a commitment to being educated about gay and lesbian issues. It is important that all current and prospective therapists examine their conscious and unconscious levels of heterosexist bias to ensure that they do not intrude into their client's therapy.

Consistent with the mandate of the APA, it is essential that the treatment of gay and lesbian clients and research with this special population be given formal and explicit attention in the training of all psychologists. This can assume many different forms, including the incorporation of required course work and clinical supervision. The active recruitment of psychologists with research, supervision, teaching, and other forms of expertise and interest in this area and the inclusion of openly gay or lesbian faculty and staff members in academic and training institutions must also be accomplished to meet the goals of competent practice. APA accreditation teams must be serious in their efforts to hold training institutions accountable for upholding standards consistent with APA policy in this area. The establishment of requirements for demonstrating proficiency, as an integral requirement for licensure and certification, should be undertaken as well by means of examination items on lesbian and gay issues.

Conclusion

Sexual orientation is an important and complex psychological variable. To promote its accurate understanding, reductionistic attempts to explain it must be abandoned. A new line of inquiry must include an acknowledgment, exploration, and understanding of the role of heterosexist bias in psychological practice, research, and development of theoretical paradigms. It must also include assessments of the role of negative attitudes toward lesbian and gay sexual orientations on the development of identities in lesbians, gay men, bisexuals, and heterosexuals. We are challenged with the task of developing broader questions that explore the complex origins and determinants of affectional/erotic attraction as reflections of a healthy range of human diversity.

References

Bell, A. P., Weinberg, M. S., & Hammersmith, S. K. (1981). *Sexual preference: Its development in men and women.* Bloomington: Indiana University Press.

Bigner, J. J., & Bozett, F. W. (1989). Parenting by gay fathers. *Marriage and Family Review, 14,* 155-175.

Brown, L. S. (1988). Lesbians, gay men and their families: Common clinical issues. *Journal of Gay and Lesbian Psychotherapy, 1,* 65-77.

Brown, L. (1989). New voices, new visions: Toward a lesbian and gay paradigm for psychology. *Psychology of Women, 13,* 445-458.

Buhrke, R. A. (1989a). Female student perspectives on training in lesbian and gay issues. *Counseling Psychologist, 17,* 629-636.

Buhrke, R. A. (1989b). Incorporating lesbian and gay issues into counselor training: A resource guide. *Journal of Counseling and Development, 68,* 77-80.

Cass, V. C. (1984). Homosexual identity formation: A theoretical model. *Journal of Sex Research, 20,* 143-167.

Coleman, E. (1981-1982). Developmental stages of the coming out process. *Journal of Homosexuality, 7,* 31-43.

Clunis, D. M., & Green, G. D. (1988). *Lesbian couples.* Seattle: Seal Press.

Committee on Lesbian and Gay Concerns. (1986). *APA policy statement on lesbian and gay issues.* Washington, DC: American Psychological Association.

Crawford, S. (1987). Lesbian families: Psychosocial stress and the family building process. In Boston Lesbian Psychologies Collective (Eds.), *Lesbian psychologies* (pp. 195-214). Chicago: University of Illinois Press.

Dahlheimer, D., & Feigal, J. (1991, January-February). Bridging the gap. *The Family Therapy Networker,* pp. 26-29, 31-35.

Dworkin, S., & Gutierrez, F. (Eds.). (1989). Gay, lesbian and bisexual issues in counseling [Special issue]. *Journal of Counseling and Development, 68,* 6-96.

Dworkin, S., & Gutierrez, F. (1992). Opening the closet door. In S. Dworkin & F. Gutierrez (Eds.), *Counseling gay men and lesbians: Journey to the end of the rainbow* (pp. xvii-xxvii). Alexandria, VA: American Association of Counseling and Development.

Falk, P. J. (1989). Lesbian mothers: Psychosocial assumptions in family law. *American Psychologist, 44,* 941-947.

Garnets, L., Hancock, K. A., Cochran, S. D., Goodchilds, J., & Peplau, L. A. (1991). Issues in psychotherapy with lesbians and gay men: A survey of psychologists. *American Psychologist, 46,* 964-972.

Garnets, L., & Kimmel, D. (1991). Lesbian and gay male dimensions in the psychological study of human diversity. In J. Goodchilds (Ed.), *Psychological perspectives on human diversity in America: Master lectures* (pp. 143-192). Washington, DC: American Psychological Association.

Giusti, I., & Katz, R. (1992). *The history of the organization of gay and lesbian psychology: How it all began.* Unpublished manuscript.

Glassgold, J. (1992). New directions in dynamic theories of lesbianism: From psychoanalysis to social contructionism. In J. Chrisler & D. Howard (Eds.), *New directions in feminist psychology: Practice, theory, and research* (pp. 154-164). New York: Springer.

Gonsiorek, J. (1982). The use of diagnostic concepts in working with gay and lesbian populations. In J. Gonsiorek (Ed.), *Homosexuality and psychotherapy: A practitioner's handbook of affirmative models* (pp. 9-20). Beverly Hills, CA: Sage.

Gonsiorek, J. (1988). Mental health issues of gay and lesbian adolescents. *Journal of Adolescent Health Care, 9,* 114-122.

Gonsiorek, J., & Weinrich, J. (1991). The definition and scope of sexual orientation. In J. Gonsiorek & J. Weinrich (Eds.), *Homosexuality: Research implications for public policy* (pp. 1-12). Newbury Park, CA: Sage.

Graham, D., Rawlings, E. I., Halpern, H. S., & Hermes, J. (1984). Therapists' needs for training in counseling lesbians and gay men. *Professional Psychology, 15,* 482-496.

Green, G. D., & Bozett, F. (1991). Lesbian mothers and gay fathers. In J. Gonsiorek & J. Weinrich (Eds.), *Homosexuality: Research implications for public policy* (pp. 197-214). Newbury Park, CA: Sage.

Greene, B. (1990a). Sturdy bridges: The role of African American mothers in the socialization of African American children. *Women & Therapy, 10,* 205-225.

Greene, B. (1990b, December). African American lesbians. *BG Magazine,* pp. 6, 26.

Greene, B. (1992, May). An African American perspective on racism and antisemitism within feminist organizations. In *Catalogue of the seventh black international cinema—Berlin* (pp. 9-15). Berlin: Fountainhead Tranz Theater.

Greene, B. (1994a, April). Ethnic minority lesbians and gay men: Mental health and treatment issues. *Journal of Consulting and Clinical Psychology.*

Greene, B. (1994b). Lesbian women of color. In L. Comas-Diaz & B. Greene (Eds.), *Women of color.* New York: Guilford.

Greene, B. (in press). African American lesbians: Triple jeopardy. In A. Brown-Collins (Ed.), *The psychology of African American women.* New York: Guilford.

Haldeman, D. (1991). Sexual orientation conversion therapy for gay men and lesbians: A scientific examination. In J. Gonsiorek & J. Weinrich (Eds.), *Homosexuality: Research implications for public policy* (pp. 149-160). Newbury Park, CA: Sage.

Herdt, G. (1989). Gay and lesbian youth. *Journal of Homosexuality, 17,* 1-4.

Herek, G. M. (1989). Hate crimes against lesbians and gay men. *American Psychologist, 44,* 948-955.

Herek, G. M., & Berrill, K. (Eds.). (1992). *Hate crimes: Confronting violence against lesbians and gay men.* Newbury Park, CA: Sage.

Hersch, P. (1991, January-February). Secret lives: Lesbians and gay teens in fear of discovery. *The Family Therapy Networker,* pp. 36-39, 41-43.

Hooker, E. (1957). The adjustment of the male overt homosexual. *Journal of Projective Techniques, 21,* 18-31.

Kanuha, V. (1990) Compounding the triple jeopardy: Battering in lesbian of color relationships. In L. S. Brown & M. P. P. Root (Eds.), *Diversity and complexity in feminist therapy* (pp. 169-184). New York: Haworth.

King, N. (1988). Teaching about lesbians and gays in the psychology curriculum. In P. A. Bronstein & K. Quina (Eds.), *Teaching a psychology of people: Resources for gender and sociocultural awareness* (pp. 168-174). Washington, DC: American Psychological Association.

Kinsey, A., Pomeroy, W. B., & Martin, C. E. (1948). *Sexual behavior in the human male.* Philadelphia: W. B. Saunders.

Kinsey, A., Pomeroy, W. B., Martin, C. E., & Gebhard, P. H. (1953). *Sexual behavior in the human female.* Philadelphia: W. B. Saunders.

Markowitz, L. M. (1991, January-February). Homosexuality: Are we still in the dark? *The Family Therapy Networker,* pp. 26-29, 31-35.

Money, J. (1988). *Gay, straight and in between: The sexology of erotic orientation.* New York: Oxford University Press.

Morin, S. (1977). Heterosexual bias in psychological research on lesbianism and male homosexuality. *American Psychologist, 32,* 629-637.

Morin, S., & Rothblum, E. (1991). Removing the stigma: Fifteen years of progress. *American Psychologist, 46,* 947-949.

Peplau, L. A. (1991). Lesbian and gay relationships. In J. Gonsiorek & J. Weinrich (Eds.), *Homosexuality: Research implications for public policy* (pp. 177-196). Newbury Park, CA: Sage.

Renzetti, C. (1992). *Violent betrayal: Partner abuse in lesbian relationships.* Newbury Park, CA: Sage.

Savin-Williams, R. (1989). Gay and lesbian adolescents. *Marriage and Family Review, 14,* 197-216.

Stone, G. L. (Ed.). (1991). Counseling lesbian women and gay men [Special issue]. *The Counseling Psychologist, 19,* 155-248.

Strommen, E. (1989). Hidden branches and growing pains: Stressful aspects of negotiating their lives. Homosexuality and the family tree. *Marriage and Family Review, 14,* 9-34.

Weinberg, T. S. (1983). *Gay men, gay selves: The social construction of homosexual identities.* New York: Irvington.

Woolley, G. (1991, January-February). Beware the well intentioned therapist. *The Family Therapy Networker,* p. 30.

Youngstrom, N. (1991, July). Lesbians and gay men still find bias in therapy. *APA Monitor,* pp. 24-25.

2

When Perceptions Meet Reality

Individual Differences in Reactions to Lesbians and Gay Men

MARY E. KITE

Stereotypes have captured the interest of social psychologists since journalist Walter Lippmann's (1922) now-classic analysis of this topic. More recent conceptualizations, heavily influenced by Tajfel's (1969) seminal paper, have focused on the cognitive aspects of stereotyping and prejudice (Ashmore & Del Boca, 1981; Fiske & Neuberg, 1990; Hamilton & Trolier, 1986). These works offer explanations for category-based reactions to persons of color, gay persons, and other stereotyped groups. Perhaps more important, they also address how stereotypes influence behavior toward individual members of these groups. Although the present body of knowledge about the content of these stereotypes is considerable and recent work in social cognition has provided insight about stereotypic information processing, little is understood about individual differences in stereotypic beliefs or how these differences lead to differential treatment of members of stereotyped groups.

The paucity of research examining individual differences in stereotyping is somewhat surprising, particularly because classic theorists such

AUTHOR'S NOTE: The author thanks Tina Coleman for her help in preparing this chapter and Michael Stevenson and Bernard Whitley, Jr., for their helpful comments on an earlier version of this manuscript.

as Brigham (1971) noted the importance of the issue. Even more noteworthy is that the attitude and personality literatures contain numerous examples of researchers attempting to predict behavior from an individual's attitudes or traits. This tradition dates back to such well-known work as the LaPiere (1934) study on the discrepancy between reported intention and actual acceptance of a Chinese couple in various hotels and restaurants. In many ways, the focus of these literatures is similar to the question of how individual variation relates to stereotyping and prejudice; indeed, there appears to be a straightforward relationship between stereotypes about and attitudes toward subgroups (e.g., Eagly & Mladinic, 1989).

Although the overall success of these efforts has been questioned (cf. McGuire, 1968; Mischel, 1968; Wicker, 1969), the fervor with which this research continues has not lessened, demonstrating researchers' beliefs that individual differences are key to understanding the complexities of human behavior. More intuitively, it is easy to think of individuals who hold well-delineated stereotypes as well as people who seem unwilling to categorize others. Similarly, some experimental participants readily make inferences about a person based on almost no information, whereas others eschew such a task. Even Lippmann (1922) recognized that although stereotyping appeared to be inevitable and functional there were those "whose consciousness is peopled thickly with persons rather than types, who know us rather than the classification into which we might fit" (p. 88).

The purpose of this chapter is to examine the issue of individual differences in beliefs about and reactions to the specific subgroup of gay persons. The perspective taken here is based on the premise that heterosexuals' affective and behavioral reactions to gay men and lesbians are influenced by a generalized belief system (Deaux & Kite, 1987) that includes, but is not limited to, their beliefs and opinions about gay individuals and their affective reactions to homosexuality. It also is proposed that this belief system is related to heterosexuals' perceptions of and stereotypes about women and men and their ideas about appropriate gender roles.

The discussion begins with a brief comment about terminology, followed by an historical overview of research on stereotyping and prejudice, with a focus on perspectives taken in research on antigay prejudice. Next, specific beliefs about and attitudes toward gay men and lesbians are discussed. Finally, evidence is presented that individual differences influence reactions to gay persons, and factors that might facilitate prediction of these reactions are discussed.

Comments on Terminology

The American Psychological Association's Committee on Lesbian and Gay Concerns (1991) has set forth guidelines for avoiding heterosexual bias in language. Those guidelines recommend that authors use the terms *gay male* and *lesbian* rather than *homosexual.* Such usage is intended to reduce the perpetuation of negative stereotypes associated with the word *homosexual* and to clarify its ambiguous nature, which has been used both to refer to gay men exclusively and to gay men and lesbians collectively. These guidelines are followed whenever possible and, as has been suggested, the term *gay persons* is used when referring to lesbians and gay men as a group. At times, however, strict adherence to these guidelines is problematic because much of the research summarized in this chapter was published before the guidelines were formulated. In some of the studies cited below, for example, the researchers used *homosexual* as a stimulus term; in other cases, nonparallel terms such as *homosexual male* and *lesbian* are employed. In such instances, the original terminology is preserved, because failing to do so might lead to an inaccurate interpretation of those studies. Finally, the parallel terms *homosexual* and *heterosexual* are used occasionally, because doing so better represents the original authors' intent.

In addition, problems with the term *homophobia* are recognized (see Herek, 1986a; Hudson & Ricketts, 1980). Defined as explicit hostility or prejudice toward gay men and lesbians (Herek, 1986b) or as an irrational, persistent fear or dread of homosexuals (MacDonald, 1976), the term appears routinely in both scientific research and the popular press. Extensive discussion of the problems with its usage is beyond the scope of this chapter, but they can be briefly summarized as follows.

First, as Herek (1986a) notes, the term itself is unfortunate. Technically, homophobia means fear of sameness, yet its usage implies a fear of homosexuals. Although negativity toward gay men and lesbians is no doubt based on fear to some extent, the *–phobia* suffix implies a specific kind of fear—one that is irrational and characterized by a desire to remove oneself from the object of the fear. Because some people labeled homophobic not only fail to avoid homosexuals but also seek them out to harass and physically assault them, this term does not accurately represent negativity toward gay persons (cf. Herek, 1986a). In addition, because such fear-based reactions to homosexuals appear to be more common among males than females (Herek, 1986b; Morin & Garfinkle, 1978), the term may be more applicable to heterosexual men than to heterosexual women.

Another problem is that attitudes toward gay men and lesbians are likely to be multifaceted and complex (e.g., Millham, San Miguel, & Kellogg, 1976; Plasek & Allard, 1984; Weinberger & Millham, 1979), and holding negative attitudes toward homosexuality likely serves different functions for different people (Herek, 1986a). Hence fear or aversion may comprise one component of beliefs about homosexuality, but other factors are unquestionably important.

Finally, the specific nature of the term implies that prejudice toward lesbians and gay men differs in form from prejudice toward other groups. Although expression of hostility toward gay persons may be more socially acceptable than similar acts directed at other groups (a point discussed below), it is unlikely that the process by which this stereotyping and prejudice occurs is unique. Indeed, negative attitudes toward homosexuals have been consistently linked to negative attitudes toward women and racial and ethnic minorities (cf. Brigham, 1971; Henley & Pincus, 1978; Kite, 1992b; Kurdek, 1988), suggesting that the mechanisms driving prejudicial reactions are similar across categories and are more likely a function of the perceiver than of the target group.

Several alternative terms have been offered to better reflect the antecedents of prejudicial attitudes toward gay men and lesbians and to sidestep the problems inherent with the term *homophobia.* These include *homonegativism* (Hudson & Ricketts, 1980), *homosexism* (Hansen, 1982), and *heterosexism* (Herek, 1986a). Unfortunately, none has gained widespread acceptance. This chapter considers heterosexuals' attitudes and behaviors toward homosexuals in a more global sense, labeling those with less negative attitudes and beliefs as tolerant or nonprejudiced and those espousing negative attitudes and beliefs as intolerant or prejudiced. Although these terms lack the panache of *homophobia,* they are less ambiguous and allow consideration of reactions to lesbians and gay men as part of a broader framework of stereotyping and prejudice. Using these terms also encourages a shift from the predominant focus on negative attitudes toward homosexuality to a balanced perspective that includes acceptance (cf. Stevenson, 1988).

Historical Perspectives on Stereotyping and Prejudice

A detailed analysis of the theoretical orientations social psychologists have adopted toward stereotyping and prejudice is beyond the scope of this chapter; however, a brief summary is provided. The discussion is derived from the historical perspectives outlined by Ashmore and Del Boca (1976, 1981; see also Ashmore, 1990; Deaux & Kite, in press) and describes three general viewpoints on the study of stereotyping and prejudice: sociocultural, motivational, and cognitive. Although the cognitive perspective now dominates social psychological research on this topic, each point of view offers a slightly different lens though which the issues can be viewed. Peering through these lenses reveals the differing assumptions of each perspective that, in turn, direct attention to slightly different questions, answered through somewhat differing methodologies. As each framework is examined, the discussion focuses specifically on how that perspective addresses prejudice toward gay persons and, more generally, on the role of individual differences in that perspective.

Sociocultural Perspective

The sociocultural perspective assumes that stereotypes are provided by the culture and form patterns that are consistently linked to prejudice across time and region of the country. Two major models underlie this perspective: the structural-functionalist view and the conflict perspective (cf. Ashmore & Del Boca, 1981; Deaux & Kite, in press). The structural-functionalist view asserts that there is societal consensus about the characteristics of groups. This model thus deemphasizes individual differences, assuming instead that most individuals incorporate the culture's stereotype to gain social approval. In contrast, the conflict perspective assumes that society contains groups with different values and interests and that people adopt the viewpoint of their particular subgroup. This implies that individuals can and do differ in their opinions about stereotyped groups. Much of the research with a sociocultural perspective surveys the content of stereotypes (cf. Broverman, Vogel, Broverman, Clarkson, & Rosenkranz, 1972; Katz & Braly, 1933; Williams & Best, 1982, 1990). Recently, however, theoretical work from this perspective has linked stereotypes to the social roles that regulate behavior in adult life. The social role theory (Eagly, 1987; Eagly & Crowley, 1986;

Eagly & Steffan, 1984) holds that stereotypes are derived, at least in part, from observing individuals in their societal roles. Hence stereotypes are linked to the differential roles that groups occupy rather than group membership in and of itself. For example, employed people are regarded as more agentic (e.g., assertive and independent) and less communal (e.g., warm and helpful) than are people in the domestic role, regardless of gender (Eagly & Steffan, 1984) or age (Kite, 1990).

Eagly's perspective provides an interesting explanation for individual differences in perceptions of gay men and lesbians. Consider first that heterosexuals who report that they do not know a gay person are more likely than others to hold negative attitudes toward homosexuality (e.g., Hansen, 1982; Millham et al., 1976; Weis & Dain, 1979). Note next that unlike membership in most other basic categories sexual orientation is not readily discernible and disclosure of this information is typically voluntary. It is unlikely, then, that a gay person would reveal his or her sexual orientation to a highly prejudiced individual (see Garnets & Kimmel, 1991, for a detailed discussion of the conditions under which disclosure is likely). For highly prejudiced heterosexuals, therefore, the mass media may well be the sole provider of observable group stereotypes of lesbians and gay men. Unfortunately, gay persons are rarely portrayed in the electronic media (Gross, 1991; Russo quoted in Herek, 1990) and when they are, the depiction is usually negative or the protagonist is dying. This restricted range of observable behaviors provides intolerant heterosexuals with limited information about gay persons and may well serve to perpetuate their negative attitudes. Conversely, heterosexuals with less prejudicial attitudes are more likely to know a gay man or lesbian personally and, accordingly, have more positive, realistic models on which to base their beliefs. For these individuals, any available negative information is probably integrated into a more balanced perspective on the characteristics and behaviors of gay persons.

Motivational Perspective

According to the motivational perspective, prejudice is motivationally based and serves to strengthen one's personal identity. The benchmark work in this viewpoint is that of Adorno, Frenkel-Brunswik, Levinson, and Sanford (1950) on the authoritarian personality and its relationship to prejudice. Related research on tolerance for ambiguity also takes a motivational perspective (Frenkel-Brunswik, 1949; Larsen, 1984). In each case, there is an attempt to show that certain stable personality dispositions predict a person's willingness to evaluate negatively members of some outgroup. Demonstrations that outgroup derogation is related to an individual's self-esteem or level of depression (e.g., Crocker & Schwartz, 1985; Crocker, Thompson, McGraw, & Ingerman, 1987) also reflect this perspective.

Functional theories of attitudes emphasize motivational factors, stressing that people can hold similar attitudes for very different reasons (Katz, 1960; Smith, Bruner, & White, 1956). For example, two heterosexuals may view gay persons negatively, but the psychological mechanisms underlying their beliefs can be quite dissimilar. In redirecting attention to functional causes, Herek (1986a, 1987) suggested that some heterosexuals' attitudes toward homosexuality are derived from their past interactions with gay persons and are shaped by whether those interactions were rewarding or punishing. Others' attitudes stem from the benefits realized through expressing the attitude, such as affirming one's sense of self and increasing self-esteem. Because negative beliefs about gay persons are widespread and socially sanctioned, lesbians and gay men provide an easy target for those wishing to enhance their self-worth by derogating others. Not surprisingly, then, theorists have offered motivational explanations for prejudicial reactions to gay persons. These include Herek's writings on functional attitude theory discussed above, and the often-tested hypothesis that fear of contact (or homophobia) underlies prejudice toward gay persons (e.g., Gentry, 1987; Hudson & Ricketts, 1980; Leitner & Cado, 1982; MacDonald, 1976). Arguments that certain demographic variables and personality variables are associated with intolerance toward gay persons (see Herek, 1984, for a review) also reflect this viewpoint. Interestingly, although this literature implicitly assumes an individual difference perspective, often the focus is on intolerance, rather than acceptance, of gay persons (cf. Stevenson, 1988). Researchers, for example, describe the personality profile of prejudiced persons (e.g., that intolerant individuals are religious and authoritarian) but seldom explicitly outline characteristics of tolerant individuals (e.g., well-educated and sexually permissive). Perhaps because of this, relatively little attention has been paid to heterosexuals who profess tolerance of homosexuality and to whether these overarching personality differences directly relate to behavior toward gay men and lesbians.

Cognitive Perspective

From a cognitive perspective, stereotypes are useful mechanisms for helping sensory-overloaded people interpret a complex world. From this viewpoint, stereotyping is not considered to be fundamentally different from other cognitive processes. Rather, stereotypes provide a heuristic through which individuals can comprehend all available information at a given point in time. Because all humans have limited capacities for information, stereotypes are not thought to be bad or invalid, rather stereotyping and prejudice are viewed as unfortunate consequences of human information processing. This perspective can be traced to the writings of early theorists, including Lippmann (1922) and Allport (1954). Yet it was not until Tajfel's (1969) landmark paper that it received widespread attention. The subsequent escalation of research with a cognitive perspective has emphasized stereotypic processing, with less interest in the specific content of beliefs (cf. Fiske & Neuberg, 1990; Fiske & Taylor, 1991; Hamilton, 1979). The impact of cognitive theories on the stereotyping literature has been tremendous; even so, the cognitive perspective has not been widely adopted by researchers in the homosexuality literature (for exceptions, see Devine, Monteith, Zuwerink, & Elliot, 1991; Kite & Deaux, 1987; Whitley, 1990).

Categorization mechanisms are seen as essential for efficient information processing and, at first glance, stereotypic processing appears to be inevitable, with little room for individual differences. Indeed, there appears to be considerable agreement about the characteristics associated with stereotyped groups (e.g., Broverman et al., 1972; Devine, 1989; Williams & Best, 1982, 1990). Moreover, this agreement appears to affect stereotypic processing consistently: Reactions to a member of a stereotyped group appear to be stable, automatic, and to some extent, outside of the perceiver's awareness (Devine, 1989; Fiske & Neuberg, 1990). When decisions have little consequence or importance, perceivers readily rely on stereotypic information to form judgments of others (Fiske & Neuberg, 1990). When situations call for more accurate evaluation, however, evidence suggests that individual differences can and do come into play. In such cases, prejudiced and nonprejudiced people employ different strategies to form a detailed impression. These strategies lead nonprejudiced people to temper their stereotypic reactions and to respond to others as individuals rather than merely as members of a minority group (e.g., Devine, 1989; Kite, 1992a; Kite & Deaux, 1986). This less pessimistic approach suggests that heterosexuals' reactions to individual gay men and lesbians should, at least sometimes, be affected by their general attitudes toward homosexuality and, therefore, that prejudiced and nonprejudiced heterosexuals should respond differently to known gay persons.

Before this matter is considered in detail, the research on stereotypes about and reactions to gay men and lesbians is summarized. When reviewing this research, the reader should be aware that participant sexual orientation was assessed in very few of the studies. Therefore, unless otherwise noted, it should be assumed that most participants were heterosexual but that the samples likely included some gay male, lesbian, and bisexual persons. It can be further assumed that members of the latter groups usually responded positively to gay persons (and thus were categorized as nonprejudiced). Accordingly, the results, if affected, would likely have been more negative and more stereotypical if all of the participants had been heterosexual. Although the decision to include heterosexuals and homosexuals in a particular study depends, in part, on the issues addressed, researchers should attend more carefully to the impact of this decision on subsequent interpretations of their results. If the implied question is heterosexuals' attitudes toward or reactions to gay persons, selecting only those who report exclusive heterosexuality might be desirable (Herek, Kimmel, Amaro, & Melton, 1991).

Content of the Gay Male and Lesbian Stereotype

Early research on beliefs about homosexuals focused primarily on the deviance of homosexuality, with *sexually abnormal, perverted, mentally ill,* and *maladjusted* as the traits most commonly attributed to homosexuals (Simmons, 1965). More recent work suggests that little has changed; heterosexuals readily endorse statements such as "Homosexuality is a mental illness" (Kite & Deaux, 1986; Leitner & Cado, 1982; Steffensmeier & Steffensmeier, 1974). In addition, undergraduates view male homosexuals and, to a lesser extent, lesbians as significantly different from "normal healthy adults" (Page & Yee, 1985).

It also is clear that beliefs about gay men and lesbians are linked to general beliefs about women and men in important ways. When describing male and female homosexuals, undergraduates overwhelmingly rely on gender-linked attributes (e.g., Kite & Deaux, 1987), and both these open-ended descriptions and their ratings on a gender stereotype measure reflect an implicit belief in inversion theory (i.e., that homosexuals possess cross-sex characteristics). In one U.S. national survey, nearly 70% of the respondents reported that male homosexuals acted like women (Levitt & Klassen, 1974). Similarly, a study of stereotypic beliefs held by a sample of Scottish citizens found that lesbians were seen to resemble more closely the average man on a standard set of traits, whereas homosexual men were thought to be more similar to the average woman (Taylor, 1983). There is evidence that these inferences work in the other direction as well and that information about specific characteristics can lead to inferences about sexual orientation. Women described as masculine are perceived as more likely to be homosexual than are women described as feminine (Storms, Stiver, Lambers, & Hill, 1981), and role or trait information that is gender inconsistent (e.g., feminine traits ascribed to a man) leads to a sharp increase in the estimated probability of that person being homosexual (Deaux & Lewis, 1984).

Such stereotypic beliefs about appropriate gender roles are clearly linked to antigay prejudice; heterosexuals who endorse traditional sex roles are typically negative toward homosexuality (e.g., McDonald, Huggins, Young, & Swanson, 1973; Newman, 1989; Whitley, 1987). Moreover, gay men and lesbians are disliked, at least in part, because of their perceived sex role deviance (Laner & Laner, 1979, 1980), particularly by those who hold traditional sex role attitudes (Krulewitz & Nash, 1980). In addition, when sharing information in a getting-acquainted interaction, intolerant men describe themselves as lower in femininity and higher in agency (e.g., assertive, independent) than do tolerant men (Kite, 1992a; Kite & Deaux, 1986), a pattern that emerges regardless of the other person's sexual orientation. That these effects hold even when controlling for pretest ratings obtained in a noninteractive situation suggests that intolerant men want to make certain that others know they are not sex role deviant.

Taken together, such findings support the hypothesis that beliefs about gay persons are part of a larger, more generalized gender belief system (see Herek, 1986b, for a discussion of how these factors affect heterosexual masculinity). Yet the structure of this belief system is poorly understood, and perhaps as a consequence, researchers in this area often fail to make clear distinctions between gender-linked beliefs and beliefs related to homosexuality per se. Measures of attitudes toward homosexuality, for example, often include items such as "Homosexual males tend to be very effeminate" (e.g., Kite & Deaux, 1986; Leitner & Cado, 1982; Steffensmeier & Steffensmeier, 1974), and one extant measure is a composite of attitudes toward women's roles and attitudes toward homosexuality (e.g., Dew, 1985). That the blurring of the lines between gender and sexual orientation may be justifiable still makes it difficult to evaluate how these factors interrelate and to determine how this generalized belief system affects prejudicial reactions to lesbians and gay men. Accordingly, this area is one that deserves future attention. The discussion now turns to the specific ways in which antigay prejudice emerges.

Summary of Past Research on Attitudes Toward Homosexuals

The literature on attitudes toward homosexuality is extensive, yet relatively little attention has been paid to behavioral reactions to known gay persons. The available findings outline a general pattern wherein gay men and lesbians are consistently treated differently, and typically more harshly, than their heterosexual counterparts. Research participants speak more rapidly to a believed gay male or lesbian (Cuenot & Fugita, 1982), label gay men as less masculine and less preferred as fellow participants in future experiments (Karr, 1978), are likely to decline when given the opportunity to meet a lesbian or gay man (Kite, 1992a), and are unlikely to help a person wearing a progay T-shirt (Gray, Russell, & Blockley, 1991). Laboratory studies show that in interactions with a supposed gay person participants like homosexuals less than heterosexuals (e.g., Gross, Green, Storck, & Vanyur, 1980; Gurwitz & Marcus, 1978; Krulewitz & Nash, 1980) and remember less about them (Kite & Deaux, 1986). Moreover, introductory psychology students believe that both gay male and lesbian couples are less satisfied and less in love than are heterosexual couples (Testa, Kinder, & Ironson, 1987). Finally, homosexuals who have contracted the human immunodeficiency virus (HIV) from an uncontrollable source are evaluated more harshly than are infected heterosexuals (Anderson, 1992; Kite, Whitley, Simon, & Michael, 1991), and undergraduates report less willingness to interact with a homosexual person with AIDS (PWA) than a heterosexual PWA (Fish & Rye, 1991; Stevenson, 1991).

These findings are based largely on college students' reactions to gay persons and hence results may not generalize to heterosexuals' interactions with an individual gay person in a real-world setting, an issue that is returned to later in this chapter. Nonetheless, the pattern of results is consistent with the public's generally negative view of gay men and lesbians. A recent Gallup poll indicated that 53% of Americans believe that the homosexual lifestyle is unacceptable (Turque, 1992). Further evidence that this negativity is widespread comes from considering the number of lesbians and gay men who are the victims of antigay violence. In a review of 23 surveys conducted with convenience samples of lesbians and gay men, Berrill (1992) found that the median proportion of respondents who had been physically assaulted was 17%. A median of 44% had been threatened with violence and 80% had been verbally harassed. Moreover, there is arguably more open hostility toward gay men and lesbians than toward any other stereotyped group, and the U.S. public's equating of gay men and AIDS may have intensified this negativity (cf. Herek & Glunt, 1988). This again raises the issue of whether prejudice toward homosexuals is distinct from bias toward other underrepresented groups.

Certainly, whites' prejudice against people of color and men's prejudice against women are now often indirect, and people appear to be less willing to publicly express racist and sexist attitudes than before (e.g., Dovidio & Gaertner, 1986; Sigall & Page, 1971; Virginia Slims, 1990). Consequently, researchers now examine more subtle forms of whites' prejudice toward blacks, labeled modern racism (Gaertner & Dovidio, 1986; McConahay, 1986), or men's attitudes toward women, labeled the "chilly climate" (e.g., Sandler & Hall, 1986; Spertus, 1991). In contrast, concern for social desirability is rarely evident in expressed attitudes toward homosexuals (Kite, 1992b; Kite, Whitley, & Michael, 1992). Rather, highly prejudiced heterosexuals feel global discomfort but not compunction for perceived discrepancies between how they believe they should and would behave toward homosexuals (Devine et al., 1991). These findings are not surprising given the continued refusal on the part of Congress to include sexual orientation in the antidiscrimination legislation of the Civil Rights Act (see Sullivan, 1984, for a bibliography), the Supreme Court's decision to uphold Georgia's sodomy law (*Bowers v. Hardwick*, 1986), and the recent passage of an amendment to the Colorado state constitution that bars local governments from prohibiting discrimination on the basis of sexual orientation (Zeman, Meyer, & Keene-

Osborn, 1992). These events, along with the debate over whether allowing gay persons to serve in the armed forces threatens morale and unit cohesion (Herek, 1993), send the message that gay men and lesbians are second-class citizens and that prejudice against them is acceptable. On the other hand, a similar antigay amendment failed to pass in Oregon in 1992, and the Colorado amendment, which passed by a small majority, may well be ruled unconstitutional; at this writing (summer 1993), a national boycott of Colorado tourism is in place (Zeman et al., 1992). That many heterosexuals openly oppose discrimination against gay persons again raises the issue of individual differences in attitudes toward homosexuality and their moderating role in reactions to lesbians and gay men.

Research on Individual Differences in Attitudes Toward Homosexuality

Perhaps because the attitudes-toward-homosexuality literature has emphasized prejudice rather than tolerance (cf. Stevenson, 1988), evidence that individual differences moderate the research findings described above is sparse. The discussion focuses now on those studies that provide support for an individual difference perspective. This is followed by a discussion of the author's work in this area (Kite, 1992a; Kite & Deaux, 1986), and data from a new study are presented. Overall, the data support the assertion that general attitudes toward homosexuality moderate negative reactions to specific gay persons and that delineating the impact of this variable is essential to understanding antigay prejudice.

Judgments of Physical Appearance

Dew (1985) investigated whether attitudes toward homosexuality moderate the tendency to infer that physically unattractive women are lesbian. In her study, male and female introductory psychology students viewed 22 photographs of different women. For each photograph, participants evaluated the accuracy of a series of 11 statements (e.g., "This woman has a pretty face."). Of particular interest was the tendency to endorse the statement "This woman is gay." Once the initial ratings were completed, participants learned that half of the women photographed were homosexual; they then chose which women they believed were lesbians. Finally, respondents completed a 15-item scale assessing opinions of homosexuality, civil rights, and the women's rights movement.

Results showed that women who were seen as homosexual also were seen as less extroverted and generally less attractive. Moreover, when asked to choose which photographs were homosexual, men consistently chose the unattractive models. For women, however, this tendency was moderated by attitudes toward homosexuality and women's rights (assessed by a composite index of those variables). Those with more negative attitudes were likely to believe the unattractive women were lesbian, whereas those with more accepting attitudes did not consistently do so.

Discrepancies Between Actual and "Ought" Responses

Devine, Monteith, Zuwerink, and Elliot (1991) and Monteith, Devine, and Zuwerink (1993) explored the relationship between level of prejudice and discrepancies between how heterosexual college students believed they should and would respond in contact situations with homosexual men. In one study (Devine et al., 1991), high-, moderate-, and low-prejudice respondents, selected on the basis of pretest scores on the Heterosexual Attitudes Toward Homosexuals Scale (HATH) (Larsen, Reed, & Hoffman, 1980), read four scenarios that described interactions with a homosexual target (e.g., having a gay person sit next to you on the bus). They then indicated how, based on their own personal standards, they should respond and how they actually would respond in those situations. Finally, participants reported their affective reactions to discrepancies between their should and would responses. Results showed that at all levels of prejudice discrepancies emerged between how heterosexuals believed they should behave and how they actually would behave. However, feelings about these discrepancies differed. Low-prejudice students reacted with global discomfort, guilt, and self-criticism, whereas high-prejudice students reacted only with global discomfort.

Employing a similar procedure, Monteith et al. (1993) replicated and extended this work, adding thought scenarios (e.g., thinking an effeminate man must be gay) and behavior scenarios (e.g., leaving a restaurant after learning the waiter was gay) to the feeling scenarios used in the earlier work. As before, for low-prejudice respondents, discrepancies between should and would behavior resulted in guilt and self-criticism. For high-prejudice respondents, these discrepancies instead produced feelings of anger and disgust for others. Results also indicated that low-prejudice students used internal standards to respond to the scenarios, whereas high-prejudice students responded in the way they believed significant others would expect them to respond.

Liking for and Affective Reactions to Gay Persons

The discussion now turns to studies by Kite and Deaux (1986) and Kite (1992a) and a new study, all of which examine individual differences in reactions to a gay male, lesbian, or person of unknown sexual orientation. In all studies, the target either was or was not identified as gay; however, the experiments differ somewhat in their focus. Kite and Deaux (1986) examined men's reactions to another male with whom they did or did not expect to interact. Kite (1992a) examined men's reactions to a gay male or lesbian. The new study examined women's reactions to those targets. In no case did participants indicate their own sexual orientation; hence it can be assumed that the sample was predominantly heterosexual but also included some gay men, lesbians, and bisexuals.

Introductory psychology students were selected on the basis of pretest scores on the Homosexuality Attitude Scale (HAS) (Kite & Deaux, 1986). Respondents in the upper third (intolerants) and lower third (tolerants) of the distribution were contacted by phone and asked to participate, but they were not informed of the connection between the experiment and the pretest until they were debriefed.

All studies employed the "imagined stranger paradigm." In this approach, two participants complete the experiment at the same time but do not see or meet one another. Both are placed in adjoining cubicles and both learn that the other person is their experimental partner. This procedure is advantageous because participants can hear the experimenters enter and leave the cubicles, and thus the presence of the other person is obvious. This cover story is quite effective; available data showed that only 2.5% of the participants questioned the existence of a partner.

Participants were told that the experiment was designed to determine how differing amounts of information affect first impressions. They also were informed that during the early part of the experiment they would exchange information with their partner via the experimenter. Respondents then received a handwritten self-description, allegedly written by their partner. This self-description included statements about the partner's background, classes, and personal interests. In addition, a random half of the participants learned that their partner was gay, information presumably volunteered in response to one of the suggested topics for self-description. The remaining participants received no information about their partner's sexual orientation. A manipulation check indicated that people either assumed that the alleged partner was heterosexual or they made no judgment about sexual orientation. Ratings were collected on a variety of dependent measures that varied by experiment. The measures assessing affective reactions to the alleged partner are described here.

Liking

In all three studies, liking was measured by a 20-item questionnaire assessing overall evaluation of the partner (e.g., intelligence and dependability) and desire to interact with the partner. This measure is highly reliable (Cronbach's $\alpha > .90$); hence analyses were based on the respondents' mean score on these items. Only the data from the female participants are depicted in Table 2.1. However, the pattern of results is strikingly similar across the three studies. Intolerant participants disliked their partner—including the partner with unknown sexual orientation—more than did tolerant participants, a pattern consistent with earlier findings that intolerant individuals are generally prejudiced against others (cf. Henley & Pincus, 1978; Kurdek, 1988). In addition, intolerant individuals particularly disliked known gay men and lesbians, whereas tolerant individuals liked their partner regardless of sexual orientation. It is also noteworthy that neither the men's nor the women's liking was affected by target sex (e.g., whether the alleged partner was male or female), a point that will be returned to later.

Affective Reactions to Partner

Positive and negative affective reactions to the partner were assessed by Kite (1992a) and in the new data reported here. The measure employed was adapted from Abelson, Kinder, Peters, and Fiske (1982). On this instrument, participants responded to the query "Could your partner ever make you feel . . ." by rating 22 adjectives (e.g., afraid, happy,

Table 2.1 Female Respondents' Liking by Tolerance Level and Target Sexual Orientation

	Tolerance Level		
Target Sexual Orientation	*Intolerant*	*Tolerant*	*Totals*
Homosexual	4.34 (31)	5.35 (31)	4.85 (62)
Unknown	5.20 (31)	5.23 (32)	5.22 (63)
Totals	4.77 (62)	5.29 (63)	

NOTE: Higher numbers indicate greater liking. Numbers in parentheses indicate n per cell. Analyses of variance revealed significant main effects for tolerance level, $F(1, 117) = 32.22$ ($p < .0001$), and sexual orientation, $F(1, 117) = 15.92$ ($p < .0001$). The Tolerance Level × Sexual Orientation interaction was also significant, $F(1, 117) = 28.27$ ($p < .0001$).

Table 2.2 Female Respondents' Positive Affect by Tolerance Level and Target Sexual Orientation

	Tolerance Level		
Target Sexual Orientation	*Intolerant*	*Tolerant*	*Totals*
Homosexual	3.55 (31)	4.73 (31)	4.14 (62)
Unknown	4.96 (31)	4.80 (32)	94.92 (63)
Totals	4.25 (62)	4.81 (63)	

NOTE: Higher numbers indicate greater positive affect. Numbers in parentheses indicate n per cell. Analyses of variance revealed significant main effects for tolerance level, $F(1, 117) = 11.83$ ($p < .001$), and for sexual orientation, $F(1, 117) = 24.09$ ($p < .0001$). The Tolerance Level × Sexual Orientation interaction was also significant, $F(1, 117) = 14.69$ ($p < .0001$).

and disgusted). The measure contains two independent, reliable factors (Cronbach's $\alpha > .88$), hence mean scores reflecting both positive and negative affect were analyzed. The means for the male respondents are available elsewhere (Kite, 1992a), but the pattern of results for the positive affect measure was similar to those for female respondents depicted in Table 2.2. In those data, intolerant women reported less positive affect (e.g., were less happy and less excited) when they believed their partner was homosexual than when sexual orientation was unknown, whereas tolerant women's positive affect did not differ by perceived sexual orientation of their partner.

Results of the negative affect measure showed that intolerant women also responded more negatively (e.g., were disgusted and tense) when the partner was known to be homosexual (mean = 4.30) than when the person did not state sexual orientation (mean = 3.19). Tolerant women's negative affect did not differ by sexual orientation (mean = 2.88 for homosexual, mean = 2.82 for unknown sexual orientation). Conversely, both tolerant and intolerant men (see Kite, 1992a) reported more negative affect for a homosexual than for a person of unknown sexual orientation.

Sex-of-Target Effects

As noted earlier, in those experiments in which sex of target was varied, this variable did not significantly affect liking. On the negative affect measure, however, target sex did have an impact. For male participants (Kite, 1992a), negative affect was most pronounced for gay male targets (compared with lesbians), regardless of the participant's attitudes toward homosexuality. For the female participants (Table 2.3), these effects were reversed: Negative affect was most pronounced for lesbian targets. Finally, although only marginally significant, a similar pattern emerged for the female respondents on the positive affect measure. Positive affect ratings were lowest for lesbians and highest for women of unknown sexual orientation, with positive affect ratings for gay men and men of unknown sexual orientation falling in between.

These findings raise the issue of whether the sexes differ in their attitudes toward and reactions to gay males and lesbians. The bulk of the evidence shows that heterosexual men hold more negative attitudes toward homosexuality than do heterosexual women (cf. Kite, 1984) and that men's attitudes are particularly negative when the target is a gay male rather than a lesbian (e.g., Gentry, 1987; Herek, 1988; Kite, 1984; Whitley, 1988). Less clear is whether heterosexual women's attitudes differ by sex of target. Some research shows that women sometimes evaluate gay males and lesbians similarly (Herek, 1988; Kite, 1984), whereas other data (including that described above) show that women rate lesbians more negatively than they do gay men (Gentry, 1987; Whitley, 1988). These effects may well depend on the type of measure employed. In the study reported here, for example, results showed no sex-of-target effects on the liking measure, yet both women and men reported more negative emotions such as fear and disgust in reaction to a gay person of the same sex.

More detailed evaluation of and explanations for sex differences in attitudes and behavior toward gay persons are available elsewhere (e.g., Herek, 1986b; Morin & Garfinkle, 1978; Whitley, 1988). Briefly, however, it should be noted that evaluating these findings is difficult because of

Table 2.3 Female Respondents' Negative Affect by Target Sex and Target Sexual Orientation

Target Sexual Orientation	*Target Sex*		
	Male	*Female*	*Totals*
Homosexual	3.30 (32)	3.91 (30)	3.59 (62)
Unknown	3.13 (31)	2.88 (32)	3.00 (63)
Totals	3.21 (63)	3.38 (62)	

NOTE: Higher numbers indicate higher negative affect. Numbers in parentheses indicate *n* per cell. The main effect for sexual orientation was significant, $F(1, 117) = 10.81$ ($p < .001$), as was the Sexual Orientation × Target Sex interaction, $F(1, 117) = 6.19$ ($p < .05$). The main effect for target sex was not significant ($F < 1$).

the relative inattention paid to lesbian targets in this literature (for exceptions, see Dew, 1985; Herek, 1988; Newman, 1989; Whitley, 1988), the general lack of theory-based research on this topic (but see Herek, 1987; Whitley, 1990), the tendency to rely on self-reported attitude rather than behavior, and the failure to link this issue with sex differences in other areas of psychology. The last limitation is particularly problematic because, as is often the case, the obtained sex differences have been small in magnitude and affected by other factors such as sample size, year of publication, and sex of author (cf. Kite, 1984). Thus many questions remain, and although the overall pattern is currently more fuzzy than clear, future research will no doubt resolve some of these issues. The discussion turns to other variables that may moderate reactions to gay persons and may also override sex differences in those reactions.

Predicting Prejudicial Behavior

Ultimately, the goal of understanding attitudes toward gay persons (or any stereotyped group) is to predict prejudicial behavior toward members of that group. The difficulties of finding relationships between attitudes and behavior are well-known (see Wicker's [1969] classic treatise on the attitude-behavior relationship and Mischel's [1968] writings on trait-behavior consistency) and much has been written on ways to improve the attitude-behavior link. Perhaps most prominent has been the work of Fishbein and Ajzen (1974) and Ajzen and Fishbein (1977, 1980), who proposed that attitudes can indeed predict behavior but that this connection is not as easily explicated as previous researchers have supposed.

Fishbein and Ajzen (1984) and Ajzen (1982) pointed to psychometric considerations that should maximize behavior prediction. They argued that researchers should pay more attention to the accurate measurement of behavior and should be less willing to accept almost any measure as a valid assessor of the behavioral domain in question. In the area of heterosexuals' reactions to homosexuality, empirical research certainly has focused more on accurately measuring attitudes (e.g., Herek, 1988; Kite & Deaux, 1986; Millham et al., 1976) than on behavioral indices. To remedy this problem, Fishbein and Ajzen (1974) and Ajzen (1982) proposed that behaviors toward an object should reflect general behavioral tendencies in the same way that global attitude measures assess general attitudes. Hence general measures of attitudes toward homosexuality are more likely to relate to general patterns of behavior toward gay males and lesbians than to any specific action toward a given person. Multiple-act criteria can be developed to assess this general tendency by examining a variety of behaviors in a variety of contexts across a series of occasions to determine the overall pattern of this relationship (see Epstein, 1980, 1983, for discussion of the similar principle of aggregation).

These measurement issues have clear implications for increasing the ability to predict prejudiced behavior. Other theorists and researchers, however, have proposed that these largely psychometric issues cannot totally account for attitude-behavior inconsistency (cf. Mischel & Peake, 1982; Wicklund, 1982). As Allport (1935) noted, any given behavior is likely to be affected by more than one attitude, and prediction of which attitude will influence how an individual will respond is very difficult. Although the domain of variables that might moderate the attitude-behavior relationship seems endless (cf. Wicker, 1969), contextual factors certainly play an important role. In the next section, their potential impact is briefly considered.

Situational Factors

Social psychologists have paid surprisingly little attention to contextual variables and, in particular, their utility in increasing behavioral prediction (but see Deaux & Major, 1987; Eagly, 1987). Yet context most certainly influences behavior and, in many situations, carries more weight than individual attitudes or traits (see Mischel, 1977; Monson,

Hesley, & Chernick, 1982). Specifically, when situations are highly constrained there is little latitude for individual differences compared with situations without clear norms in which individual responses are more free to vary (e.g., Abelson, 1982).

Abelson's (1982) ideas are derived from script theory, which hypothesizes that everyday knowledge is organized around hundreds of stereotyped situations involving routine activities. A script, then, refers to the memory structure a person has for encoding his or her general knowledge of certain routine situations and activities (Abelson, 1976, 1981; Schank & Abelson, 1977). Most script research has examined rules for mundane activities such as going to a restaurant or visiting a dentist, but scripts may have an impact on the attitude-behavior relationship as well. Inasmuch as behavioral expectations have been clearly learned and a situation is well structured, people can be expected to do little thinking about their personal beliefs and attitudes, falling instead into the less taxing mode of responding with well-learned action rules. The idea here is that the actor will adopt the strategy that involves the least effort and best fits the script for that situation. Alternatively, in individuated situations in which attention is self-focused, people are likely to consider their attitudes and beliefs and are likely to behave in accordance with those ideals (see also Wicklund, 1982).

The implications of this perspective for the antigay prejudice literature are obvious. Much of this research involves the highly scripted situation of being an undergraduate participant in a psychology experiment—a role that may have little to do with an individual's actual beliefs and behaviors. It is, of course, well known that participants often respond to demand characteristics (cf. Aronson, Ellsworth, Carlsmith, & Gonzales, 1990) and to experimenter expectancies (Rosenthal, 1966, 1969). It is also well known that laboratory studies can bear little relation to real-world interactions (Aronson & Carlsmith, 1968). Any of these factors can result in such strong alternative scripts that attitudes and beliefs never become relevant to the individual at all (see Eagly, 1987, for a review of how experimental factors may influence outcomes of a variety of gender-related research studies).

Contextual factors are seldom addressed in the homosexuality attitude literature, yet careful consideration of their impact would advance understanding in this area. If research participants believe, for example, that negative attitudes toward gay persons are the norm, they may well respond more negatively than they would in a real-world situation. Similarly, heterosexuals may readily report negative attitudes toward a lesbian or a gay man on a paper-and-pencil measure but may be reluctant to display prejudiced behavior in direct interaction. The importance of contextual factors is illustrated by considering the impact of merely expecting to meet another person on behavior; this expectation typically increases liking for the other person (e.g., Berscheid, Boyd, & Darley, 1968; Layton & Insko, 1974). However, when the target is a gay male, men rate him less favorably when anticipating interaction (Gurwitz & Marcus, 1978). Paradoxically, this latter pattern may hold only for tolerant men; intolerant men actually like a male partner better when they expect interaction, regardless of his sexual orientation (Kite & Deaux, 1986). Although the reasons for these varied effects are not clear, the pattern of results illustrates how different experimental situations and their interaction with other variables can produce very different results.

Somewhat surprisingly, research further suggests that both tolerant and intolerant people are usually willing to meet a gay person; only 26.2% declined to do so in Kite's (1992a) study. Although this is significantly more than the 8.3% who declined to meet a person of unknown sexual orientation (Kite, 1992a), the numbers suggest that people do not always want to avoid interaction with gay persons, and in fact, they may seek out the opportunity to do so. Even so, prejudiced and nonprejudiced people may bring different expectations and goals to an interaction. Accordingly, members of these groups may well behave differently during an actual interaction. Unfortunately, it is in such interactions that research is sorely lacking, leaving open the question of how the laboratory research described earlier applies to everyday life. Overall, the impact of either anticipated or actual interaction on reactions to gay persons is poorly understood and both topics deserve further attention.

Contextual issues no doubt also influence the effectiveness of other manipulations and the care with which participants respond to the task at hand. For example, impressions formed on the fly are more stereotypic than those more carefully constructed (e.g., Devine, 1989; Fiske & Neuberg, 1990), suggesting that the paper-and-pencil measures often employed in this literature may overestimate heterosexuals' negative affect toward gay persons. Context may also account for the inconsistent findings about heterosexuals' reactions to same- or other-sex gay persons. As noted above, sometimes gender issues appear to matter and other times they do not. Perhaps in situations in which contact is of a more personal nature (e.g., sharing living quarters), heterosexuals avoid same-sex more than other-sex gays, but in settings in which interactions are less intimate, lesbians and gay men are viewed similarly. Or perhaps gender issues affect reactions to gay men and lesbians only in those less-scripted situations described earlier. Systematic exploration of these possibilities is in order.

Conclusions and Future Directions

The problems presented in exploring whether individual differences in attitudes toward homosexuality can be linked to prejudiced behaviors are many and complex. Although theoretical and empirical work from the social psychological literature suggests paths that may allow insightful discovery, a great deal of empirical work is needed before conclusions can be confidently drawn. This chapter provides a review of the literature on reactions toward gay persons and notes that in general heterosexuals' reactions to lesbians and gay men are negative. However, individual differences are evident and tolerant individuals can and do choose to treat heterosexuals and homosexuals similarly. Finally, the importance of moderating variables when considering prejudicial reactions to gay men and lesbians should not be overlooked. Although the issues raised here are by no means exhaustive, it is hoped that this discussion highlighted some areas in which both empirical and theoretical work are needed and suggested possible avenues for exploration.

References

Abelson, R. P. (1976). Script processing in attitude formation and decision making. In J. S. Carroll & J. W. Payne (Eds.), *Cognition and social behavior* (pp. 33-45). Hillsdale, NJ: Lawrence Erlbaum.

Abelson, R. P. (1981). Psychological status of the script concept. *American Psychologist, 36,* 715-729.

Abelson, R. P. (1982). Three modes of attitude-behavior consistency. In M. P. Zanna, E. T. Higgins, & C. P. Herman (Eds.), *Consistency in social behavior: The Ontario symposium* (Vol. 2, pp. 131-146). Hillsdale, NJ: Lawrence Erlbaum.

Abelson, R. P., Kinder, D. R., Peters, M. D., & Fiske, S. T. (1982). Affective and semantic components in political person perception. *Journal of Personality and Social Psychology, 42,* 619-630.

Adorno, T. W., Frenkel-Brunswik, E., Levinson, D. J., & Sanford, R. N. (1950). *The authoritarian personality.* New York: Harper & Row.

Ajzen, I. (1982). The attitude behavior relation: On behaving in accordance with one's attitudes. In M. P. Zanna, E. T. Higgins, & C. P. Herman (Eds.), *Consistency in social behavior: The Ontario symposium* (Vol. 2, pp. 3-15). Hillsdale, NJ: Lawrence Erlbaum.

Ajzen, I., & Fishbein, M. (1977). Attitude-behavior relations: A theoretical analysis and review of empirical research. *Psychological Bulletin, 84,* 888-918.

Ajzen, I., & Fishbein, M. (1980). *Understanding attitudes and predicting social behavior.* Englewood Cliffs, NJ: Prentice-Hall.

Allport, G. W. (1935). Attitudes. In C. Murchinson (Ed.), *Handbook of social psychology* (pp. 798-844). Worcester, MA: Clark University Press.

Allport, G. W. (1954). *The nature of prejudice.* Cambridge, MA: Addison-Wesley.

Anderson, V. N. (1992). For whom is this world just?: Sexual orientation and AIDS. *Journal of Applied Social Psychology, 22,* 248-259.

Aronson, E., & Carlsmith, J. M. (1968). Experimentation in social psychology. In G. Lindzey & E. Aronson (Eds.), *Handbook of social psychology* (Vol. 2, 2nd ed., pp. 1-79). Reading, MA: Addison-Wesley.

Aronson, E., Ellsworth, P.C., Carlsmith, J. M., & Gonzales, M. H. (1990). *Methods of research in social psychology* (2nd ed.). New York: McGraw-Hill.

Ashmore, R. D. (1990). Sex, gender, and the individual. In L. A. Previn (Ed.), *Handbook of personality: Theory and research* (pp. 486-526). New York: Guilford.

Ashmore, R. D., & Del Boca, F. K. (1976). Psychological approaches to understanding intergroup conflict. In P. Katz (Ed.), *Toward the elimination of racism* (pp. 73-123). New York: Pergamon.

Ashmore, R. D., & Del Boca, F. K. (1981). Conceptual approaches to stereotypes and stereotyping. In D. L. Hamilton (Ed.), *Cognitive processes in stereotyping and intergroup behavior* (pp. 1-35). Hillsdale, NJ: Lawrence Erlbaum.

Berrill, K. T. (1992). Anti-gay violence and victimization in the United States: An overview. In G. M. Herek & K. T. Berrill (Eds.), *Hate crimes: Confronting violence against lesbians and gay men* (pp. 19-45). Newbury Park, CA: Sage.

Berscheid, E., Boyd, D., & Darley, J. M. (1968). Effect of forced association upon voluntary choice to associate. *Journal of Personality and Social Psychology, 8,* 13-19.

Bowers v. Hardwick, 106 S.Ct. 2841 (1986).

Brigham, J. C. (1971). Ethnic stereotypes. *Psychological Bulletin, 76,* 15-38.

Broverman, I. K., Vogel, S. R., Broverman, D. M., Clarkson, F. E., & Rosenkrantz, P. S. (1972). Sex-role stereotypes: A current appraisal. *Journal of Social Issues, 28,* 59-78.

Committee on Lesbian and Gay Concerns, APA. (1991). Avoiding heterosexual bias in language. *American Psychologist, 46,* 973-974.

Crocker, J., Thompson, L. L., McGraw, K. M., & Ingerman, C. (1987). Downward comparison, prejudice, and evaluations of others: Effects of self-esteem and threat. *Journal of Personality and Social Psychology, 52,* 907-916.

Crocker, J., & Schwartz, I. (1985). Prejudice and ingroup favoritism in a minimal intergroup situation: Effects of self-esteem. *Personality and Social Psychology Bulletin, 11,* 379-386.

Cuenot, R. G., & Fugita, S. S. (1982). Perceived homosexuality: Measuring heterosexual attitudinal and nonverbal reactions. *Personality and Social Psychology Bulletin, 8,* 100-106.

Deaux, K., & Kite, M. E. (1987). Thinking about gender. In B. B. Hess & M. M. Ferree (Eds.), *Analyzing gender: A handbook of social science research* (pp. 92-117). Newbury Park, CA: Sage.

Deaux, K., & Kite, M. E. (in press). Gender stereotypes. In F. Denmark & M. Paludi (Eds.), *Handbook on the psychology of women.* New York: Greenwood.

Deaux, K., & Lewis, L. L. (1984). Structure of gender stereotypes: Interrelationships among components and gender label. *Journal of Personality and Social Psychology, 46,* 991-1004.

Deaux, K., & Major, B. (1987). Putting gender into context: An interactive model of gender-related behavior. *Psychological Review, 94,* 369-389.

Devine, P. G. (1989). Stereotypes and prejudice: Their automatic and controlled components. *Journal of Personality and Social Psychology, 56,* 5-18.

Devine, P. G., Monteith, M. J., Zuwerink, J. R., & Elliot, A. J. (1991). Prejudice with and without compunction. *Journal of Personality and Social Psychology, 60,* 817-830.

Dew, M. A. (1985). The effects of attitudes on inferences of homosexuality and perceived physical attractiveness in women. *Sex Roles, 12,* 143-155.

Dovidio, J. F., & Gaertner, S. L. (Eds.). (1986). *Prejudice, discrimination, and racism: Theory and research.* Orlando, FL: Academic Press.

Eagly, A. H. (1987). *Sex differences in social behavior: A social-role interpretation.* Hillsdale, NJ: Lawrence Erlbaum.

Eagly, A. H., & Crowley, M. C. (1986). Gender and helping behavior: A meta-analytic review of the social psychological literature. *Psychological Bulletin, 100,* 309-330.

Eagly, A. H., & Mladinic, A. (1989). Gender stereotypes and attitudes toward women and men. *Personality and Social Psychology Bulletin, 15,* 543-558.

Eagly, A. H., & Steffan, V. J. (1984). Gender stereotypes stem from the distribution of women and men into social roles. *Journal of Personality and Social Psychology, 46,* 735-754.

Epstein, S. (1980). The stability of behavior: II. Implications for psychological research. *American Psychologist, 35,* 790-806.

Epstein, S. (1983). Aggregation and beyond: Some basic issues on the prediction of behavior. *Journal of Personality, 51,* 360-392.

Fish, T. A., & Rye, B. J. (1991). Attitudes toward a homosexual or heterosexual person with AIDS. *Journal of Applied Social Psychology, 21,* 651-667.

Fishbein, M., & Ajzen, I. (1974). Attitudes towards objects as predictors of single and multiple behavioral criteria. *Psychological Review, 81,* 59-74.

Fiske, S. T., & Neuberg, S. (1990). A continuum of impression formation, from category-based to individuating processes: Influences of information and motivation on attention and interpretation. In M. P. Zanna (Ed.), *Advances in experimental social psychology* (Vol. 23, pp. 1-74). New York: Academic Press.

Fiske, S. T., & Taylor, S. (1991). *Social cognition* (2nd ed.). New York: McGraw-Hill.

Frenkel-Brunswik, E. (1949). Intolerance of ambiguity as an emotional and perceptual personality variable. *Journal of Personality, 18,* 108-143.

Gaertner, S. L., & Dovidio, J. F. (1986). The aversive form of racism. In J. F. Dovidio & S. L. Gaertner (Eds.), *Prejudice, discrimination, and racism: Theory and research* (pp. 61-89). Orlando, FL: Academic Press.

Garnets, L., & Kimmel, D. (1991). Lesbian and gay male dimensions in the psychological study of human diversity. In J. D. Goodchilds (Ed.), *Psychological perspectives on human diversity in America* (pp. 137-192). Washington, DC: American Psychological Association.

Gentry, C. S. (1987). Social distance regarding male and female homosexuals. *Journal of Social Psychology, 127,* 199-208.

Gray, C., Russell, P., & Blockley, S. (1991). The effects upon helping behaviour of wearing pro-gay identification. *British Journal of Social Psychology, 30,* 171-178.

Gross, A. E., Green, S. K., Storck, J. T., & Vanyur, J. M. (1980). Disclosure of sexual orientation and impressions of male and female homosexuals. *Personality and Social Psychology Bulletin, 6,* 307-314.

Gross, L. (1991). Out of the mainstream: Sexual minorities & the mass media. *Journal of Homosexuality, 21,* 19-46.

Gurwitz, S. B., & Marcus, M. (1978). Effects of anticipated interaction, sex and homosexual stereotypes on first impressions. *Journal of Applied Social Psychology, 8,* 47-56.

Hamilton, D. L. (1979). A cognitive-attributional analysis of stereotyping. In L. Berkowitz (Ed.), *Advances in experimental social psychology* (Vol. 12, pp. 53-81). New York: Academic Press.

Hamilton, D. L., & Trolier, T. K. (1986). Stereotypes and stereotyping: An overview of the cognitive approach. In J. F. Dovidio & S. L. Gaertner (Eds.), *Prejudice, discrimination and racism* (pp. 127-163). Orlando, FL: Academic Press.

Hansen, G. L. (1982). Measuring prejudice against homosexuality (homosexism) among college students: A new scale. *Journal of Social Psychology, 117*, 233-236.

Henley, N. M., & Pincus, F. (1978). Interrelationship of sexist, racist, and antihomosexual attitudes. *Psychological Reports, 42*, 83-90.

Herek, G. M. (1984). Beyond "homophobia": A social psychological perspective on attitudes toward lesbians and gay men. *Journal of Homosexuality, 10*(1-2), 1-21.

Herek, G. M. (1986a). The social psychology of homophobia: Toward a practical theory. *Review of Law and Social Change, 14*, 923-934.

Herek, G. M. (1986b). On heterosexual masculinity. *American Behavioral Scientist, 29*, 563-577.

Herek, G. M. (1987). Can functions be measured? A new perspective on the functional approach to attitudes. *Social Psychology Quarterly, 50*, 285-303.

Herek, G. M. (1988). Heterosexuals' attitudes toward lesbians and gay men: Correlates and gender differences. *Journal of Sex Research, 25*, 451-477.

Herek, G. M. (1990). The context of anti-gay violence. *Journal of Interpersonal Violence, 5*, 316-333.

Herek, G. M. (1993). Sexual orientation and military service: A social science perspective. *American Psychologist, 48*(5), 538-547.

Herek, G. M., & Glunt, E. K. (1988). An epidemic of stigma: Public reactions to AIDS. *American Psychologist, 43*, 886-891.

Herek, G. M., Kimmel, D. C., Amaro, H., & Melton, G. B. (1991). Avoiding heterosexist bias in psychological research. *American Psychologist, 44*(9), 957-963.

Hudson, W. W., & Ricketts, W. A. (1980). A strategy for the measurement of homophobia. *Journal of Homosexuality, 5*, 357-372.

Karr, R. G. (1978). Homosexual labeling and the male role. *Journal of Social Issues, 34*, 73-83.

Katz, D. (1960). The functional approach to the study of attitudes. *Public Opinion Quarterly, 24*, 163-204.

Katz, D., & Braly, K. (1933). Racial prejudice and racial stereotypes. *Journal of Abnormal and Social Psychology, 28*, 280-290.

Kite, M. E. (1984). Sex differences in attitudes towards homosexuals: A meta-analytic review. *Journal of Homosexuality, 10*(1-2), 69-81.

Kite, M. E. (1990, August). *Age, gender, and employment: A test of social role theory.* Paper presented at the meeting of the American Psychological Association, Boston.

Kite, M. E. (1992a). Individual differences in males' reactions to gay males and lesbians. *Journal of Applied Social Psychology, 22*, 1222-1239.

Kite, M. E. (1992b). Psychometric properties of the homosexuality attitude scale. *Representative Research in Social Psychology, 19*(2), 3-18.

Kite, M. E., & Deaux, K. (1986). Attitudes toward homosexuality: Assessment and behavioral consequences. *Basic and Applied Social Psychology, 7*, 137-162.

Kite, M. E., & Deaux, K. (1987). Gender belief systems: Homosexuality and the implicit inversion theory. *Psychology of Women Quarterly, 11*, 83-96.

Kite, M. E., Whitley, B. E., Jr., & Michael, S. T. (1992, May). *Are attributions about AIDS victims affected by the social desirability of the source of infection?* Paper presented at the meeting of the Midwestern Psychological Association, Chicago.

Kite, M. E., Whitley, B. E.. Jr., Simon T., & Michael, S. (1991, May). *Response to AIDS victims: The roles of source of infection and victim sexual orientation.* Paper presented at the meeting of the Midwestern Psychological Association, Chicago.

Krulewitz, J. E., & Nash, J. E. (1980). Effects of sex role attitudes and similarity on men's rejection of male homosexuals. *Journal of Personality and Social Psychology, 38,* 67-74.

Kurdek, L. A. (1988). Correlates of negative attitudes toward homosexuals in heterosexual college students. *Sex Roles, 18,* 727-738.

Laner, M. R., & Laner, C. A. (1979). Personal style or sexual preference: Why gay men are disliked. *International Review of Modern Sociology, 9,* 215-228.

Laner, M. R., & Laner, C. A. (1980). Sexual preference or personal style? Why lesbians are disliked. *Journal of Homosexuality, 5,* 339-356.

LaPiere, R. T. (1934). Attitudes vs. action. *Social Forces, 13,* 230-237.

Larsen, K. S., Reed, M., & Hoffman, S. (1980). Attitudes of heterosexuals toward homosexuality: A Likert-type scale and construct validity. *Journal of Sex Research, 16,* 245-257.

Larsen, R. J. (1984). *Tolerance for ambiguity in the personality attributes of others.* Unpublished manuscript, University of Illinois.

Layton, B. D., & Insko, C. A. (1974). Anticipated interaction and the similarity-attraction effect. *Sociometry, 37,* 149-162.

Leitner, L. M., & Cado, S. (1982). Personal constructs and homosexual stress. *Journal of Personality and Social Psychology, 43,* 869-872.

Levitt, E., & Klassen, A. (1974). Public attitudes toward homosexuality: Part of the 1970 national survey by the Institute for Sex Research. *Journal of Homosexuality, 1,* 29-43.

Lippmann, W. (1922). *Public opinion.* New York: Harcourt, Brace.

MacDonald, A. P., Jr. (1976). Homophobia: Its roots and meanings. *Homosexual Counseling Journal, 3*(1), 23-33.

MacDonald, A. P., Jr., Huggins, J., Young, S., & Swanson, R. A. (1973). Attitudes toward homosexuality: Preservation of sex morality or the double standard? *Journal of Consulting and Clinical Psychology, 40,* 161.

McConahay, J. B. (1986). Modern racism, ambivalence, and the modern racism scale. In J. F. Dovidio & S. L. Gaertner (Eds.), *Prejudice, discrimination, and racism: Theory and research* (pp. 91-125). Orlando, FL: Academic Press.

McGuire, W. J. (1968). The nature of attitudes and attitude and attitude change. In G. Lindzey & E. Aronson (Eds.), *The handbook of social psychology* (2nd ed., pp. 136-314). Reading, MA: Addison-Wesley.

Millham, J., San Miguel, C. L., & Kellogg, R. (1976). A factor-analytic conceptualization of attitudes toward male and female homosexuals. *Journal of Homosexuality, 2,* 3-10.

Mischel, W. (1968). *Personality and assessment.* New York: Wiley.

Mischel, W. (1977). The interaction of person and situation. In D. Magnusson & N. S. Endler (Eds.), *Personality at the crossroads: Current issues in interactional psychology* (pp. 333-352). Hillsdale, NJ: Lawrence Erlbaum.

Mischel, W., & Peake, P. (1982). In search of consistency: Measure for measure. In M. P. Zanna, E. T. Higgins, & C. P. Herman (Eds.), *Consistency in social behavior: The Ontario symposium* (Vol. 2, pp. 187-207). Hillsdale, NJ: Lawrence Erlbaum.

Monteith, M. J., Devine, P. G., & Zuwerink, J. R. (1993). Self-directed versus other-directed affect as a consequence of prejudice-related discrepancies. *Journal of Personality and Social Psychology, 64,* 198-210.

Monson, T. C., Hesley, J. W., & Chernick, L. (1982). Specifying when personality traits can and cannot predict behavior: An alternative to abandoning the attempt to predict single-act criteria. *Journal of Personality and Social Psychology, 43,* 385-399.

Morin, S. F., & Garfinkle, E. M. (1978). Male homophobia. *Journal of Social Issues, 34,* 29-47.

Newman, B. S. (1989). The relative importance of gender role attitudes to male and female attitudes toward lesbians. *Sex Roles, 21,* 451-465.

Page, S., & Yee, M. (1985). Conception of male and female homosexual stereotypes among university undergraduates. *Journal of Homosexuality, 12,* 109-118.

Plasek, J. W., & Allard, J. (1984). Misconceptions of homophobia. *Journal of Homosexuality, 10*(1-2), 23-37.

Rosenthal, R. (1966). *Experimenter effects in behavioral research.* New York: Appelton-Century-Crofts.

Rosenthal, R. (1969). Interpersonal expectations: Effects of the experimenter's hypothesis. In R. Rosenthal & R. L. Rosnow (Eds.), *Artifact in behavioral research* (pp. 181-277). New York: Academic Press.

Sandler, B. R., & Hall, R. M. (1986). *The campus climate revisited: Chilly for women faculty, administrators, and graduate students.* Washington, DC: Association of American Colleges, Project on the Status and Education of Women.

Schank, R. C., & Abelson, R. P. (1977). *Scripts, plans, goals and understanding: An inquiry into human knowledge structures.* Hillsdale, NJ: Lawrence Erlbaum.

Sigall, H., & Page, R. (1971). Current stereotypes: A little fading, a little faking. *Journal of Personality and Social Psychology, 18,* 247-255.

Simmons, J. L. (1965). Public stereotypes of deviants. *Social Problems, 13,* 223-332.

Smith, M. B., Bruner, J. S., & White, R. W. (1956). *Opinions and personality.* New York: Wiley.

Spertus, E. (1991, August), *Why are there so few female computer scientists?* (Report. No. AITR1315). Cambridge: MIT Artificial Intelligence Lab.

Steffensmeier, D., & Steffensmeier, R. (1974). Sex differences in reactions to homosexuals: Research continuities & further developments. *Journal of Sex Research, 10,* 52-67.

Stevenson, M. R. (1988). Promoting tolerance for homosexuality: An evaluation of intervention strategies. *Journal of Sex Research, 25,* 500-511.

Stevenson, M. R. (1991). Social distance from persons with AIDS. *Journal of Psychology and Human Sexuality, 4,* 13-20.

Storms, M. D., Stivers, M. L., Lambers, S. M., & Hill, C. A. (1981). Sexual scripts for women. *Sex Roles, 7,* 699-707.

Sullivan, G. (1984). A bibliographic guide to government hearings and reports, legislative action, and speeches made in the House and Senate of the United States Congress on the subject of homosexuality. *Journal of Homosexuality, 10*(1-2), 135-189.

Tajfel, H. (1969). Cognitive aspects of prejudice. *Journal of Social Issues, 25,* 79-97.

Taylor, A. T. (1983). Conceptions of masculinity and femininity as a basis for stereotypes of male and female homosexuals. *Journal of Homosexuality, 9,* 37-53.

Testa, R. J., Kinder, B. N., & Ironson, G. (1987). Heterosexual bias in the perception of loving relationships of gay males and lesbians. *Journal of Sex Research, 23,* 163-172.

Turque, B. (1992, September 14). Gays under fire. *Newsweek,* pp. 35-40.

Virginia Slims. (1990). *The 1990 Virginia Slims opinion poll: A 20-year perspective of women's issues.* Chicago: Author.

Weinberger, L. E., & Millham, J. (1979). Attitudinal homophobia and support of traditional sex roles. *Journal of Homosexuality, 4*(3), 237-245.

Weis, C. B., & Dain, R. N. (1979). Ego development and sex attitudes in heterosexual and homosexual men and women. *Archives of Sexual Behavior, 8*(4), 341-356.

Whitley, B. E., Jr. (1987). The relationship of sex-role orientation to heterosexuals' attitudes toward homosexuals. *Sex Roles, 17,* 103-113.

Whitley, B. E., Jr. (1988). Sex differences in heterosexuals' attitudes towards homosexuals: It depends upon what you ask. *Journal of Sex Research, 24,* 287-291.

Whitley, B. E., Jr. (1990). The relationship of heterosexuals' attributions for the causes of homosexuality to attitudes toward lesbians and gay men. *Personality and Social Psychology Bulletin, 16,* 369-377.

Wicker, A. W. (1969). Attitudes vs. actions: The relationship of verbal and overt behavioral responses to attitude objects. *Journal of Social Issues, 25,* 41-78.

Wicklund, R. A. (1982). Self-focused attention and the validity of self reports. In M. P. Zanna, E. T. Higgins, & C. P. Herman (Eds.), *Consistency in social behavior: The Ontario symposium* (Vol. 2, pp. 149-172). Hillsdale, NJ: Lawrence Erlbaum.

Williams, J. E., & Best, D. L. (1982). *Measuring sex stereotypes: A thirty nation study.* Beverly Hills, CA: Sage.

Williams, J. E., & Best, D. L. (1990). *Sex and psyche: Gender and self viewed cross-culturally.* Newbury Park, CA: Sage.

Zeman, N., Meyer, M., Keene-Osborn, S. (1992, November 23). No special rights for gays. *Newsweek,* p. 32.

3

Our Politics and Choices

The Feminist Movement and Sexual Orientation

CARLA GOLDEN

Sexuality has been one of the central concerns of feminism as a social and political movement. Feminists have considered it important to understand women's sexuality, both in the interest of knowing more about human sexuality and in discerning how its multiple forms of expression and repression are related to women's liberation. Since the earliest days of the second wave, feminists have examined sex, sexual desire, and intimate relationships, especially as these relate to gender in its cultural and historical context. While the particulars of the analyses have differed across various feminist groups and have shifted over time, they typically include prescriptions for women's sexual and relational behavior. Implicit in such statements is a causal analysis of sexuality itself.

Early radical feminist groups, such as Cell 16, Redstockings, and The Feminists, articulated distinct points of view not only about the causes of women's oppression and the best strategies for overcoming it but also regarding what kinds of sexual relationships women should have (or whether they should have them at all) and about how such relationships

AUTHOR'S NOTE: This chapter was originally presented at the symposium Social and Ethical Implications of Causal Explanations for Sexual Orientation at the 1990 annual meeting of the American Psychological Association, Boston.

related to feminist politics. Echols (1989) provided a fascinating account of the development of radical feminism on the East Coast of the United States in the 1960s. The members of Cell 16 are characterized as the movement heavies, known for their emphasis on celibacy, separatism, and karate as well as the work shirt, combat boots, and short-hair look. Although they advocated that women withdraw from men both personally and politically, and encouraged members to live in women's communities, this was by no means a prescription for lesbianism. As a group committed to social activism, they saw lesbianism as nothing more than a personal solution. When Rita Mae Brown was critical of Cell 16 for ignoring lesbians, Roxanne Dunbar apparently replied that the point was to get women "out of bed" and that it was okay for women to love each other as long as they didn't sleep together! Cell 16's position was decidedly antisex. They claimed that what women needed was to be liberated from sex—both heterosexual and lesbian.

Along with such prescriptions about women's sexual behavior were explanations of women's sexuality. In the Cell 16 journal, *No More Fun and Games,* one can find articulation of the point of view that there is nothing natural or necessary about sex. The group's contention was that people were conditioned to have sexual needs, and that they could be unconditioned. Dana Densmore wrote that "happy, healthy self-confident animals and people don't like being touched, don't need to snuggle and huggle. They are really free and self contained and in their heads" (quoted in Echols, 1989, p. 162). She claimed that women engage in sex not for any physical pleasure but for the "human kindness, communication, back-to-the-womb merging and oblivion" (p. 162). Abby Rockefeller argued that "the real issue is simply that women don't like [sex] either with the same frequency or in the same way as men" (quoted in Echols, 1989, p. 163). With respect to lesbianism, she claimed that it "muddles what is the real issue for women by making it appear that women really like sex as much as men—that they just don't like sex *with* men" (p. 163). In short, Cell 16 maintained the position that sexual desire was all in the head.

The Redstockings, in contrast, did not advocate that women abandon men and marriage, because they believed that relations between men and women were the battlefield on which the feminist revolution would and should be waged. If women demanded equality in their relationships with men, then men would have to change. The problem was not with marriage per se but with unequal sex roles within marriage (Echols, 1989).

While other radical feminist groups, like Cell 16, argued that women married as a result of false consciousness, the Redstockings asserted that they did so out of economic necessity. They wanted to promote and maintain solidarity with the masses of women, and not, in their analysis of women's oppression, end up dividing women into the "brainwashed" and the "liberated." As a result, they took a negative stance toward the development of alternative lifestyles, because they saw them both as personal solutions and as creating greater distance between feminists and the masses of women. The Redstockings tended to view women who were experimenting with women's communities, lesbianism, celibacy, or bisexuality as "retreating from the sexual battlefield" (Echols, 1989, p. 156).

In taking the position that heterosexuality could be used to advance the struggle for women's liberation, the Redstockings accepted women's desire for genital sexuality with men as an instinctive rather than socially constructed need. There was, however, a minority faction who questioned the dependence of women and men on each other and who suggested that heterosexual desire was a social construct designed by men to keep women subordinate.

The Feminists, founded by Ti-Grace Atkinson, viewed women as having collaborated in their own oppression. Their manifesto proclaimed "we must change women's ideas of themselves and in that way change what women want" (The Feminists, 1970). One of the ideas they saw as most in need of change was that women desired sex with men. According to The Feminists, sexual desire itself was male. The essence of their argument was that women needed to be liberated from sex, not that women needed to become sexually liberated. This was in contrast to the position of other radical feminists who considered the repression of female sexuality to be a serious problem and its perpetuation central to the maintenance of women's oppression.

The Feminists argued that women who thought that sexual pleasure was necessary or important had merely been deceived into believing that. As far as they were concerned, masturbation could take care of whatever sexual needs women had. They saw lesbianism as "merely sexual" and lesbians as women who were victims of the false consciousness that women need sex. In their view, lesbianism and feminism were contradictory. It is a striking indication of the evolution of feminist thinking that years later, none other than Ti-Grace Atkinson claimed that "feminism is the theory, lesbianism the practice" (quoted in Abbot & Love, 1972, p. 117).

The Feminists voiced some rather explicit prescriptions for relational behavior. They saw marriage as inherently unequal and asserted that "the rejection of this institution both in theory and practice was a primary mark of the radical feminist" (quoted in Echols, 1989, p. 176). Along with this proclamation, they adopted a membership requirement that no more than one-third of their membership could be married or living with a man. Two years later, in 1971, they voted to exclude all married women from membership in The Feminists.

It is clear that among early radical feminist groups on the East Coast, there was a certain antagonism (if not outright homophobia) toward lesbianism. The early radical feminists either ignored discussion of it, or viewed lesbianism as nothing more than a personal and sexual concern. Such views were countered by radical activism on the part of lesbians (like Rita Mae Brown and Charlotte Bunch) and lesbian-feminist groups like The Furies.

Radicalesbians (1973) defined lesbianism as a political choice and as the ultimate form of solidarity between women. While the characterization of lesbianism as a political choice has since generated much debate about the centrality of eroticism in definitions of lesbianism (Ferguson, 1981; Rich, 1980; Zita, 1981), Radicalesbians did not deny its sexual aspects. They asserted that "until women see in each other the possibility of a primal commitment which includes sexual love, they will be denying themselves the love and value they readily accord to men, thus affirming their second-class status" (p. 243).

Within many feminist communities, attitudes toward lesbianism slowly began to change. As lesbians became more visible, it was more difficult to deny that they were often at the forefront of the women's movement. Attitudes shifted to the point at which Ti-Grace Atkinson's suggestion that feminism was the theory and lesbianism the practice generated intense debate about whether heterosexual women could be fully committed to feminism.[1] Many women personally lived through the "lesbian/straight split" that rocked the feminist community. Vestiges of this division are still apparent today, and there has even emerged a new manifestation of it in the lesbian/bisexual split (Orlando, 1984; Shuster, 1987).[2]

The purpose of this brief sketch is to highlight that within feminist communities there is a history of discussion and prescription regarding women's sexuality, specifically about the relation between women's politics and their sexual and relational choices. Feminism as a movement and feminist psychology as a discipline have both encouraged women to self-consciously examine their lives and experiences as women and to make conscious, informed decisions about what they need and want. Implicit in this encouragement is the view that women can choose how to live, sexually and otherwise. This belief is as apparent in the 1990s as it was earlier.

An explicit statement of this position can be seen in a workshop offered in June 1990 at the Fourth International Congress on Women (held at Hunter College in New York). A flyer distributed by two German women announced the workshop titled "Two Women Together: Intensive Relationships Between Women and How They Can Develop." The small print was a direct invitation to women to think about the possibility of choosing other women as life and sexual partners:

> It is the dominating view in our society that relationships between women are of inferior value. Relationships between men and women, however, are fundamentally accepted and institutionalized. Our aim is to inspire women to free themselves from these conceptions. We want to show that marriage is not the only way of living together (marriage is a possible way, there are more ways beside it!). By discussing and sharing our own experiences with other women we want to encourage them to reflect intensively on their relationships with women. Women should realize that connections and friendships between women are as valuable and rich as connections between men and women.

And yet among psychologists who study sexual orientation, the factor of choice is either not seriously considered or viewed as erroneous (Money, 1988). This results from the failure to include women and to consider the feminist movement when theorizing about the nature and origins of sexuality. The author's research, composed of discussions and interviews with dozens of women, makes clear that issues of choice and preference are salient to many women. This is true for both college students who are in the process of exploring and defining their sexuality and older feminists reflecting on their sexuality.

The interviews consisted of asking women how they identify their own sexuality, both for themselves and for the world, and how they understand it to have developed. The research focused on the extent to which women conceptualize their sexual orientation and identity as something that they shape and create or as something beyond their control and about which they have little choice.[3] In a study of a Southern lesbian community, Ponse (1978) identified a sample of women who felt that they had always been lesbian, in fact had been born that way. Ponse called these women primary lesbians and distinguished them from elective lesbians who felt that they had chosen their lesbian lifestyle and identity.

Research with college women found that the same distinction emerged for both heterosexual and lesbian women. The primary lesbians believed that they were true lesbians, because they had always been attracted to girls and women for as long as they could remember and were sure that this would be the case for life. The elective lesbians described themselves as having made a conscious decision to consider lesbianism. They often said this was prompted by their developing feminist consciousness and/or as a result of exposure to lesbian role models. This does not mean that their lesbianism had strictly political dimensions; for most of these women it was also an erotic choice (Golden, 1987).

Although the primary lesbians held an essentialist view of their sexual orientation (believing that they had been lesbian for as long as they could remember and that this was a fixed and unchanging aspect of who they were), some of the elective lesbians held this view as well. If they had elected lesbianism after some heterosexual experience, they often expressed the view that there was something unreal about their previous heterosexuality. They seemed to reinterpret their past history so as to see themselves as having really been lesbians all along; in other words, despite their choice to be lesbians, they conceptualized their sexual orientation as essential, or fixed and unchanging. Though there had been a change from the past, they denied the possibility that their sexuality could change again in the future.

Other elective lesbians did not reconstruct their pasts as implicitly lesbian. In fact, they did not view sexual attraction to women as an essential and unchangeable aspect of who they were, although most expressed the belief that they would probably continue to have their primary (if not all) relationships with women. Some women said they identified as lesbians but felt that their sexual feelings could be more accurately characterized as bisexual. These women were distinguishing between their sexual identity and their sexual orientation, viewing the latter as fluid and potentially changeable over the course of their lives.

Having found these differences in a population of young lesbians, the author then interviewed women who were in their late 20s to early 50s and found some interesting age-related shifts in their thinking about the nature of their lesbianism. When they first came out and for years thereafter, some elective lesbians had believed their sexuality was essential and fixed, but later in their development, these women had come to realize that their sexuality was in fact more fluid. For a few, this shift resulted from bisexual feelings and experiences later in life that had, in some cases, taken them quite by surprise. Others who felt this way had continued to have relationships only with women. They attributed their earlier position to their more adamant lesbian feminist politics or to what (in retrospect) they considered was a developmental phase some lesbians go through.

Alternatively, some elective lesbians thought that in their younger years, when they were engaged in sexual exploration and discovery, their sexuality was more fluid, but that in the context of lesbian culture and relationships, they had developed a very explicit preference for women. These women thought of their sexuality as having become more fixed as they got older. The issue of choice emerged again: Some women said that while their sexuality was probably actually fluid, they had chosen to consider it fixed, because after so many years of being part of lesbian culture and community, they could not imagine living outside of it.

Interviews with heterosexual women on these same issues revealed that similar distinctions apply to the way they think about their sexuality. Most of the college students who were interviewed simply assumed that they were heterosexual and that their heterosexuality was a given, meaning biologically determined and fixed. They typically had not given the topic much thought and reacted with astonishment when asked, "When did you first know that you were heterosexual?" The most common response was "It never even occurred to me that I could be anything else."

There were, however, other students who *had* previously given some thought to sexual preference issues, usually because their curiosity was prompted by a discussion in a women's studies class or by a book that made reference to the social construction of sexuality or more informally by talking with a lesbian friend. Upon exposure to the concept of sexual fluidity, some heterosexual women rejected its applicability to themselves. They could not imagine themselves having anything but heterosexual attractions and relationships (i.e., they viewed their sexuality as both determined and fixed). Some of these women openly acknowledged that the notion that their sexuality might be fluid made them distinctly uncomfortable; others conveyed their discomfort nonverbally. For some women, however, the belief in the fixed nature of their sexuality didn't seem at all defensive. These women were primary heterosexuals who believed in the central and enduring quality of their sexuality.

In contrast to those who maintained that their sexuality was essentially heterosexual, there were other college women who acknowledged that although they had always considered themselves to be heterosexual they had either been, or could imagine being, attracted to and getting involved with a woman. It was striking how powerful the idea of sexual fluidity was to this subgroup of heterosexual women. When asked when and how the possibility had first occurred to them, they mentioned women's studies classes; exposure to lesbians within feminist groups; or more discrete events such as viewing a film or TV program, hearing a lecture, reading an article, or having a discussion with a lesbian friend. These had often prompted ongoing reflection on their part. Sometimes this included their reinterpreting close female friendships and/or attachments to teachers and camp counselors as evidence of the possibility that they had been sexually attracted to women but had never recognized it as such until now. They expressed the view that their sexuality did in fact involve a choice that they had not realized until recently. In this sense they are similar to the elective lesbians described previously.

Compared with the elective lesbians, however, their thinking about sexuality had led them to make a conscious choice in the opposite direction, that is, not to explore their lesbian or bisexual potential. They said, in effect, that choosing to be lesbians would make their lives more difficult in a variety of ways but particularly with respect to having to tell their families. Although they were aware they had a choice, it was one they were choosing not to make. These women can be characterized as elective heterosexuals, who believe in the potential fluidity of their sexuality but who have chosen not to act on it.

A different strand of elective heterosexuality was among older feminist women (aged 25 to 55). Some women said they had been attracted to women (or could imagine the possibility) as well as to men and were open to involvement in a lesbian relationship, but it had not happened yet. They expressed the view that although they were currently heterosexual, they still considered their sexuality to be fluid. There were other women who were involved in long-term marriages or relationships with men who said that if anything should happen to their partner (e.g., if he died or they separated), they would prefer to be involved with women.

Although most had never had previous lesbian experience, they did not anticipate difficulty in such a switch. Quite a few mentioned that they found women sexually attractive, and almost all remarked that they preferred women as emotional partners.

Clearly, some women feel that choice has played a role in their sexual orientation, and some experience their sexuality as fluid. Some lesbians talk about choosing openly to accept and embrace a sexuality they believe they were born with; other women talk about choosing to be lesbians because they prefer women and because the feminist movement has legitimated that choice. Among some heterosexual women, there also is a language of possibility and preference. Although most have never questioned their heterosexuality, some have considered the options and chosen to pursue the road most traveled. Others leave open the possibility of change in the future, when the right woman comes along or the current male partner is not around. Women's choices about their sexuality are evident not only in the acceptance and adoption of a stigmatized lifestyle and identity but also in the conscious and implicitly homophobic rejection of such a possibility because it would make life too difficult.[4]

These interviews with women have shown that the visibility of the feminist movement in the 1970s and 1980s had a powerful influence on how many women conceptualize and make choices about their sexuality. The research also highlighted the importance of considering the cultural and historical context in specifying what is meant when talking about sexual orientation and causal attributions. A brief consideration of the psychological literature on this topic reveals the problems generated by ignoring cultural variables.

In this period of postmodern skepticism about the universality of any category, psychologists are in fuzzy territory when discussing sexual orientation as if it represented something that can be clearly defined and to which causality can be attributed. For one thing, the way sexual orientation is conceptualized by (many) psychologists differs from the way lay people understand it. In contrast to the widespread popular assumption that there are two discrete categories of sexual orientation (or three, depending on the recognition of bisexuality), there is scholarly recognition that sexual orientation is more of a continuous variable than a dichotomous one (De Cecco, 1982; Ellis, Burke, & Ames, 1987). Although Kinsey, Pomeroy, and Martin first made the suggestion in 1948, it has not been until recently that it has been widely acknowledged, and this is more evident at the level of theory than in the conduct of research.

Furthermore, there has been the important recognition that sexual orientation is multifaceted and that different dimensions of behavior, emotions, preferences, and fantasy need to be considered. Kinsey et al. (1948) used only two indicators—actual sexual experience, and erotic attractions and fantasies—to assess a person's sexual orientation. But other researchers have considered additional dimensions. Shively and De Cecco (1977) identified three different components of sexual orientation: sexual behavior, fantasies, and affectional preference. Klein's (1990) sexual orientation grid added four variables: sexual attraction, social preference, self-identification, and lifestyle choice, each of which is assessed in terms of a time dimension, including consideration of a person's past, present, and ideal state. Money (1988) argued that the definitive criterion for sexual orientation is falling in love: A homosexual person is one who falls in love with someone of the same sex; heterosexuals and bisexuals fall in love with people of the other sex and both sexes, respectively. Money also referred to additional criteria, like "being sexually attracted to" and "aroused by," as if somehow these always occurred in concert, a dubious assumption.

The author's discussions with women identified a similar range of components as contributive to their sexual orientation, including (1) sexual fantasies, (2) sexual attractions, (3) falling in love, (4) emotional and affectional preferences, (5) actual sexual experience, (6) the quality of that sexual experience, and most important, (7) self-identification.[5] The interviews with college women revealed striking variability in the criteria they used to define their sexuality. There were women who identified as lesbian even though they had never been sexual with other women, and others who identified as heterosexual even though they had engaged in sexual relations with women. There is no simple relation here between sexual experience, orientation, and identity, and even if there were, there are still other elements that cannot be ignored.[6]

The identification of multiple components of sexual orientation complicates the definition, because not only may there be internal inconsistencies in how a person experiences different components but there may also be changes over time in the way they are experienced (Richardson, 1984; Suppe, 1984). Human sexual and relational behavior is even richer and more diverse than is suggested by multicomponent definitions and sexual-orientation grids. It is known that the fantasies of heterosexual people are not always heterosexual ones and that lesbians sometimes fall in love with men. It is not an uncommon woman who has had sex with only men but who has had sexual fantasies about women and who in her lifetime has fallen in love with both women and men. How then is her sexual orientation defined and explained? And, perhaps more important, how does she define and understand herself (Cass, 1984)? Does consideration of this issue leave room for an assessment of the impact of the feminist movement on her sexual self-definition?

As argued in the first half of this chapter, feminism does have something to do with the way women define themselves. The element of conscious decision making and choice is something that must be considered when talking about sexual orientation and its causes. Although some researchers have moved away from discussions and research about what causes homosexuality or heterosexuality, the question still persists. The role of prenatal and postnatal hormones has been hotly debated, and the impact of gender-related and sexual experiences in childhood and adolescence has been considered and woven into various theories of homosexuality (Bell, Weinberg, & Hammersmith, 1981; Money, 1987, 1988; Storms, 1981).

The idea that homosexuality is set early and probably biologically based is prominent even though the literature does not easily support such a conclusion. Some have argued that stressing biological causation might be politically expedient in that the nongay public would be more tolerant if they believed that people were born gay and that it was not a socially transmitted condition. This position is evident in the literature produced by the National Gay and Lesbian Task Force, particularly in pamphlets designed for parents of lesbian and gay youth.

Within this context, most researchers do not actively consider choice to be a significant factor in sexual orientation. Either the issue is never raised or it is explicitly rejected. Money (1988) clearly articulated such a position and asserted that the term *sexual preference* is incorrect because people do not choose their sexuality. Rather, it "is something that happens . . . like being tall or short, left-handed or right-handed, color-blind or color-seeing" (p. 11). According to Money, no one prefers to be homosexual rather than heterosexual or bisexual rather than monosexual. One's sexuality is a status or orientation, not a preference. He considered the concept of choice to be not only erroneous but also politically dangerous; if people choose their sexual preference, the intolerant would consider themselves justified in punishing those who made the "wrong" choice.

Given Money's claim that sexuality is something that happens, like being tall or short, one might incorrectly assume that he is a biological determinist. This is not the case; rather he believes that all behavioral expressions are both biological and social and that the correct paradigm is to think in terms of nature/critical period/nurture. Considering himself a developmental determinist and acknowledging that psychologists do not know the origins of homosexuality, Money suggested that the critical programming probably takes place during the prenatal and early postnatal (childhood) periods, rather than at puberty. His comparison of homosexuality to left-handedness was meant to make several points. Even though left-handedness is not statistically normative, it is not in itself pathological. Furthermore, infants do not choose to be right- or left-handed, and parental attempts to push the child beyond his or her natural inclinations usually fail.

Money also compared sexual orientation to language. Although individuals are born without a specific language and the environment is obviously the definitive factor, people do not choose their native tongue. The infant's brain is prewired to respond to the native language he or she is exposed to, and once assimilated ("through the ears into the brain"), the language "becomes securely locked in" (Money, 1988, p. 11). The brain's wiring and readiness to acquire language means that once it is picked up, it is fixed and the individual cannot get rid of it (except through brain damage).

According to Money, sexual orientation similarly becomes locked in and it stays immutable and irreversible. He claimed that people never lose their native language and that if a second language is acquired, it never matches the fluency or ease of the native language. However, this brushes over some important aspects of bilingual language acquisition and expression and limits its use as an analogy for sexual orientation. There are bilingual children who acquire two languages simultaneously without major difficulty; there are children who learn one language before puberty, then move to another country and eventually become more fluent in the "second" language; and there are adults who learn a second language and attain almost equivalent fluency with frequent use (Harley, 1986).

In Money's view, sexual orientation, like handedness and language, is not chosen, even though it depends on environmental input for its expression. He conceptualized the relevant input as sensory stimulation in infancy and sexual rehearsal play in childhood, which are assimilated and developmentally integrated into what he called a *lovemap* (a template in the brain depicting the "idealized program of sexuoerotic activity"). From Money's perspective, this lovemap and the sexual orientation to which it gives rise are more or less fixed and not amenable to attempts to change it.

Based on Money's speculations, it can be expected that more people (especially females) have what he calls an ambiphilic lovemap and a bisexual orientation. If the relevant input is from sensory stimulation in infancy (a significant amount of which is sensually experienced in relation to the female caregiver) and childhood sexual rehearsal play (a significant amount of which is between same-sex playmates), many people might have the relevant programming to be bisexual. This is where the expanded language analogy, especially with respect to bilingualism, becomes interesting. Just as an African-American child who is exposed to black English and standard English becomes fluent in both languages and chooses when to use each one, it seems plausible that the infant who is held, cuddled, and loved by a mother and a father (or by women and men) would develop the potential to express both sexual orientations and to choose either, depending on the circumstances. To the extent that infants and young children are primarily nurtured by women (and depending on the importance one attaches to this experience as a contributor to later sexuality), one might expect boys to be more predisposed toward heterosexuality and girls to be more directed toward lesbianism. Adding in the cultural imperative toward heterosexuality, one might expect a greater incidence of bisexuality among women, or at least the expression of interest in the possibility.

When one incorporates the experiences and words of women into one's theories, it is no longer possible to ignore or reject notions of sexual choice and preference. This is not to suggest that sexuality is experienced as a choice by all women or even by most. That it is salient for some women is enough to consider its relevance and application to psychological work. In both the teaching and counseling of students and clients, psychologists take as a legitimate goal to encourage women to think about their lives and choices and to make decisions that will best meet their needs and enrich their lives. If a lesbian (primary or elective) seeks counseling and needs affirmation for her lifestyle, it should not cause any psychologist pause to support her choice. Or if a woman of whatever self-identification is actively questioning her choices in regard to sexuality, therapists should comfortably support her in that process.

What is the appropriate response to women who are not directly confronting issues of sexual orientation and identification per se but who are grappling with their sexual choices? Specifically, think of women (and, as a college professor, I see many) who consider themselves heterosexual and are either struggling to find a compatible partner or to create an egalitarian relationship with a male partner who is actively resisting; or women who may have given up the struggle to find or create a compatible relationship but are miserably unhappy. Do psychologists ask such women if they have considered the alternative of relationships with women? Do therapists teach about sexual fluidity and the possibility of choice with respect to sexual orientation? Undoubtedly, such a psychologist would be accused of trying to recruit or convert students.[7] The worst fears about students being led into deviance by gay or lesbian teachers would be fueled. Taking women's voices and the feminist movement into account when thinking about sexual orientation raises both social and ethical issues. If important aspects of human behavior and lifestyle are influenced by choice, first one must acknowledge it, then incorporate it into research, and finally think carefully about what it means for work with students and clients.

Notes

1. While working on this paper, I received the August-September 1990 issue of *Off Our Backs,* the international feminist newspaper. I was quite surprised to see the headline "Do You Have to Be a Lesbian to Be a Feminist?" The accompanying article was a reprint of Marilyn Frye's paper that was delivered at the 1990 National Women's Studies Association Meeting. Frye identified this question as one commonly asked by heterosexual students in women's studies courses. In her talk, she argued that all feminist theory leads to the proposition that the "key mechanism of the global phenomenon of male domination, oppression and exploitation of females, is near-universal female heterosexuality" (p. 22). This, along with the position that female heterosexuality is neither biological nor inevitable but "a concrete historical reality," led Frye to the familiar contention that "if the institution of female heterosexuality is . . . central to the continuous replication of patriarchy, then women's abandonment of that institution recommends itself as one strategy (perhaps among others) in the project of dismantling patriarchal structures" (p. 22). Her use of the word *perhaps* suggests that she questioned whether there are other strategies at all. With respect to the relationship between one's politics and one's sexuality, it was her inclination to maintain that feminism and heterosexuality are incompatible. However, because she did not want to suggest a hopeless social determinism, she allowed for the possibility that women involved in heterosexual relationships might be able to create heterosexuality in forms not compatible with patriarchy. She defined such forms of heterosexual relations in terms of virginity, a state of being that involves a "creative defiance of patriarchal definitions." In a powerful sequence of images, she pictured what virgin lives might look like. Then she posed the title question along with her response to it: "Are these things possible? Can you fuck without losing your virginity? I think everything is against it, but it's not my call. It's up to those who want to live it" (p. 23).

2. This is exemplified in the controversy that erupted in 1990 in Massachusetts during the planning of the Northampton Pride March. The march had been called the Lesbian, Bisexual, and Gay Liberation March, but that year, bisexuals were consciously excluded from both the steering committee and the march title. A sense of the depth of the split as revealed in the varied responses to this action has been published ("Northampton," 1990).

3. There is an important distinction that must be made between sexual orientation and sexual identity. It is commonly assumed that one's sexual identity will be consistent with one's sexual orientation, as assessed in terms of sexual behavior. But there is not always a congruent relationship between sexual experience, orientation, and identity, and furthermore sexual behavior is not the sole criterion by which sexual orientation should be assessed. Through interviews, it was found that women sometimes made a distinction between their sexual identity (how they identified themselves both personally and politically) and their sexuality, by which they seemed to mean orientation. In the discussions of the interviews presented here, the term *sexuality* is used to mean sexual orientation, and *sexual identity* is used when referring to self-labeling.

4. Various discussions and interviews seem to indicate that there are many more women who have considered a lesbian lifestyle and rejected it than have elected to adopt it. Given the particular tensions around intimacy in heterosexual relationships (Chodorow, 1978; Eichenbaum & Orbach, 1984; Rubin, 1983; Stiver, 1984), one might expect lesbianism to be an obvious choice for women. A relevant question is why so many women avoid it. One answer might be an argument in favor of the position that sexual orientation is locked in early and neither changeable nor subject to choice. Another might have to do with the compulsory nature of heterosexuality (Rich, 1980) and with rampant homophobia. The latter seems more likely to me.

5. Each of these seven components can be considered continuous rather than dichotomous variables, and furthermore, they can be considered in terms of separate homosexual and heterosexual dimensions. Just as masculinity and femininity are now considered orthogonal dimensions as opposed to polar ends of a unidimensional scale, so too can each of these seven components be considered in terms of the degree to which the person expresses homosexual and heterosexual orientations. Conceptually, bisexuality would be evident in moderate to high scores on the measured dimensions. In the same way that it is possible to conceive an androgynous person as one who expresses moderate to high degrees of both masculine and feminine characteristics, so too it is possible consider the bisexual person to be one whose placement on the seven components is made up of moderate to high degrees of both homosexual and heterosexual orientation. The relative weight of each of these components in an overall assessment of a person's sexual orientation is an open question. So too is whether these seven components are equivalently applicable to women and to men. Several factors that might contribute to substantial dissimilarities are women's early homoerotic experience, the impact of the feminist movement, and women's homoemotionality.

6. In her autobiography, Near (1990) clarified why she resists calling herself bisexual even though she has had significant relationships with both women and men. She explained that she is "too closely linked to the political perspectives of lesbian feminism. . . . It is part of my world view, part of my passion for women and central in my objection to male domination" (p. 205).

7. Is this situation analogous to the way professors advise students/clients on career options? If a student who I think is capable of doing graduate work in clinical psychology comes to me with a stated desire to pursue a degree in social work, I am interested in whether she has explored all the options or has simply been channeled into a field deemed more suitable for women. Some of my students have consciously rejected the possibility

of getting a Ph.D. in psychology because they do not want to spend five more years in school and do not want the kind of research training they will get in a Ph.D. program. They prefer social work training. But other highly capable students had not really considered the choice of graduate school, because they did not realize it was an option. I consider it my responsibility as an adviser to explore with the student her options. And should the student end up deciding to pursue a graduate degree in psychology, I would probably be considered to have done my job well (if anyone were paying attention!).

References

Abbot, S., & Love, B. (1972). *Sappho was a right-on woman: A liberated view of lesbianism.* New York: Stein & Day.

Bell, A., Weinberg, M., & Hammersmith, S. (1981). *Sexual preference: Its development in men and women.* Bloomington: Indiana University Press.

Cass, V. (1984). Homosexual identity: a concept in need of definition. *Journal of Homosexuality, 7*(2-3), 31-43.

Chodorow, N. (1978). *The reproduction of mothering: Psychoanalysis and the sociology of gender.* Berkeley: University of California Press.

De Cecco, J. (1982). Definition and meaning of sexual orientation. *Journal of Homosexuality, 6*(4), 51-67.

Echols, A. (1989). *Daring to be bad: Radical feminism in America: 1967-1975.* Minneapolis: University of Minnesota Press.

Eichenbaum, L., & Orbach, S. (1984). *What do women want: Exploding the myth of dependency.* New York: Berkley Books.

Ellis, L., Burke, D., & Ames, M. (1987). Sexual orientation as a continuous variable: A comparison between the sexes. *Archives of Sexual Behavior, 6,* 523-529.

Golden, C. (1987). Diversity and variability in women's sexual identities. In Boston Lesbian Psychologies Collective (Ed.), *Lesbian psychologies: Explorations and challenges* (pp. 19-34). Urbana: University of Illinois Press.

Ferguson, A. (1981). Compulsory heterosexuality and lesbian existence: Defining the issues. *Signs: Journal of Women in Culture and Society, 7,* 158-172.

Frye, M. (1990, August-September). Do you have to be a lesbian to be a feminist? *Off Our Backs,* pp. 21-23.

Harley, B. (1986). *Age in second language acquisition.* San Diego: College-Hill Press.

Kinsey, A., Pomeroy, W., & Martin, C. (1948). *Sexual behavior in the human male.* Philadelphia: Saunders.

Klein, F. (1990). The need to view sexual orientation as a multi-variable dynamic process: A theoretical perspective. In D. S. McWhirter, S. A. Sanders, & J. M. Reinisch (Eds.), *Homosexuality/heterosexuality: Concepts of sexual orientation.* New York: Oxford University Press.

Money, J. (1987). Homosexual gender identity and psychoneuroendocrinology. *American Psychologist, 42,* 384-399.

Money, J. (1988). *Gay, straight, and in between: The sexology of erotic orientation.* New York: Oxford University Press.

Near, H. (1990). *Fire in the rain . . . singer in the storm.* New York: William Morrow.

Northampton: The story so far . . . . (1990, June-July). *Bi Women,* pp. 1, 5-9.

Orlando, L. (1984, February 25). Loving whom we choose: bisexuality and the lesbian/gay community. *Gay Community News.*

Ponse, B. (1978). *Identities in the lesbian world.* Westport, CT: Greenwood.

Radicalesbians. (1973). Woman identified woman. In A. Koedt, E. Levine, & A. Rapone (Eds.), *Radical feminism* (pp. 240-245). New York: Quadrangle Books.

Rich, A. (1980). Compulsory heterosexuality and lesbian existence. *Signs: Journal of Women in Culture and Society, 5,* 631-660.

Richardson, D. (1984). The dilemma of essentiality in homosexual theory. *Journal of Homosexuality, 9*(2-3), 79-90.

Rubin, L. (1983). *Intimate strangers: Men and women together.* New York: Harper & Row.

Shively, M., & de Cecco, J. (1977). Components of sexual identity. *Journal of Homosexuality, 3,* 41-48.

Shuster, R. (1987). Sexuality as a continuum: The bisexual identity. In Boston Lesbian Psychologies Collective (Ed.), *Lesbian psychologies* (pp. 56-71). Urbana: University of Illinois Press.

Stiver, I. (1984). The meanings of "dependency" in female-male relationships. In J. Jordan, A. Kaplan, J. Baker Miller, I. Stiver, & J. Surrey (Eds.), *Women's growth in connnection: Writings from the Stone Center* (pp. 143-161). New York: Guilford.

Storms, M. (1981). A theory of erotic orientation development. *Psychological Review, 88,* 340-353.

Suppe, F. (1984). In defense of a multi-dimensional approach to sexual identity. *Journal of Homosexuality, 10*(3-4), 7-13.

The Feminists. (1970, June 5-19). Feminist resolutions. *Rat,* p. 9.

Zita, J. (1981). Compulsory heterosexuality and lesbian existence: Defining the issues. *Signs: Journal of Women in Culture and Society, 7,* 172-187.

4

Sexual Pride and Shame in Lesbians

SUZANNA ROSE

The euphoric views of lesbian sexuality accompanying 1970s feminism recently have been tempered by concerns about lesbians' sexual functioning. As a result, two contradictory attitudes concerning lesbian sexuality prevail currently. One celebrates lesbian sexuality as being highly physically and emotionally gratifying; the second holds that low sexual desire is often a problem in lesbian relationships. Both views have support. Findings that lesbians are more orgasmic in their relationships than heterosexual women confirm the idea that lesbian sex tends to be very satisfying (Masters & Johnson, 1979; Peplau & Amaro, 1982). In contrast, the low rate of sexual contact among lesbian couples compared with heterosexual and gay male couples (Blumstein & Schwartz, 1983) has caused alarm about "lesbian bed death," or the loss of passion in long-term relationships (McLaughlin, 1987). Proponents of the first view have countered by pointing out that what heterosexuals are counting as sexual relations are more likely to involve male orgasm than female; thus heterosexual sex may be more frequent but is not necessarily more fulfilling for women than lesbian sex (Frye, 1990). Those focusing on the lack of passion have emphasized the clinical evidence that identifies lack of sexual contact as a common problem among lesbians seeking couple therapy (Clunis & Green, 1988; Nichols, 1987; Rothblum & Brehony, 1993).

These two attitudes can be viewed as reflecting issues of sexual pride and shame, respectively, in lesbian relationships. Sexual pride results from a combination of feelings of joy and expressions of personal adequacy (Nathanson, 1987). In contrast, sexual shame underlies many of the psychological factors believed to inhibit desire, including intrapsychic conflicts, internalized homophobia, fear of failure, and responses to traumatic sexual experiences. Shame and the associated emotions of embarrassment and humiliation occur when perceived defects in the self are exposed (Kohut, 1971, 1977). Thus the issue of how sexual pride and shame develop and are expressed is important for understanding lesbian sexuality.

Self-psychology provides a useful starting point for exploring sexual pride and shame in more depth from a feminist perspective (Gardiner, 1987; Kohut, 1977). This framework, in turn, may be used to organize and examine current research on lesbian sexuality to determine the circumstances under which the two emotions are demonstrated.

Self-Psychology and Sexuality

Self-psychology posits that the development of the self involves two central psychological structures: (a) the grandiose self and (b) the idealized other (idealized parental imago) (Kohut, 1971). Each structure, in turn, may be linked hypothetically to specific areas of sexual expression. Extending self-psychology theory according to the following reasoning, the development of the grandiose self is predicted to affect bodily pride or shame; processes associated with the idealized other will affect interpersonal aspects of sexuality, such as feelings of entitlement to sexual pleasure and sexual self-confidence.

The grandiose self refers to the infant and young child's perception of himself or herself as the center of the universe and as all powerful. The responsiveness of parents and other self-objects (those who provide the psychological and material nurturant supplies the child needs for survival) to the child serves to shape the self. If parents are able to reflect, echo, approve, confirm, and admire the greatness and perfection of the child's grandiose self in an age-appropriate way, the child will develop a sense of pride and a mature, cohesive self. However, shame arises when the boundless exhibitionism of the grandiose self is not mirrored and approved by the self-objects.

In terms of sexuality, the theory can be extended to predict that bodily pride or shame will depend on how the self-objects respond to the child's physical and sexual self. If adults confirm the child's sense of physical perfection and competence and respond empathically to his or her natural exhibitionism and sexual curiosity, it is likely that bodily pride will result. In adulthood, bodily pride may be expressed in sexual terms via a positive body image and sexual curiosity. On the other hand, if children are deprived of adequate mirroring in the physical realm or are responded to inappropriately, as in the case of sexual abuse, bodily shame will develop.

In a separate but parallel process, the idealized other also affects the development of the self. As the child begins to confront his or her own vulnerability, the child will seek an idealized other who can make him or her feel safe and calm. If an adequate idealized other is available, the child will eventually be able to internalize parental soothing and regulating functions and so construct an internal emotional thermostat that provides stability. If the child is deprived of an idealized other by traumatic loss or disappointment, these characteristics would be weak or absent. The failures or inadequacies of self-objects will be attributed to perceived defects in the self, producing a sense of shame.

In terms of sexuality, it may be conjectured from theory that an internal emotional thermostat, if developed, would enable the individual to determine whether sexual problems originated in the self, partner, or other sources and to maintain a sense of entitlement to sexual pleasure independent of a partner's response. Sexual entitlement may be expressed in adulthood in terms of sexual self-confidence and positive attitudes toward initiating and receiving sexual pleasure. In contrast, deficits in the idealized other function might be expressed through self-blame for sexual problems or by adjusting sexual needs to suit the partner's level of interest.

Lesbian Sexuality

The question to be addressed here concerns to what extent sexual pride and shame are revealed by current research on lesbian sexuality. A self-psychology approach has been used above to identify two major areas in which these emotions are likely to be expressed and that provide a convenient way to organize specific findings. Although it is not possible from the available research to determine whether behaviors are linked to the developmental processes proposed, the framework provides insight as to what variables might be explored in future research.

Bodily Pride or Shame

The first area of sexual expression believed to result from the development of the grandiose self is bodily pride or shame. Specific sexual behaviors that could be classified as manifesting this aspect of sexuality include masturbation, oral sex practices, sexual curiosity, and body image. Each aspect will be discussed to determine whether pride or shame is associated with it.

One index of lesbians' bodily pride or shame may be reflected by masturbation practices. Most lesbians appear to engage in masturbation, suggesting that more pride than shame is associated with this act. Loulan (1987) reported that 89% of lesbians masturbate and that 86% usually experience orgasm through masturbation. These findings do not prove conclusively that lesbians are at ease with masturbation, however, because neither survey explored lesbians' attitudes toward the behavior.

Willingness to engage in oral sex is a second indicator of lesbians' attitudes about their bodies. Research indicates that a majority of lesbians are comfortable about performing or receiving oral sex, suggesting acceptance of or lack of shame about their genitalia. However, there is still a large percentage of lesbians who report being embarrassed by oral sex and seldom or never engage in it. Bell and Weinberg (1978) reported that 38% of the 228 white and 34% of the 64 black middle-class lesbians they surveyed had oral sex only a few times or not at all within the previous year. About 44% of the approximately 1,000 middle-class lesbians surveyed by Jay and Young (1979) had oral sex infrequently. Almost 33% of the 1,566 lesbians in Loulan's (1987) study did not ever receive oral sex from their partners. Blumstein and Schwartz (1983) reported that oral sex was not a usual sexual behavior for the majority of the 772 predominantly white middle-class lesbians they studied, although lesbians were more at ease about oral sex than heterosexual women. About 57% of lesbian couples had oral sex infrequently, and 4% never had oral sex. In addition, infrequent oral sex was associated with a less happy sex life and more arguments about sex (Blumstein & Schwartz, 1983). Thus a slim majority of lesbians appear to express sexual pride as evidenced by oral sex practices, but shame-related emotions such as embarrassment accompany the act for a large minority.

Sexual curiosity is a third behavior that might reflect bodily pride or shame. One rough measure of sexual curiosity about which there is some information on lesbians concerns the breadth of their sexual techniques. The evidence available suggests that many lesbians have a limited sexual repertoire. As stated earlier, a large number of lesbians infrequently or never engage in oral sex. Jay and Young (1979) also indicated that most lesbians had never engaged in "talking dirty" (64%), used a vibrator (75%), looked at pornography (71%), used a dildo (82% to 93%), or engaged in analingus (68%), to name a few options. Loulan (1987) found that less than 10% of the lesbians she sampled had ever acted out a sexual fantasy with their partners, engaged in manual vaginal or anal penetration, or used a vibrator; only 55% had masturbated their partners.

The narrow sexual repertoire of many lesbians implies that discomfort or shame may be associated with trying new techniques. Despite an increase in the availability of sex toys and erotic lesbian magazines and videotapes, sexual experimentation does not appear to be widely practiced even among the white, middle-class, urban lesbians that typically have been studied. Indeed, many of these behaviors are viewed as politically incorrect within the lesbian feminist community. For example, a majority of lesbians (59% to 67%) have negative attitudes about using dildos (Jay & Young, 1979). Consequently, it may be embarrassing for many lesbians to express an interest in such behaviors.

The question of how sexually curious lesbians are remains to be answered more fully, however. What is known is limited by what has been asked. Jay and Young (1979) included the most comprehensive list of sexual behaviors studied to date, but other research has not been as thorough. For instance, Loulan (1987) did not include tribadism (i.e., grinding, or clitoral stimulation obtained by pressing against a partner's body) in her list of sexual behaviors, even though it is the third most common sex technique used among lesbians as reported by Jay and Young (1979). Approximately 28% very frequently or always have orgasm by this means. Incidence of multiple orgasm also was not investigated. Bell and Weinberg (1978) and Blumstein and Schwartz (1983) either did not ask or did not report prevalence of anal stimulation among lesbians, although they did ask gay men. Duration of sex and types of sexual positions also have not been evaluated. Nor has research focused on lesbians' attitudes toward trying new behaviors, which might more accurately tap sexual curiosity than behavioral measures. Nevertheless, based on current research, the range of sexual techniques used by lesbians implies that more shame than pride is present.

A last indicator of bodily pride or shame concerns lesbians' body image. Little is known about this dimension of sexuality, but positive attitudes have been indicated more often than negative ones. Lesbians (83%) tend to be positive about their general physical appearance; only 38% report being negative about their weight (Jay & Young, 1979). Perceived attractiveness to others also appears to be high. Approximately 50% of white and 62% of black lesbians rated themselves as having above average homosexual sex appeal (Bell & Weinberg, 1978). Furthermore, Blumstein and Schwartz (1983) found that lesbians' happiness and satisfaction with their relationships were unaffected by their partners' physical beauty.

Other sources demonstrate that lesbians' body image is not uniformly positive. For instance, very few of the lesbians among thousands Loulan (1987) has addressed "absolutely loves her body" (p. 41). The androgynous lesbian sexual ideal, which deemphasizes noticeable breasts and hips, also hints at some rejection of female sex characteristics. For instance, although 68% of white and 52% of black lesbians emphasize body type and frame as important in selecting a partner, only 3% and 13%, respectively, preferred a partner with distinguishable hips (Jay & Young, 1979). Noticeable breasts were somewhat more acceptable to a minority; about 29% of white and 45% of black lesbians preferred partners with this attribute. Although there is clearly more to be learned about how lesbians feel about their own and their partner's sexual appearance, the research indicates that most lesbians, if not proud, are at least fairly comfortable with their body image.

Overall, in terms of the indications of bodily pride and shame explored here, lesbians exhibit pride. Most appear to be comfortable with masturbation, oral sex, and body image. Even so, a large minority report discomfort with these practices and a majority do not appear to express sexual curiosity by trying new techniques.

Entitlement to Sexual Pleasure

The second area of sexual expression believed to result from the development of the idealized other concerns feelings of entitlement (pride) or lack of entitlement (shame) to sexual pleasure. These feelings are likely to arise in an interpersonal context. An internal sense of sexual competence or a lack of confidence in the face of relationship problems also is hypothesized to originate from the idealized other structure. Specific behaviors that might tap this area include expectations about sexual satisfaction and orgasm, the ability to initiate and receive sex, and the ability to attend to a partner's needs.

Evidence concerning the importance of sexual satisfaction and orgasm in lesbian relationships is contradictory, implying that conflict along the pride-shame continuum exists. Unlike other couple types, low rates of sex did not affect overall satisfaction with the relationship among lesbians in the Blumstein and Schwartz (1983) study. Other research confirms the finding that sexual satisfaction is unrelated to relationship satisfaction among lesbians (Duffy & Rusbult, 1985-1986; Kurdek & Schmitt, 1986). On the other hand, sexual dissatisfaction and conflict over sex were more highly related to breakups among lesbians together more than 2 years than other couple types (Blumstein & Schwartz, 1983). The ambivalence about the role of sexuality in relationships implies that lesbians may feel shame about overtly and consciously valuing it.

Lesbian attitudes about orgasm appear to be somewhat more prideful. Of those surveyed by Jay and Young (1979), 49% said it was very important and 42% rated it somewhat important to achieve an orgasm during sex. Most appeared to be successful at reaching that goal: 89% frequently or always had an orgasm and 46% were frequently or always multiorgasmic. Almost 94% of Loulan's (1987) respondents were orgasmic with a partner. Other views of orgasm are less positive. Some lesbians think that having an orgasm as a goal of sex is male identified or too goal oriented. Loulan (1984) claimed orgasm was overrated and chastised lesbians for their "preoccupation with this particular muscle spasm" in a chapter called "The Tyranny of the Orgasm" (p. 71). In addition, most lesbians interviewed by Blumstein and Schwartz (1983) preferred nongenital physical contact such as hugging and cuddling to genital sex.

In terms of initiating sex, strong feelings of entitlement do not typify lesbians. A reluctance to initiate sex appears to be a major cause of the low rate of sexual contact among lesbians (Blumstein & Schwartz, 1983). Shame is not necessarily solely responsible for an unwillingness to take the lead, but it may be implicated partially. Some lesbians equate simply wanting or asking for sex with being sexually coercive or aggressive

(Blumstein & Schwartz, 1983; Nichols, 1987); others may have learned to ignore their sexual desires. For example, Nichols (1987) documented a case of a lesbian couple in sex therapy who had not had sex for the past 7 of their 10 years together. Although one woman was upset about the lack of sex, the couple had never fought about it. Her unwillingness to raise her concerns out of consideration for her partner or fear of conflict suggests a discomfort with meeting her own sexual needs. A more complete investigation would be needed to clarify motives, but the findings suggest that some lesbians view pursuing their own sexual satisfaction as inappropriate behavior.

The ability to attend to a partner's sexual needs seems to be a major area of pride among lesbians. They are much more concerned that their partner have an orgasm than that they have one themselves (Jay & Young, 1979). The stone-butch role, in which self-worth is derived from pleasing the partner, not the self, exemplifies this pattern. Although the stone-butch role appears to be on the decline, it still occurs among working-class lesbians (Nichols, 1987). Placing a partner's needs first may have some positive effects on a relationship, but it is likely that a woman who will not allow her partner to make love or touch her has feelings of shame concerning her sexuality that may have a detrimental effect as well.

Not all lesbians perceive their partners to be as responsive to them as the above research suggests. About 18% of white and 19% of black lesbians reported that their partners' failure to respond to their sexual requests was a serious sexual problem (Bell & Weinberg, 1978). About 17% of both groups also reported having difficulty responding to their partners' sexual requests. These results might indicate shame.

In sum, pride is more strongly revealed in lesbians' desire to please a partner than in the other three behaviors associated with feelings of entitlement to sexual pleasure. Ambivalence is more often associated with the importance of sexual satisfaction, orgasm, and initiating sex.

Developmental Issues

The self-psychology framework used here to examine lesbian sexuality revealed that bodily pride was more strongly in evidence than feelings of entitlement to sexual pleasure. This suggests that the development of the grandiose self is more secure than the idealized other function for many lesbians. Moreover, sexual shame across all behaviors was found for a large proportion of lesbians, indicating ruptures in both areas of the self. Whether the specific developmental processes proposed by self-psychology are implicated in pride or shame for the behaviors discussed is open to question. However, it is possible to speculate about how lesbians' development of self is affected by gender role socialization and how it may differ from that of other women as well as to suggest directions for future research based on the theory.

It is perhaps not surprising that shame in both areas of the sexual self was found for lesbians. What is of more interest is why lesbians appear to exhibit more pride in some areas than heterosexual women, even though they presumably share the same socialization. The gender socialization of girls and women virtually guarantees that outcomes connected to the grandiose self and idealized other are more likely to cause shame, regardless of a woman's sexual orientation. Girls and women are taught to be ashamed of their bodies and sexuality (Resneck-Sannes, 1991). Exhibitionistic strivings in females are usually severely and narrowly restricted to sexual attractiveness and caring for others (Boden, Hunt, & Kassoff, 1987).

The emphasis on sexual attractiveness is believed to distort girls' body image by failing to confirm their full physical grandiosity. Girls' physical competency is less encouraged than boys. As early in life as 24 hours postpartum, parents are significantly more likely to describe daughters as little, beautiful, pretty, and cute than sons, even when the infants do not differ in birth weight, length, or other measures of physical health (Rubin, Provenzano, & Luria, 1974). Parents are more likely to play vigorously with sons' arms and legs than daughters' and to treat girls as if they were more fragile (Maccoby & Jacklin, 1974). Boys are encouraged to engage in large motor activities, whereas parents are likely to criticize girls for running, jumping, and climbing (Fagot, 1978). Parents also give preschool- and elementary-school-age boys more freedom to roam in the physical environment than they do girls of the same age (Saegert & Hart quoted in Russo, 1985). In addition, adults, in general, are more likely to encourage large muscle activity in a child they believe to be male, rather than female (Sagert & Hart quoted in Russo, 1985). Shame concerning body weight also has been well-documented in girls and women (Silberstein, Striegel-Moore, & Rodin, 1987). Furthermore, inappropriate adult responses to girls' bodies are frequent. An estimated 31% of girls have been sexually abused by the age of 18 (Russell, 1984).

Girls' sexual curiosity and voyeuristic tendencies—aspects of the grandiose self—are curtailed strongly as well. Galenson and Roiphe (1980) reported an increase in girls' sexual curiosity by the age of 16 months; all 70 girls had expressed curiosity about mothers' bodies and somehow managed to see fathers' genitals by the age of three, even in modest families. Thereafter, however, girls usually confront a blockade of silence about female sexuality. The author reviewed 15 sex education books for young children available in public libraries and noted that none identified the clitoris on anatomical diagrams or discussed female orgasm. Few parents provide this information, leaving girls to learn about orgasm primarily through self-discovery, usually long past the age they are capable of it physically (Laws & Schwartz, 1977). Only 33% have masturbated by age 13 (Hunt, 1975), and some women never realize their capacity for orgasm.

The distorted mirroring girls receive for caring for others affects different aspects of sexuality. Girls learn that physically self-affirming behaviors are likely to embarrass their parents and that sexual needs conflict with parents' wishes. Thus girls learn that having sex without marriage or without love will disappoint parents. Because girls are primarily reinforced for caring for parents and, later on, partners, they learn to suppress their physical and sexual grandiosity and expect other girls and women to do so as well (Resneck-Sannes, 1991).

Women are also more likely to experience shame than men due to the lack of or disappointments in an idealizable other (Boden et al., 1987). Women generally are limited in the amount of safety and calm they can provide to a child, because women lack power as a group. However, if girls turn to the father as an idealized self-object, they usually are not supported in identifying with masculine values or goals. Deprived of an adequate idealized self-object and encouraged to care for others, girls will tend to attribute the inadequacies of the self-objects to perceived defects in the self. For instance, sexually abused girls often assume the blame for their abuse, thereby retaining what little attention is offered by parents as well as preserving the image of the idealized other (Miller, 1984). As adults, then, women have been groomed to place their partner's sexual needs above their own and to conform to the partner's sexual ideal rather than an internally produced one.

Although all women share many sexually shame-producing experiences, the degree to which lesbian sexuality conforms to the pattern described above has not yet been determined. Empirical evidence indicates that lesbians are more likely to be orgasmic than heterosexual women (Masters & Johnson, 1979; Peplau & Amaro, 1982). Other research has found that the use of large muscle groups is a correlate of sexual satisfaction in women (Fischer & Osofsky, 1967). Does this imply that lesbians develop more physical competency as children than heterosexual women? Obviously, more research would need to be done to establish a connection between sexual shame, orgasmic potential, and the antecedents of sexuality elaborated here. Questions about lesbians' sexual histories that need to be asked include parental responses to physical attributes and activities in childhood, sources of sex education and sexual values, incidence of sexual abuse, attributions about parental attitudes about sex and sexual abuse, and characteristics of idealized sexual images.

The extent to which shame or pride originates in lesbians' early developmental histories, as predicted by self-psychology, or is modified by self-objects later in life, is not possible to determine from existing sources. The interplay of personal and cultural influences also is difficult to sort out. The self-psychology framework used here is not intended to imply that pride or shame originates independent of cultural forces. These, too, would need to be more fully investigated.

In addition to possible differences in lesbians' and heterosexual women's developmental histories, pride-shame outcomes may be affected by at least four other cultural influences. First, heterosexual women enjoy heterosexual privilege, which ensures that their choice of partner and sexual behaviors are celebrated, whereas lesbians experience the shame or denial of such privileges. Second, lesbians have partners who have had similar gender-based shame-producing experiences regarding sex; heterosexual women do not. Third, lesbians do not have a power difference based on gender built into their relationships, which might reduce shame about some aspects of sexuality. Fourth, lesbian culture, as well as childhood development, may play a role in the observed differences. For instance, lesbians who are willing to participate in research are likely to be feminists. They may be more likely to have been affected by the freeing influence feminism has had on women's sexuality via the positive sexual images promoted by Dodson's celebration of masturbation and vulvas, Chicago's *Dinner Party,* and recent discoveries about the anatomy of the clitoris (Federation of Feminist Women's Health Centers, 1981), to name a few.

Conclusions

This self-psychology analysis reveals that sexual pride in lesbians is more likely to be expressed in terms of self-image than in the interpersonal realm, although many lesbians are inhibited in both areas. Difficulties in saying "I want, I need, I require, I deserve" sexual pleasure are hypothesized to stem from the failure of self-objects (parents and lovers) to affirm the exhibitionistic strivings of the grandiose self (Boden et al., 1987). Attributing blame for self-object failures to the self and wishing to please the partner more than the self are believed to result from deficiencies in the idealizing function. Thus exploring the origins of pride and shame has been shown to be a useful approach for understanding lesbian sexuality, particularly in terms of classifying behaviors, making predictions, and developing avenues for future research.

References

Bell, A. P., & Weinberg, M. S. (1978). *Homosexualities.* New York: Simon & Schuster.

Boden, R., Hunt, P., & Kassoff, B. (1987, March). *The centrality of shame in the psychology of women.* Paper presented at the Association for Women in Psychology conference, Denver, CO.

Blumstein, P., & Schwartz, P. (1983). *American couples.* New York: William Morrow.

Chicago, J. (1979). *The dinner party: A symbol of our heritage.* Garden City, NY: Doubleday.

Clunis, D. M., & Green, G. D. (1988). *Lesbian couples.* Seattle: Seal Press.

Dodson, B. (1974). *Liberating masturbation: A meditation on self love.* New York: Body Sex Designs.

Duffy, S. M., & Rusbult, C. E. (1985-1986). Satisfaction and commitment in homosexual and heterosexual relationships. *Journal of Homosexuality, 12,* 1-23.

Fagot, B. (1978). The influence of sex of child on parental reactions to toddler children. *Child Development, 49,* 462.

Federation of Feminist Women's Health Centers. (1981). *A new view of a woman's body.* New York: Simon & Schuster.

Fischer, S., & Osofsky, H. (1967). Sexual responsiveness in women. *Archives of General Psychiatry, 17,* 214-226.

Frye, M. (1990). Lesbian sex. In J. Allen (Ed.), *Lesbian philosophies and cultures* (pp. 305-315). New York: SUNY.

Galenson, E., & Roiphe, H. (1980). Some suggested revisions concerning early female development. In M. Kirkpatrick (Ed.), *Women's sexual development* (pp. 83-106). New York: Plenum.

Gardiner, J. K. (1987). Self psychology as feminist theory. *Signs: The Journal of Women in Culture and Society, 12*(4), 761-780.

Hunt, M. (1975). *Sexual behavior in the 1970s.* New York: Dell.

Jay, K., & Young, A. (1979). *The gay report.* New York: Summit.

Kohut, H. (1971). *The analysis of self.* New York: International Universities Press.

Kohut, H. (1977). *The restoration of self.* New York: International Universities Press.
Kurdek, L. A., & Schmitt, J. P. (1986). Early development of relationship quality in heterosexual married, heterosexual cohabiting, gay, and lesbian couples. *Developmental Psychology, 22,* 305-309.
Laws, J. L., & Schwartz, P. (1977). *Sexual scripts.* Washington, DC: University Press of America.
Loulan, J. (1984). *Lesbian sex.* San Francisco: Spinsters Ink.
Loulan, J. (1987). *Lesbian passion.* San Francisco: Spinsters Ink.
Maccoby, E. E., & Jacklin, C. M. (1974). *The psychology of sex differences.* Stanford, CA: Stanford University Press.
Masters, W., & Johnson, V. (1979). *Homosexuality in perspective.* Boston: Little, Brown.
McLaughlin, J. (1987, October 10). *Sex and politics town meeting.* Speech presented at the Lesbian and Gay March on Washington, DC.
Miller, A. (1984). *Thou shalt not be aware.* New York: New American Library.
Nathanson, D. M. (1987). The shame-pride axis. In H. B. Lewis (Ed.), *The role of shame in symptom formation* (pp. 183-206). Hillsdale, NJ: Lawrence Erlbaum.
Nichols, M. (1987). Lesbian sexuality: Issues and developing theory. In Boston Lesbian Psychologies Collective (Ed.), *Lesbian psychologies* (pp. 97-125). Chicago: University of Illinois Press.
Peplau, A., & Amaro, H. (1982). Understanding lesbian relationships. In W. Paul, J. D. Weinrich, J. C. Gonsiorek, & M. E. Hotvedt (Eds.), *Homosexuality: Social psychological and biological issues* (pp. 233-247). Beverly Hills, CA: Sage.
Resneck-Sannes, H. (1991). Shame, sexuality, and vulnerability. *Women and Therapy, 11,* 111-126.
Rothblum, E. D., & Brehony, K. A. (1993). *Boston marriages: Romantic but asexual relationships among contemporary lesbians.* Amherst: University of Massachusetts.
Rubin, J., Provenzano, F., & Luria, Z. (1985). The eye of the beholder: Parents' views on sex of newborns. In J. H. Williams (Ed.), *Psychology of women: Selected readings* (2nd ed., pp. 147-154). New York: Norton. (Original work published 1974)
Russell, D. (1984). *Sexual exploitation.* Beverly Hills: Sage.
Russo, N. F. (1985). Sex role stereotyping, socialization and sexism. In A. G. Sargent (Ed.), *Beyond sex roles* (pp. 150-167). New York: West.
Silberstein, L. R., Striegel-Moore, R., & Rodin, J. (1987). Feeling fat: A woman's shame. In H. B. Lewis (Ed.), *The role of shame in symptom formation* (pp. 89-108). Hillsdale, NJ: Lawrence Erlbaum.

5

Lesbians and Physical Appearance

Which Model Applies?

ESTHER D. ROTHBLUM

Lesbians are women who wear comfortable shoes.
—Robin Williams in *Good Morning, Vietnam!*

Being female means being told how to look. The overwhelming majority of television and magazine advertisements are related to products that enhance the physical attractiveness of women (Dermer & Thiel, 1975; Downs & Harrison, 1985). Social psychologists have developed a large body of literature on physical attractiveness (see Berscheid & Walster, 1984, for a review). Feminist scholars have critically examined the relationship between gender and appearance (e.g., Brownmiller, 1984; Chapkis, 1986; Daly, 1978; Wolf, 1991).

There has been little emphasis on how lesbians are affected by society's emphasis on physical appearance for women. Given this lack of research, this chapter speculates on six ways in which appearance may affect lesbians. First, lesbians, as all women, grow up surrounded by institutions that value physical appearance. Second, lesbians are not in sexual relationships with men, and this may lessen the importance of standard appearance norms. Third, research on stereotypes indicates that the dominant culture has extremely negative attitudes about lesbians, including lesbians' appearance. Fourth, the process of identifying with the lesbian culture may depend on the ability to recognize and be recognized by other lesbians, and thus on physical appearance. Fifth, lesbians who are also members of other minority groups may be invisible or may need to choose which group to identify with. Finally, the lesbian community itself has norms for physical appearance and these have changed over the course of the century.

The Value of Physical Appearance

Women are socialized to value their physical appearance, and lesbians are women. There is an enormous psychological literature on the effects of physical appearance. Berscheid and Walster (1984) introduced the phrase "what is beautiful is good" to describe the fact that people who are physically attractive are perceived as having a number of positive personality characteristics, occupations of greater prestige, and more fulfilling lives than are unattractive people. Berscheid and Walster also found physical attractiveness to be more important for women than for men. Appearance norms for women include most facial features (e.g., eyes, eyebrows, nose, lips, and cheeks), body parts (breasts, thighs, waist, and hips), weight, skin color, age, clothing, makeup, and posture (see Rothblum, in press, for a review of this literature). As Dworkin (1988) stated:

> Women and men in our society undergo a different socialization process. From early childhood women are taught that their appearance is a crucial aspect of their lives whereas men are taught that their accomplishments are what counts. Not only is appearance important for a woman but the appearance must come as close as possible to whatever the current media image of women happens to be. Often that image can only be achieved by a minority of the population. The end result of this impossible quest is that most women are unhappy with their bodies and suffer from negative body image. (p. 27)

Lesbians, too, are socialized as girls and women to value physical attractiveness. Most lesbians work and socialize with heterosexual people and are influenced by appearance norms in the media. Dworkin (1988) described how lesbians' occupational roles are affected by the privilege that comes with an acceptable physical appearance. As lesbians work, relax, and live, their coworkers, supervisors, neighbors, biological relatives, teachers, and friends may be unaware of their sexual orientation. Thus lesbians may be as restricted by the appearance mandates for women as are heterosexual women. Brand, Rothblum, and Solomon (1992) found, for example, that both lesbians and heterosexual women were more likely to experience dissatisfaction with their bodies, greater concern with their weight, and more frequent dieting than did gay and heterosexual men. In that study, gender was more salient than sexual orientation.

Physical Appearance and Sexual Relationships

Women's physical appearance is important in sexual relationships with men, and lesbians are not in relationships with men. Lesbians differ from heterosexual women in the crucial fact that they are not involved in sexual relationships with men. This is true for all women who are exclusively lesbian, no matter how closeted they are and no matter how integrated they are into occupational and social roles with heterosexual people.

The research on physical attractiveness has found that the reason why physical attractiveness is important, particularly for women, is that it is related to social and sexual attractiveness. Physical attractiveness for women affects number of dates and overall popularity (see Rothblum, in press, for a review), and physically attractive women report having been in love more often and having had more sexual partners than do women who are not physically attractive (Berscheid & Walster, 1984). Men's social status often results more from the physical attractiveness of the women they are with than with their own attractiveness (Berscheid & Walster, 1984). When men were asked how much they liked their dates and how much they would like to date their partner again, the only variable determining these factors was the physical attractiveness of their dates (Walster, Aronson, Abrahams, & Rottman, 1966).

The fact that lesbians are sexually independent from men would argue that societal pressures regarding physical attractiveness may be less salient for lesbians. In this vein, Brown (1987) described lesbians' greater acceptance with body weight and with personal power. Brand et al. (1992) speculated that heterosexual women and gay men (two groups that are sexually involved with men) would be more concerned with their weight than lesbians and heterosexual men (two groups that are not sexually involved with men). Their results provided some partial support for this hypothesis, with heterosexual women and gay men more preoccupied with their weight and reporting lower ideal weights than did lesbians or heterosexual men.

The idea that lesbians are less affected by physical appearance norms has also been borne out by studies of personal ads. A study by Deaux and Hanna (1984) examined 800 personal advertisements by lesbians, gay men, and heterosexual women and men. Gay men were more likely to seek physical attractiveness, other specified physical characteristics (e.g., height, weight, and hair color), and sexual characteristics. They were also more likely to offer financial assets, indicate their race or ethnicity, and describe their physical characteristics. Lesbians were more likely to describe and to seek specific personality traits (e.g., intelligent, sense of humor, loving, and caring), to seek sincerity, and to suggest the potential of a long-term relationship. Heterosexual women were most likely to offer physical attractiveness, and lesbians were least likely to do so. Heterosexual women were also least likely to indicate their age, and most likely to seek financial security and status, occupational information, and sincerity. Lesbians were least likely to ask for a photograph and also least likely to offer or ask for other physical characteristics. Gay men were most likely to offer and seek physical and sexual characteristics, and were second to heterosexual women in offers of physical attractiveness. It seems that heterosexual women and gay men are somewhat similar in that the group they are trying to attract (i.e., men) seems to demand more physical attractiveness and physical characteristics. Deaux and Hanna (1984) concluded:

> In terms of general sex differences, our results suggest that men are more concerned with objective and physical characteristics, while women are more interested in the psychological aspects of a potential relationship. . . . We might suggest that the heterosexual relationship sets up certain expectations for women, and the woman who chooses a different (homosexual) type of relationship is free to define herself in different ways, responding to a lessened (or at least a different) set of role demands. (p. 374)

Webbink (1981) noted that lesbian images in photography often portray lesbians as assuming a relaxed and casual stance, with their hands in their pockets. This stance indicates that lesbians may be more comfortable with their bodies and themselves than are heterosexual women.

Attitudes About the Appearance of Lesbians

The dominant culture holds negative attitudes about the appearance of lesbians. Surveys indicate that society at large holds extremely negative attitudes toward lesbians. The majority of people in the United States consider homosexuals—including lesbians—to be immoral, unhappy, and harmful (see Rothblum, 1988, for a review). People who have the most favorable attitudes toward lesbians are college-educated, under age 30, and live in urban areas (Nyberg & Alston, 1976-1977).

The dominant society also holds negative stereotypes about the appearance of lesbians. Dew (1985) asked college students to rate the attractiveness of photographs of women. She then told the raters that half the women were lesbians and asked them to determine which ones were. Raters generally selected photographs of unattractive women as lesbians. They also tended to rate lesbians as less attractive than, not dressing as well as, not having as pretty a face as, not having as attractive a hair style as, and as not being as desirable to meet as heterosexual women.

Nyberg and Alston (1976-1977) found that lesbians who were described as masculine were more disliked by heterosexual college students than were lesbians described as feminine or neutral; in contrast, heterosexual women had more latitude so that even women described as masculine were liked. In this study, the group that received the highest ratings were heterosexual feminine women, who were often described as normal, agreeable, and nice. The group that received the lowest ratings were masculine lesbians, who were often described as unappealing, disagreeable, and hostile.

A study by Unger, Hilderbrand, and Madar (1982) asked college students to sort photographs of women and men into groups. Some of the students were told to sort the photographs into homosexuals versus heterosexuals. Generally, female and male college students chose the less attractive photographs of women for the homosexual group, whereas female students (but not males) chose the less attractive photographs of men for the homosexual group.

Dew's (1985) study found that female students with intolerant attitudes about homosexuality were more likely to select unattractive women as lesbians than were female students with tolerant attitudes. Male students, regardless of their tolerance for homosexuality, chose unattractive women as lesbians. Dew (1985) stated:

> One explanation (for this gender difference) may lie in the observation that, unlike men, women have an organized social movement which brings both homosexual and heterosexual women together and encourages them to be more aware of certain social issues which affect all women. For those who become involved in, or at least aware of, this movement, the importance of differences in sexual orientation may be reduced. . . . Men may not currently have the same opportunity for contact with homosexual men or women. (p. 152)

Laner and Laner (1980) examined variables that seem to increase or decrease college students' liking of lesbians and gay men. They found that lesbians who were most liked were those whose physical appearance was most conventional, according to heterosexual standards; that is, they appeared moderately feminine. This increases the pressure for lesbians to fit in with heterosexual appearance norms.

Lesbians and Biculturality

Most lesbians function in two environments: the heterosexual macrostructure and the lesbian community. Lukes and Land (1990) have described how members of minority groups become bicultural within the majority and minority cultures. They point out that lesbians and gay men differ from members of other minority groups in this process. Most minority groups first become acculturated within their own group and then later are socialized (by schools, media, and church) within the dominant culture. Lesbians and gay men, however, are first socialized by the dominant culture and later identify with the minority culture. One of the factors that aids in bicultural socialization is physical appearance (de Anda, 1984; Lukes & Land, 1990). Again, unlike members of some minority groups (e.g., African-Americans and people with physical disabilities), lesbians and gay men are not identifiable as such. Lukes and Land (1990) state:

> Those who do not fit the stereotype held by the majority culture may pass as heterosexual . . . and assume the advantages and privileges held by members of the dominant culture or other minority culture. However, because sexual minorities are not easily identifiable to those in other cultures, they also are not easily identifiable to each other. Because there is no protective coloration of the group, this can inhibit identification with their minority group members. In the complex web of when and how homosexuals decide to disclose

> their homosexuality, some may choose to do so by dressing in a stereotypical manner. Those who display stereotypical traits become publicly visible, an act that exposes them to others who share similar values. (p. 159)

Whereas members of most minority groups need to adopt the physical appearance (e.g., clothing and mannerisms) of the dominant culture, lesbians and gay men need to learn how to look like and recognize members of their minority culture. De Anda (1984) identified the following roles as part of this learning process: cultural translators (people who have successfully undergone bicultural socialization and who promote and explain the new culture), mediators (people who provide information), and models (people who identify with the culture and serve as role models). Again, for lesbians and gay men, these roles will be held by people who need to be recognizable to newly out lesbians and gay men and who need to explain the minority, rather than the dominant, culture to lesbians and gay men.

Lesbians and Multiculturality

In the dominant white male culture, lesbians are members of two minority groups: They are women as well as sexual minorities. In addition, many lesbians are members of other minority groups, for example, African-Americans, Latinas, Asian-Americans, Native Americans, Jews, refugees, immigrants, women with disabilities, older women, and/or fat women. Lesbians who are polycultural (Espin, 1987) may be more visible as members of other minority groups (e.g., Vietnamese or women with spinal cord injuries) than as lesbians. They may have had more years and even decades of experience as members of these other minority groups than with being lesbians who are out.

People who identify as African-American differ widely in the color of their skin. Since the days of slavery, African-Americans whose skin was lighter and who had Caucasian features such as straight hair, narrow noses, thin lips, and light-colored eyes had greater societal privileges (Neal & Wilson, 1989). In the early half of this century, African-Americans of differing physical features, such as skin color, came from all different socioeconomic backgrounds, but those with light skin and Caucasian features were assumed to have higher status (Neal & Wilson, 1989). This status difference was particularly salient for African-American women, whose light skin color was associated with desirability as a marital partner and with upward economic mobility. However, although light skin color was valued among African-Americans, appearing to be Caucasian was not.

After the civil rights movement of the 1960s, African-Americans began to define their own standards of beauty. Slogans such as "Black Is Beautiful" and "Black Pride" focused on the advantages of African-American heritage. The Afro hair style became a symbol of pride in African-American features, and Caucasians permed their hair to achieve a similar look (Neal & Wilson, 1989). Nevertheless, the media still portray African-Americans as models who appear nearly Caucasian. Thus, for example, Vanessa Williams, the first African-American woman to become Miss America (in 1983) had light skin, reddish hair, and green eyes (Neal & Wilson, 1989). The cosmetic industry continues to advertise products for lightening skin, straightening hair, and using tinted contact lenses to lighten eye color.

Brownmiller (1984) has speculated that men's darker skin color symbolizes men's greater freedom to be outdoors and to wear scantier clothing, whereas there is a mandate for women to be delicate and pale. It is possible that African-American lesbians have more flexibility regarding skin color than do heterosexual African-American women, due to their independence from men, but there has been no research on this. Similarly, there is little research on physical attractiveness norms affecting women of different ethnic groups other than African-Americans.

Estimates are that 1 in 10 Americans has a disability, and because some disabilities increase with age, women (who live longer than men) are disproportionately affected (Deegan & Brooks, 1985). Disabilities also affect women more than men, because women with disabilities fit neither the reproductive nor the sexualized role image of women in our society (Fine & Asch, 1985).

Women with disabilities are stereotyped as either happy, humble, and grateful or as embittered (Altman, 1985). As Thompson (1985) stated, "Our physical appearance, for example, does not fit any traditional standards: we fit neither 'mother' nor 'whore' images found in the straight world, and we are certainly a far cry from the strong, tough dyke model" (p. 80). In contrast to able-bodied women, who are objectified as sexual beings, women with disabilities are often desexualized to the degree that they are considered unmarriageable and "unfit to be mothers" (Connors, 1985, p. 104). They are ignored by the media, who perceive them as unable to engage in the many cosmetic and domestic tasks necessary for able-bodied women (Connors, 1985). Women with disabilities have been termed to experience "sexism without the pedestal" (Fine & Asch, 1985, p. 6). Among women who have disabilities, their degree of acceptability is often a direct result of how they pass as able-bodied (Thompson, 1985). As Browne, Connors, and Stern (1985) stated:

> Feminine beauty is manufactured by cosmetic and fashion industries and changes seasonally. Our self worth suffers when we respond to this sexual objectification. Disabled women have been excluded from patriarchal conceptions of beauty and sexuality. Again, we are encouraged to see our bodies and our selves as distinct. *Our* beauty is reserved for the inside. (p. 246)

Espin (1987) has described the issue of choosing between two separate minority cultures that many lesbians face. As one woman stated:

> It is a very painful question because I feel I am both [Cuban/Latin and a lesbian], and I don't want to have to choose. Clearly, straight people don't even get asked this question and it is unfair that we have to discuss it, even if it is just a questionnaire. (p. 47)

Physical Appearance and the Lesbian Community

The lesbian community has always had norms for physical appearance, and these norms have changed with times just as norms for women's appearance changed in the dominant culture (see Faderman, 1991, for a review of this literature). Appearance norms in the lesbian community have had two functions: (a) to provide a means for members of an often invisible and oppressed group to identify one another without being identifiable by the dominant culture and (b) to provide a group identity and thus separate norms from the dominant culture.

In the late 19th century, medical specialists wrote about women, particularly working-class women, who dressed in a masculine way, and connected this style of dress with same-gender sexual relations (e.g., Westphal quoted in Faderman, 1991). Because women never wore pants, those women who did passed easily as men and often lived their lives as men who were involved with or married to other women until they were discovered during medical treatment or military duty (Faderman,

1991). Before this time period and its nascent focus on women's sexuality, women who lived together and expressed love for each other were seen as engaging in normative female behavior (Faderman, 1981).

In the 1920s, being lesbian was chic for women who were bohemian, and lesbian subcultures emerged among black and white lesbians in Harlem and Greenwich Village (Faderman, 1991). However, it was World War II that was instrumental in creating a lesbian subculture in the United States. Faderman (1991) stated:

> Since hundreds of thousands of women who worked in war factory jobs during the early 1940s were actually obliged to wear pants, they had become a permanent part of American women's wardrobe, and they continued to be so after the war. The lesbian who loathed dresses felt much freer to wear pants out of doors than she had in the prewar years. Pants soon became a costume and a symbol that allowed women who defined themselves as lesbians to identify each other. (p. 126)

According to Faderman (1991), the military also was indirectly responsible for the formation of lesbian communities in large urban areas like San Francisco, Boston, and New York by discharging military personnel in these port areas.

In the 1950s, butch and femme roles for lesbians became common, and the norms for lesbians in these roles were extremely specific. Lesbians who were not clearly butch or femme were termed *kiki* and were unwelcome. Faderman (1991) stated:

> Perhaps the tyranny of "appropriate" butch and femme dress in working-class bars can be explained in part by patrons' fears: A Columbus, Ohio, woman recalls walking into a lesbian bar in the 1950s and finding that no one would speak to her. After some hours, the waitress told her it was because of the way she was dressed—no one could tell what her sexual identity was, butch or femme, and they were afraid that if she did not know enough to dress right it was because she was a policewoman. (pp. 164-165)

Middle-class and wealthy lesbians tended to avoid butch/femme appearance and were more likely to pass as heterosexual. They often condemned butch/femme roles as increasing society's negative attitudes about lesbians. The organization Daughters of Bilitis urged its middle-class readership to adopt "a mode of behavior and dress acceptable to society" (*The Ladder,* quoted in Faderman, 1991, p. 180). Middle-class lesbians were encouraged to wear feminine, professional clothing and not to appear lesbian. Faderman points out that the same message to blend in reemerged in 1989 with the publication of the book *After the Ball.* Consequently, it was poor and working-class lesbians who communicated through their appearance to the dominant culture that lesbians existed, who were portrayed in the media, and who paid for this by frequent police raids in bars and arrests.

Appearance norms in the lesbian culture remained constant in the 1960s even while the dominant culture underwent tremendous changes in dress and appearance (Faderman, 1991). In the 1970s, however, androgyny became the norm for lesbians (Loulan, 1990). Lesbian feminists wore flannel shirts, blue jeans, no jewelry, and no makeup. They wore their hair very short. To a large extent, heterosexual feminists dressed the same way (Loulan, 1990). Whereas in the past a lesbian couple often included one butch and one femme, both members of a lesbian couple in the 1970s looked alike. Loulan (1990) described a concept she referred to as "twinning" as follows:

> Twins are lesbians who bond with other women who look and act very much like themselves. You might think of couples you know that would fit this description. Women who can and do enjoy wearing each other's clothes, not because they wear the same size but because they truly share each other's taste and style. Women who have the same energy, not who just adjust to each other's pace. (p. 154)

Lesbians who did not appear androgynous were termed politically incorrect. In particular, old-culture lesbians who still played butch or femme roles were criticized (Loulan, 1990, p. 41).

Loulan (1990) described lesbian archetypes as part of the lesbian "collective unconscious" (p. 17). She argued that the butch/femme role is one of the most common lesbian archetypes and one that was revolutionary for lesbians in previous decades, yet one that lesbians today prefer to deny or about which they are embarrassed. In her public lectures, she has found that fewer than 5% of lesbians have never rated themselves or been rated by others as butch or femme. Despite this near-universal experience, lesbians dismiss the butch/femme archetype. Interestingly, lesbians who practiced S-M (sadomasochism) in the 1980s reclaimed role-playing in their dress by wearing leather and other symbols indicating their preference for sadism or masochism (see Faderman, 1991, for a review). Nevertheless, lesbian S-M became a major controversy in the 1980s, pitting lesbians who were politically correct against those who were sexually adventurous.

The 1970s introduced a number of terms in the lesbian community that referred to appearance. *Baby dykes* were young and newly out. *Downtown dykes* wore business suits and had executive jobs. *Earth mothers* were nurturant and spiritual. *Jocks* played on the local lesbian softball team. *Bad girls* shocked the lesbian community with their nonconformity in dress and behavior. And the *lesbian police* set standards for what was appropriate (Loulan, 1990). Lesbian communities and friendship circles coined their own terminology, as did the woman in Syracuse who referred to lesbians with strict rules as "lavnecks" (lavender rednecks) (Faderman, 1991, p. 231). Lesbians wore symbols of their culture (pink triangle, labyris, interlocking women's symbols) on their clothes, and the advertising, fashion, and publishing industries used these symbols (e.g., items in lavender or purple colors) to attract lesbian customers.

The 1980s reflected greater diversity in the lesbian communities, as multicultural lesbians became more visible or established their own lesbian organizations and neighborhoods. The lesbian baby boom resulted in pregnant lesbians and lesbians rearing children. The tolerance for lesbian and gay activities on college campuses in the 1970s resulted in educated lesbians with financial and occupational power, including the power to be out in their professions. A new term, *lipstick lesbian,* referred to lesbians who wore dresses and makeup. In their song "You Can't Tell the Girls From the Boys," the gay male performers Romanovsky and Phillips parody the old days when lesbians wore work shirts and gay men wore earrings; now, they state, lesbians wear dresses and even heterosexual men wear earrings.

Conclusion

In sum, lesbians may be affected by the appearance norms of the dominant culture to a similar, or lesser, degree than are heterosexual women. In addition, the appearance norms of the lesbian community may affect lesbians, particularly lesbians who are newly out and who are thus dependent on physical appearance to be recognized by and to recognize similar others. Multicultural lesbians may be additionally affected by appearance norms of other minority communities.

There has been little research that has investigated the influence of physical appearance on lesbians. This paucity of research is in stark contrast to the enormous literature on the factors of physical appearance among heterosexual women. There are a number of research questions that would be of interest to lesbian-affirmative psychologists and lesbian participants. First, how do lesbians perceive attractiveness? Is it important? Does it include physical attributes as well as personality characteristics (e.g., sense of humor and warmth)? How does physical attractiveness affect lesbians over the lifespan? How does it change for lesbians once they come out? How does it affect multicultural lesbians and lesbians from specific minority cultures? To what degree do lesbians change their physical appearance (e.g., clothing) when interacting with the dominant versus the lesbian cultures? This chapter presented six models that might explain the role of physical appearance among lesbians. Future research can determine the relative importance of these models in affecting physical appearance in the lesbian community.

References

Altman, B. M. (1985). Disabled women and the social structure. In S. E. Browne, D. Connors, & N. Stern (Eds.), *With the power of each breath: A disabled women's anthology* (pp. 69-76). San Francisco: Cleis.

Berscheid, E., & Walster, E. (1984). Physical attractiveness. *Advances in Experimental Social Psychology, 18,* 157-215.

Brand, P. A., Rothblum, E. D., & Solomon, L. J. (1992). A comparison of lesbians, gay men, and heterosexuals on weight and restrained eating. *International Journal of Eating Disorders, 11,* 253-259.

Brown, L. S. (1987). Lesbians, weight and eating: New analyses and perspectives. In Boston Lesbian Psychologies Collective (Ed.), *Lesbian psychologies: Explorations and challenges* (pp. 294-309). Urbana: University of Illinois Press.

Browne, S. E., Connors, D., & Stern, N. (1985). This body I love: Finding ourselves. In S. E. Browne, D. Connors, & N. Stern (Eds.), *With the power of each breath: A disabled women's anthology* (pp. 246-247). San Francisco: Cleis.

Brownmiller, S. (1984). *Femininity.* New York: Fawcett Columbine.

Chapkis, W. (1986). *Beauty secrets: Women and the politics of appearance.* Boston: South End Press.

Connors, D. (1985). Disability, sexism, and the social order. In S. E. Browne, D. Connors, & N. Stern (Eds.), *With the power of each breath: A disabled women's anthology* (pp. 92-107). San Francisco: Cleis.

Daly, M. (1978). *Gyn/ecology.* Boston: Beacon.

de Anda, D. (1984). Bicultural socialization: Factors affecting the minority experience. *Social Work, 29,* 101-107.

Deegan, M. J., & Brooks, N. A. (1985). *Women and disability: The double handicap.* New Brunswick, NJ: Transaction.

Deaux, K., & Hanna, R. (1984). Courtship in the personals column: The influence of gender and sexual orientation. *Sex Roles, 11,* 363-375.

Dermer, M., & Thiel, D. L. (1975). When beauty may fail. *Journal of Personality and Social Psychology, 31,* 1168-1176.

Dew, M. A. (1985). The effect of attitudes on inferences of homosexuality and perceived physical attractiveness in women. *Sex Roles, 12,* 143-155.

Downs, A. C., & Harrison, S. K. (1985). Embarrassing age spots or just plain ugly? Physical attractiveness stereotyping as an instrument of sexism on American television commercials. *Sex Roles, 13,* 9-19.

Dworkin, S. H. (1988). Not in man's image: Lesbians and the cultural oppression of body weight. *Women and Therapy, 8,* 27-39.

Espin, O. M. (1987). Issues of identity in the psychology of Latina lesbians. In Boston Lesbian Psychologies Collective (Ed.), *Lesbian psychologies: Explorations and challenges* (pp. 35-51). Urbana: University of Illinois Press.

Faderman, L. (1981). *Surpassing the love of men: Romantic friendships and love between women from the Renaissance to the present.* New York: William Morrow.

Faderman, L. (1991). *Odd girls and twilight lovers: A history of lesbian life in twentieth-century America.* New York: Columbia University Press.

Fine, M., & Asch, A. (1985). Disabled women: Sexism without the pedestal. In M. J. Deegan & N. A. Brooks (Eds.), *Women and disability: The double handicap* (pp. 6-22). New Brunswick, NJ: Transaction.

Laner, M. R., & Laner, R. H. (1980). Sexual preference or personal style? Why lesbians are disliked. *Journal of Homosexuality, 5,* 339-356.

Loulan, J. A. (1990). *The lesbian erotic dance: Butch, femme, androgyny and other rhythms.* San Francisco: Spinster.

Lukes, C. A., & Land, H. (1990). Biculturality and homosexuality. *Social Work, 35,* 155-161.

Neal, A. M., & Wilson, M. L. (1989). The role of skin color and features in the Black community: Implications for black women and therapy. *Clinical Psychology Review, 9,* 323-333.

Nyberg, K. L., & Alston, J. P. (1976-1977). Analysis of public attitudes toward homosexual behavior. *Journal of Homosexuality, 2,* 99-107.

Rothblum, E. D. (1988). Introduction: Lesbianism as a model of a positive lifestyle for women. *Women and Therapy, 8,* 1-12.

Rothblum, E. D. (in press). I'll die for the revolution but don't ask me not to diet: Feminism and the continuing stigmatization of obesity. In S. Woolley, M. Katzman, & P. Fallon (Eds.), *Feminist perspectives on eating disorders.* New York: Guilford.

Thompson, D. (1985). Anger. In S. E. Browne, D. Connors, & N. Stern (Eds.), *With the power of each breath: A disabled women's anthology* (pp. 78-85). San Francisco: Cleis.

Unger, R. K., Hilderbrand, M., & Madar, T. (1982). Physical attractiveness and assumptions about social deviance: Some sex-by-sex comparisons. *Personality and Social Psychology Bulletin, 8,* 293-301.

Walster, E., Aronson, V., Abrahams, D., & Rottman, L. (1966). Importance of physical attractiveness in dating behavior. *Journal of Personality and Social Psychology, 4,* 508-516.

Webbink, P. (1981). Nonverbal behavior and lesbian/gay orientation. In C. Mayo & N. M. Henley (Eds.), *Gender and nonverbal behavior* (pp. 253-260). New York: Springer-Verlag.

Wolf, N. (1991). *The beauty myth: How images of beauty are used against women.* New York: William Morrow.

6

Boundaries in Lesbian Therapist–Client Relationships

NANETTE K. GARTRELL

Introduction

Lesbian therapists who are active participants in the lesbian community face unique challenges concerning the establishment of professional boundaries. Both the relatively small size of the community and the high incidence of informal contact between lesbian therapists and clients make boundary delineation difficult. This chapter describes strategies for managing self-disclosure, physical contact with clients, "special" treatment, and client gifts. It discusses informal community contact with clients, and relationships with former clients. The difficulty of maintaining personal privacy for the therapist is also addressed.

I had invited a colleague to lunch to discuss boundaries in lesbian therapy relationships. We met at a quiet, unpopulated restaurant near her office. We were engrossed in conversation when one of her clients appeared at the next table.

"Do you mind if I sit here?" she asked.

"You may sit anywhere you wish," said my colleague, looking slightly flustered.

"She's my shrink!" proclaimed the woman to the table server before settling in for lunch alone a mere 12" away.

AUTHOR'S NOTE: The author wishes to thank Joan E. Biren (JEB), Diane W. Goldstein, Marny Hall, Judith L. Herman, Karen Johnson, Dee Mosbacher, Minnie Bruce Pratt, Barbara Sanderson, and Gary Schoener for their very helpful comments during the preparation of this chapter.

For the past 8 years, I have been involved in research and education concerning sexual exploitation of clients and patients by therapists and physicians (Gartrell, Herman, Olarte, Feldstein, & Localio, 1986, 1987, 1988; Gartrell, Herman, Olarte, Localio, & Feldstein, 1988). Unfortunately, sexual abuse of women by women has been a serious problem in the lesbian therapy community. The most recent figures indicate that female-female abuse is the second most commonly reported therapy violation (after male-female)[1], currently comprising 13% of reported cases (Schoener, Milgrom, Gonsiorek, Luepker, & Conroe, 1989). Perhaps the lesbian community is more susceptible to such violations because of the high incidence of informal contact between lesbian therapists and their lesbian clients.

Although many authors have discussed the complicated interactions that exist between lesbian therapists and clients who live and work in the same community (Brown, 1985, 1989; Subcommittees, Boundary Dilemmas Conference [Subcommittees], 1987), very little has been written about the *logistics* of establishing and maintaining clear boundaries. Lesbian therapists face unique challenges in this regard, because of the lesbian community's relatively small size, and because lesbian therapists routinely encounter their clients at community functions. Almost half (47%) of lesbian therapists responding to a recent survey expressed concern about boundaries and social encounters with their lesbian clients (Lyn, 1990). Most of us graduate from mental health training programs which offer little assistance in this area. For example, I trained at a White male heterosexist institution (without a single woman on the full-time faculty) where I was the only lesbian and the only feminist. This training offered no preparation for my subsequent efforts to establish personal and professional boundaries within the lesbian community.

There is little disagreement about the importance of boundaries in the therapeutic relationship. Boundaries define and clarify the roles of helper and helpee. They contribute to the client's sense of security as she explores difficult and painful life experiences. Since there is a substantial power differential between therapist and client, well-publicized community standards concerning appropriate therapeutic boundaries also help to protect clients from power abuse by therapists.

I have written this chapter to provide more dialogue about the process of constructing therapeutic boundaries. Every lesbian therapist struggles with these issues, and it is important to share successful strategies so that we do not continue to make the same mistakes. I am particularly hopeful that my experiences will help lesbian therapists who have not yet learned to establish boundaries, since therapy abuse is typically associated with poorly defined boundaries and limits (Schoener et al., 1989). In addition, I hope to clarify some of the boundary dilemmas that perplex those of us who actively participate in the same communities in which we work.

A Few Words About My Therapeutic Style

Although there are probably as many levels of comfort with outside-the-office client encounters as there are therapists, my preference is to keep my clinical work and my personal life completely separate. Rarely has this been possible. Not only do most of my clients and I live in the same area, but we also attend the same community functions. For example, I may encounter clients when I attend pro-choice rallies, lesbian political fund-raisers, lesbian film festivals, or lesbian music festivals. I have also crossed paths with clients hiking in nearby state parks, marching in Gay Day parades, giving lectures, teaching courses, or eating out. Creating boundaries (both within and outside my office) which provide some degree of privacy for myself and a sufficient level of clarity and comfort for my clients has taken years of trial and error, consultation and study.

My clinical style is a product of multiple microcultural and macrocultural factors—including my skin color, socioeconomic class, ethnicity, age, health status, politics, client population, research, and training. I am a white, able-bodied, Christian-raised, 42-year-old lesbian psychiatrist from a middle-class family. I was trained at a well-known psychoanalytically oriented psychotherapy program. My approach to therapy has become more eclectic over the years with the influx of feminist theory and culture/class analysis. I became progressively disenchanted with psychoanalytic theory because individuals who deviated from established norms (by virtue of class, sexual orientation, ethnicity, or culture) were either pathologized or expected to assimilate. Although I continue to utilize the less culture-bound analytic concepts (such as working with transference and countertransference phenomena), I agree with de Monteflores's (1986) assertion that psychotherapy theory and practice should incorporate both intrapsychic processes and ecopsychology, "which situates the individual within his or her context or environment."[2]

My treatment style is practical and pragmatic; I am verbally interactive during sessions. I typically see clients once or twice per week. The scope of my practice includes crisis intervention, short-term (3 to 12 sessions), and long-term (1 to 2 years on the average) psychotherapy with individuals and couples. In addition to my academic appointments at Harvard and UCSF medical schools, I have had a part-time private practice for 13 years. The percentage of lesbians in my practice ranges between 80% and 95%;[3] 73% of my clients are sexual abuse survivors.

In reviewing the boundaries I have outlined in this article, questions will undoubtedly be raised about whether my practices and policies allow for individual needs and differences among clients. It has been suggested, for example, that my style may fit most comfortably with white, middle-class women and may be experienced as cold or distant by women of other colors, ethnicities, or classes (D. Goldstein, personal communication, 1990). I make a point of exploring cultural contributions to any client's discomfort with my style. These discussions have usually deepened the therapeutic alliance with women of different cultures/ethnicities. Nevertheless, I acknowledge that my approach may not meet the needs of all clients; I also recognize that it has evolved out of my work with survivors of sexual abuse—a phenomenon which knows no class, color, or ethnic distinctions. I believe that it is my responsibility to serve as the "guardian of boundaries" in the therapeutic relationship (Subcommittees, 1987), and that creating a feeling of safety is a critical first step in establishing a therapeutic alliance with any client.

Clinical experience has shown me that the therapeutic relationship benefits tremendously from clear and consistent boundaries. Certainly I have made my share of mistakes; I also recognize the importance of re-evaluating my policies at regular intervals. What follows is a discussion of the boundaries I have established in my office and in the community.

Boundaries Within the Office

Self-Disclosure

One of the many benefits of the women's self-help movement is that clients are now asking for information about their therapists. I routinely give a rundown of my training, theoretical orientation, research interests, and specialties to new clients. New clients are also informed that I am a lesbian feminist. When I ask if they have any additional questions about my training or expertise, some respond by asking personal questions.

I trained in a traditional program which taught me to explore the issues behind such questions, rather than to answer them. It always felt strange to withhold information that could easily be obtained through other sources, such as medical or faculty directories. It also felt uncomfortable to begin therapeutic relationships with a struggle around this type of inquiry. Some clients would be willing to explore their reasons for asking, but in the end would still want a response. Others would end up deciding that therapy with me was just not worth the struggle.

Since that time, studies have shown that identification with a therapist can have a positive impact on the therapeutic process (Gartrell, 1984). Unfortunately, these studies do not provide any clarity about where to draw lines in providing personal information. I have modified my practice concerning personal disclosure to answer some questions during the initial interview, as long as the information requested is relatively public. I always follow my response with an inquiry about the reason for the questions. The three questions I am most commonly asked are (1) How old are you? (2) Do you have children? (3) Do you live here?

Most clients want to work with a therapist who is old enough to have had a variety of life experiences. During the early years of my practice, I was particularly reluctant to disclose my age, since I was both young and inexperienced. Now that I am in my 40s, I am asked my age only by clients of similar age. When I inquire about the reason for the question (after stating my age), I typically hear that I am older than I look and that the client wanted to see a therapist who was at least 40.

Inquiries about children typically come from current or prospective lesbian moms. Although I am not a mom, I explain that I have many children in my life. I also inform clients that I am particularly sensitive to issues concerning lesbian moms since I am engaged in a multicity longitudinal study of lesbian families. Despite the fact that I have first-hand knowledge of the various "choosing children" and "lesbian mom" support groups, the best local preschools and elementary schools for children of lesbian families, and the kinds of issues faced by kids with and without dads, I understand that some moms prefer to see therapists who are also moms, and I do not qualify. Being straightforward about this gives the client an opportunity to prioritize her needs in terms of my various areas of expertise.

The question about where I live relates to the fact that my office is located on the ground floor (with a separate entrance) of a residential-appearing building. Although there have been times when I have wished that some clients did not know where I lived, it would be so easy to verify that I live upstairs that I do not see the point in avoiding the question. The reasons for this inquiry range from a desire to see a therapist in a noninstitutional setting, to curiosity about flowers in the garden outside my office. Everyone who has asked has indicated that she liked the office or the setting, and knowing that I lived upstairs increased her sense of comfort.

It is interesting that I have never been asked my relationship status. I find that omission particularly curious since so many of my clients enter treatment because of relationship difficulties. Also, many of these clients aspire to long-term relationships. There is no doubt in my mind that having successfully negotiated a 15-year healthy, happy, and productive relationship has contributed tremendous insight and skill to my clinical work. Because of this, and because my lover and I are public figures (we have appeared together in books, articles, videos, and lectures), I would answer honestly if asked my relationship status during an initial interview. I would probably add that I do not discuss my personal life in any detail with clients, but firsthand experience negotiating a healthy long-term relationship has been very helpful in my clinical work.

Questions of a personal nature which arise during treatment are handled on a case-by-case basis. I consider it inappropriate to discuss personal problems (relationship difficulties, family conflicts, etc.) with clients—except when illness is involved. For example, if I were suffering from an illness which might impact on my clinical work, or if I were "on call" for an ill friend or relative, I would inform my clients. However, I would limit the discussion to a few minutes (G. Schoener, personal communication, 1990) and make sure that it occurred on my time rather than the client's. I never disclose personal information to clients with complex posttraumatic stress disorder (PTSD)[4] or clients with a history of psychotic transference, because maintaining firm boundaries is already a difficult challenge with these individuals.

I do provide some personal information on request when it seems as though it would be clinically helpful. However, I have found that I can be most helpful if I provide a more generic, rather than specific response. The following cases[5] illustrate this point.

Case A A client who had been seeing me for some time very tearfully announced that her only brother had just been diagnosed with metastatic melanoma. He was expected to live only a few months. My heart ached for this client, particularly since I had lost my only sister to cancer several years previously. When she asked if anyone close to me had died, I replied honestly that my sister had. Although she said she appreciated knowing I had had a similar experience, I had difficulty refocusing her on her own pain during the ensuing months when she inquired about my sister's illness. I felt obligated to respond, felt renewed hurt in reviewing the course of my sister's illness, and felt less effective at addressing the client's concerns about her brother. I also had difficulty concealing my pain, but felt I should since I did not want her to feel as though she had to take care of me. Ultimately, I realized that the situation could have been handled much more effectively if I had simply said, "Yes, I have had close personal losses," in response to her original question, and redirected any further inquiry back to her own issues.

Case B A client who was terrified of losing her lover of many years asked me one session whether I was monogamous or nonmonogamous. Her lover had recently become infatuated with another woman. I replied that I did not know of a single long-term successful relationship which had not had to face the issue of nonmonogamy and come to some resolution around it. She seemed settled with my response and was able to return to a discussion of her own fears.

Over the years I have learned that I can be helpfully empathic in most situations without disclosing personal information. I try to keep personal disclosures to a generic minimum, which I provide only upon request, in a limited number of situations, to healthy clients.

Physical Contact With Clients

We all know that a hug can communicate a variety of feelings. A hug can be friendly, needy, supportive, erotic, suffocating, comforting, pleasurable, or frightening. It is certainly much more intimate than a handshake. There is some evidence that therapists who engage in physical contact with clients (hugs, etc.) are more likely to become sexually involved with clients, although the researchers did not ask specifically about lesbian therapist-client contact (Brodsky, 1986; Holroyd &

Brodsky, 1977, 1980). I believe that therapy must be a safe experience for all clients, and for that reason, I do not routinely hug my clients.

When a client raises the issue of hugs, I explain that as a result of my work on sexual exploitation, and as part of my desire to make therapy safe and comfortable for everyone, I do not engage in physical contact with clients. I explain that I shake hands when I first meet them and may shake hands on termination (if they choose to), but those are the limits. I then explore feelings associated with the desire to be hugged or held as well as the client's reactions to my policy. Although I sometimes encounter significant disappointment, many clients have expressed appreciation for my clarity in boundaries. In any case, the request for physical contact usually brings up considerable transference material.

I have tried to be particularly sensitive to the responses of clients of different cultures/ethnicities when my limits on physical contact are discussed. Since each woman's level of comfort with physical contact is a product of her own personal experiences in conjunction with her ethnic/cultural background, I inquire about the multiple determinants of her feelings. I also address her response to a person of my racial/ethnic background setting limits on physical contact with a person of her racial/ethnic background. Generally, I have found these discussions very helpful in defining our cultural differences, exploring the transference, and developing the therapeutic alliance.

I do make an important exception to my policy on hugs in cases of acute profound grief. For example, a client who had been sexually abused as a child was raped when her car broke down the night before one of our appointments. She was severely traumatized. I asked in our first session after the assault if I might sit next to her and put my arm around her. She indicated that she would appreciate my holding her, and she sobbed on my shoulder for the entire session.

Some clients who have seen me for a long time forget the rule and hug me on termination. However, it is very important that any such hug be client initiated (Johnson, 1990). Physical contact initiated by the therapist comes entwined in her power. The privilege of touch in a professional relationship relates to the power of the respective individuals (Holroyd & Brodsky, 1977; M. B. Pratt, personal communication, 1989). Teachers may touch their students, therapists their clients, and physicians their patients, but the reverse is not generally acceptable. We must be fully aware of the power inherent in our role as therapists and the power which we convey when we initiate physical contact with clients. Our power may even make it impossible for some clients to say no to hugs when the hugs feel frightening or confusing (Brown, 1989). The following case illustrates some of the complications which may arise in the treatment when the therapist initiates physical contact with the client.

> **Case C** During medical school, I was in treatment with an older, very closeted lesbian therapist. I had been seeing her for about six months when she began hugging me at the end of each session. As the hugs increased in duration, I became concerned that she was having sexual feelings toward me. I dismissed these thoughts with ageist rationalizations. I then worried that the hugs were an expression of her desire for me to take care of her. Her health was poor, and she had begun asking me to look up articles about her ailments. I was afraid to address my concerns because I did not want to hurt her feelings. Since I was seeing her for a low fee, I ultimately decided that the hugs and medical advice were the price I was paying for treatment.

I began seeing this therapist at a time when I needed help with the stress of medical school and the dissolution of a relationship. I had extended my trust to her, because of the tremendous warmth, empathy, and support she had demonstrated during the early months of treatment. She had made it clear that she would be there for me. As soon as she began hugging me, a radical shift in the dynamics of the treatment occurred. I became her caretaker as she expressed more and more of her own neediness. I lost respect for her. I felt betrayed by her transgression of the therapeutic boundaries.

From my experience as a client, from my understanding of the dynamics of sexual exploitation, and from my work with survivors of sexual abuse, I believe that a general policy of "NO HUGS" for clients fits most comfortably with who I am.

"Special" Treatment

Early in my psychiatric training one of my supervisors said, "Special treatment always buys a cork." By that he meant that such treatment would put a stopper on client honesty. Reflecting on that concept I recalled my unwillingness to confront my former therapist about her hugs, because she was seeing me for a low fee. She had made it very clear that

I was the only low-fee client she was seeing. Although I could not have afforded her usual fee, I feel sad about the lost opportunity to be honest with her about an accumulation of uncomfortable feelings which began with those hugs.

I have made many mistakes over the years in granting special favors to various clients. Some of these favors undoubtedly bought corks for the clients, and others brought frustration to me. An example of the latter was a lesbian college student whose father had allegedly promised to pay for treatment.

When the first month's bill was overdue, he suddenly had a myocardial infarction. I agreed to continue working with her, and she promised that he would pay once he was back on his feet. Four months later he had still not sent a payment. I then told the client that she had to work out a way of arranging for payment on her own since her father was not keeping his promise. She did not keep her next appointment, did not answer my phone calls, and ducked to avoid eye contact with me at a $100/plate political fund-raiser we both attended a month later.

I currently make every effort to avoid giving any special favors to clients. I also consult with colleagues whenever I am tempted to do so. If I offer something in a limited way (such as prime-time appointments or low fees), I make it clear to clients that availability is on a first-come, first-served basis. I require all clients to pay at the time of each visit, and I require all clients to pay something for treatment. I initially offered free services to lesbians with AIDS, but I had a high no-show rate, for reasons such as "forgot," "overslept," rather than health. I now agree on a fee, however minimal, for these clients, and I have not had a single no-show since instituting this policy. I wonder retrospectively if not being charged for psychotherapy made some clients feel as though they did not have the right to address their dissatisfaction with or ambivalence about treatment.

As important as the policy "no favors given" is the reverse "no favors taken." I have been offered various favors over the years from clients, and I believe that it is very important to decline all such offers. Such offers have included tickets to special events, introductions to important people, and VIP treatment in certain settings. My most recent offer was to arrange tax exemption for our lesbian mother study. After a public fund-raising solicitation for this project, a well-meaning accountant client offered to set up a 501 (C) (3) for the project. Offers such as this have been sorely tempting. In some cases, clients have offered to barter for favors.

But the complexity of an already complex interaction is destined to magnify tremendously around a favor, and I would worry about how I would handle it if I were dissatisfied with the favor, or the client were dissatisfied with my response to it. When a favor is offered, my policy is to decline politely, explaining the importance of abstaining from dual relationships with clients.

Gifts

We live in a culture in which people commonly express gratitude by bestowing gifts. Although I was trained never to accept gifts from clients, I do accept them in a limited way. I never felt comfortable analyzing the meaning of a gift to the point that the client felt hurt and angry that she had ever considered it. I think it would be perfectly reasonable to decline gifts from clients if I had a written policy to that effect which was provided to each client early in treatment. In the absence of such a policy (which would feel fairly presumptuous), I accept the gifts which are occasionally offered by my clients.

I typically inquire briefly about the meaning of the gift. I would devote more time to the discussion if a client brought too many gifts or a gift at an unusual time. I am accustomed to receiving some gifts or cards from clients during the holiday season. I received a substantial number of gifts from clients when I closed my practice in Boston and moved to San Francisco. None of the gifts was extravagant or inappropriate; most were office gifts, or mementos which clients hoped would remind me of them. Other than these occasions, I have sometimes received copies of books or manuscripts from clients who are writers. I always explain that I am willing to read a client's publication *not* as a critic, but as her therapist. I add that I am interested in any information which will contribute to my understanding of her life.

Even though most of the gifts are defined as office gifts, I do not keep them in the office where I see clients. I explain to clients that I have several offices, and that the gift will find a good home in one of them. I used to keep office gifts in the office where I saw clients. One day a client who had never given me a gift recognized a small piece of art made by a former client, who happened to be a distant friend of hers. I realized then that no client gift was anonymous, and that even gifts which are purchased can be publicly discussed among friends. In addition, the last thing I wanted to do was demonstrate any special relationship with a client, or breach confidentiality, by displaying her gift. I also do not want clients to feel obligated to give gifts. Therefore, all client gifts reside outside my therapy office.

I have had to put a stop to gift giving only with a few clients. These were clients who either brought gifts too frequently (associated with an eroticized transference), or who could not talk openly about the meaning of the gift. With these clients I stressed the importance of verbalizing feelings directly, rather than concealing them behind a gift.

I did not plan to include a discussion of gift giving *to* clients in this chapter. It had not occurred to me that there would ever be a situation in which that would be appropriate until I recently discussed this issue in my peer supervision group.[6] One of my colleagues raised the issue of acknowledging the birth of a client's baby. She talked about feeling very bad that she had never sent a card congratulating a client on the birth of a child whose existence was due largely to the therapeutic work they had done together. All of us agreed that in a similar situation we would like to be able to send a congratulatory card to new moms we were seeing infrequently, and perhaps even give a small gift to those we were seeing regularly. I would consider a baby T-shirt from our lesbian family study an appropriate congratulatory gift. (The T-shirts read, "I'm here 'cause Mom's a Pioneer," for single moms, and "I was Hatched by a Couple of Chicks," for co-moms.) However, I plan to consult with a colleague whenever I am contemplating such a gift to make certain that (1) I am clear about what the gift is designed to communicate and (2) the gift seems appropriate in the context of the therapy (G. Schoener, personal communication, 1990).[7]

Boundaries in the Community

Just Say "Hi"

Since I choose to be an active participant in the lesbian community, I am destined to run into clients outside my office. I inform clients that I will just say hi, if either of us is accompanied by others, unless they prefer that I not acknowledge them. I explain that I will not stop to be introduced to their companions, nor will I introduce mine. I explain that this is the way that I maintain confidentiality. Although most clients say that they want me to acknowledge them if I see them, and that their friends know who I am, I feel a certain comfort in knowing that the boundary has been delineated concerning socializing outside the office.

I have not yet figured out the best way of handling situations in which a client is discussing her expected attendance at an upcoming event which I also plan to attend. I have deliberated about whether it is better to tell a client, and reiterate boundaries for outside contact, or attend and just say hello if I run into the client. I do not like the idea of burdening a client with worries or fantasies about seeing me, nor do I like the idea of a client having less time to prepare for a possible encounter than I do. I have tried both announcing and concealing my plans in different situations, and neither has felt very comfortable. I once had a client who became so anxious about seeing me that she decided not to attend herself. I, on the other hand, feel deceitful going to an event knowing a client will be there who does not know that I will be. I tend to err on the side of honesty about my plans, because it gives me an opportunity to remind the client that I will just say hi.

The greatest difficulty I have experienced in maintaining these boundaries has been with clients whose paths I cross in my teaching or research. I would never agree to treat someone who was a current student or research colleague. However, I have treated women who worked or studied in institutions where I have lectured or led workshops. Encountering such a client outside my office has been particularly uncomfortable when the client is determined to establish a social relationship with me, despite my attempts to the contrary. A recent case illustrates this point.

> **Case D** I accepted an invitation to speak at a nearby college. About 2 months after agreeing to this talk, I began treating a lesbian faculty member of this college with an antidepressant. I had explained my policy of not socializing with clients outside the office. Upon hearing this, the client irritably commented that I was awfully "rigid." She mentioned my upcoming talk and indicated that she planned to attend. When I arrived at the pretalk dinner, I was introduced to my client as my host for the evening. She had not only ignored my wishes, but also had put me in a very uncomfortable situation. This event led to a prolonged struggle around boundaries with this client.

I make every effort to anticipate small group situations where a client may be present. I discuss the fact that both of us are likely to feel more comfortable if we give each other as much space as possible in these situations (e.g., in order to maintain confidentiality of the therapeutic relationship, decrease performance anxiety for both of us, etc.). Insofar as possible, I try to avoid situations which would create dual relationships with clients and to address any outside-the-office encounters which do occur as thoroughly as possible in the treatment.

Personal Privacy in the Community

It is very important to me to have a personal life that is separate from my work. Taking care of distressed, sad, and anxious clients is extremely emotionally draining. I relish the time my lover and I can leave all our client responsibilities behind (and coverage to colleagues) for fun, travel, and play. I find that I can relax and play most effectively if I do not encounter clients during these activities.

How can one have a private life in the lesbian community without seeming too uptight? (M. Hall, personal communication, 1990). Granted, curiosity is a human characteristic. Most clients want to know more about their therapists' lives. In my early experiences as a therapy client I tried to glean as much information as I could about my therapist from her waiting room furniture and paintings. I also tried asking personal questions, but that rarely paid off.

Now I sit in the other chair. I have become fairly adept at redirecting client questions about my personal life. I feel comfortable with that approach, because they are not paying me to discuss my life. However, I find it very uncomfortable to deal with clients who relentlessly pursue information about my private life. All clients with whom I have had this difficulty were experiencing an eroticized transference, and some had a prior history of abuse. In addition to scouring the library for all my publications and attending every presentation I gave (which other clients have done as well), these clients parked outside my home for hours on end, followed me in my car, and sat near me at community events. They were often engaged in these activities for some time before acknowledging them, and they rarely discontinued them when asked to so do. One of my clients cleaned the snow off my car several times one winter, and I did not discover that she was responsible until months later. Another client found out who my lover was and joined her play-writing group in an effort to know her. Yet another got a job at a college health service, where she was able to obtain my unlisted home phone number from a very confidential file. She then called me at that number.

I utilized typical strategies for addressing this problem, most of which were fairly unsuccessful. The strategies included exploring the transference, setting limits, and seeking consultation. I also offered a third-party consultation, but that proposal was rejected as well. None of these clients was willing to discontinue her pursuit of greater closeness to me. Since my consultants did not consider this behavior sufficient justification to terminate treatment, my only option was to continue working with these clients—despite the ongoing invasion of my privacy.

I said at the outset of this chapter that I would prefer to have a personal life that is so separate from that of my clients that I never encounter them outside the office. Such a setup would certainly allow very clear boundaries. Not only is that unrealistic if I choose to participate in the lesbian community, but it also appears unrealistic to hope for privacy with some clients even in noncommunity activities. To know that despite my best efforts to the contrary I may be observed as I head out to jog, walk to a park with visiting nieces and nephews, or drive home from the hospital is fairly unsettling. Having to change my unlisted home phone number is frustrating and costly. One way around this dilemma has been to take frequent weekend trips out of town; traveling gives me a nice opportunity to be anonymous.

I do not participate in small social or political gatherings, if at all possible, when I know that a client is likely to be present. Even with healthier clients I find that I am likely to feel self-conscious and stilted in such an environment, and I cannot really enjoy myself—even if they can. My friends are respectful of this need for space and privacy, and one friend even arranged for two separate parties so that I could attend one, and a couple she had referred to me the other.

In sum, I do not want to be a recluse, rigid, uptight, or paranoid, but I have been working in the lesbian community long enough to understand that privacy outside the office is hard to come by. Privacy in my personal life is important for my well-being, because it gives me an opportunity to nurture myself so that I can meet the needs of my clients. I guess I should feel thankful that none of the clients who invaded my privacy were out to harm me in any way. But it is strange to realize that the private, quiet life I had envisioned for myself as a lesbian psychiatrist may be unrealistic. And that privacy can be a costly commodity.

Managing Relationships With Former Clients

On the subject of friendships with former clients, lesbian therapists are often strongly opinionated, but rarely agree. I reside in the camp which advocates friendliness with former clients, but clear limitations on friendships. I maintain this position for many reasons. First, a therapeutic relationship is not an egalitarian relationship. I, as a therapist, am privileged to enormously detailed and intimate information about my clients' lives. The reverse is not true. I obtain this information in order to serve as a caretaker, healer, insight provider, strategy creator, and obstacle remover in my clients' lives. They do not provide this service for me. When clients state a desire to establish a friendship with me after termination, they typically anticipate that I will continue to be as caring, supportive, and available as I have been as a therapist. Such clients do not desire a real friendship but rather an extension of the therapeutic relationship in a more informal way. Rarely has the expectation that the friendship would involve *mutual* caretaking and support been expressed. Even when that desire has been expressed, clients have only a one-dimensional picture of me, which has not included any opportunity to judge my potential as a friend.

An important additional consideration is the fact that many of my clients continue to see me as their therapist even though we are no longer working together. Clients who have had a positive therapeutic experience with me anticipate returning to treatment with me if new problems develop or old problems recur. The longer I have been in practice, the more I see returning clients—sometimes with a hiatus of as long as 10 years. Even my transcontinental relocation did not affect the frequency of former clients returning to treatment with me. In the 2 years that I have been working in San Francisco, I have been consulted by more than 10 former East Coast clients, some of whom commute to see me intermittently.

But just for the sake of argument, let's say that I did think it possible to establish friendships with former clients. Would I offer this option to all clients? If not, how would I select former clients for friendship? How would I feel about a former client finding out that she was *not* "chosen"? How would I erase the boundaries between my client and myself and correct the major discrepancy in shared information? Would I request "equal time" for my own disclosures? How would we eliminate the power disequilibrium?

It feels overwhelming even to contemplate the above questions, not to mention strategizing their solutions. Since it is inconceivable that I could offer friendships to all former clients (due to sheer limitations on time) and since creating a "special" category of ex-clients is completely antithetical to my work, I prefer to have a style that allows *friendliness, but not friendship.*

One of the most unfortunate situations which occurs when a therapist agrees to establish a friendship with a former client is that the client forever loses a therapist, as the following case illustrates.

> **Case E** A professional lesbian in her mid-30s entered treatment with me to work out unresolved feelings about a former therapist. This client had been in treatment with her former therapist for 5 years, and they had agreed to establish a friendship after termination. The client soon found herself initiating most of their social engagements. When they did get together, the therapist acted somewhat distant, and the client began to feel insecure about their friendship. This insecurity compounded the client's growing irritation at being the initiator of their contact. Unfortunately, she did not feel comfortable addressing these feelings with the therapist. Eventually, the client just stopped calling. By the time she began seeing me, she had had no contact with her former therapist for 2 years. "I don't know if she was just more uptight than I thought she'd be, or what the deal was," she said. "Maybe she had second thoughts about becoming friendly with a client. But one thing's for sure—I could never go back to seeing her as my therapist."

Just as a patient who has a successful surgical procedure considers that physician her surgeon should she ever require further surgery, I have found that clients who are pleased with the psychotherapeutic process anticipate returning to the same therapist should the need arise.

Finally, as Herman et al. (1987) wrote in one publication, "neither transference nor the real inequality in the power relationship ends with termination of therapy." Clients typically enter treatment at vulnerable times in their lives, when they need help and support. Inherent in the therapeutic relationship is the inequality which arises when the client's vulnerability is met by the therapist's superior knowledge and skill. This inequality is further enhanced by transference feelings, associated with childhood experiences of dependency. Expectations that transference, countertransference, client vulnerability, and power inequalities will automatically disappear with the termination of treatment reflect either a "naive romanticism or an insufficient understanding of the nature of the therapeutic relationship, or both" (Herman et al., 1987). Because it is essential that therapists abstain from using their positions of power for personal gratification, I believe that any therapist considering friendship with a client should seek consultation before agreeing to such a venture.

The Importance of Peer Consultation and Clinical Supervision

I cannot overemphasize the importance of consulting with colleagues around boundary issues. I have made it a priority in my clinical work to make liberal use of consultation. My consultants have given me invaluable advice about boundary dilemmas, helped me to clarify treatment goals, and have facilitated problem solving concerning difficult cases. For example, when treating clients with complex PTSD who are self-destructive or invasive of my privacy, I have found consultation an extremely useful avenue for venting my frustration so that I do not direct it at these clients. Also, I consult whenever I treat VIPs to make certain that the flattery to my self-esteem (of being consulted by such clients) does not result in any special treatment. Having regularly scheduled consultations gives me an opportunity to address boundary concerns before a problem occurs.

Conclusion

I realize that the strategies I have put forth in this chapter may be tailored to my therapeutic style and client population. However, they represent my attempts to establish clear boundaries in my clinical work as a lesbian psychiatrist within the lesbian community. They also reflect my long-term concern about exploitation in lesbian therapy relationships. Exploitation of women by women is a serious concern in the lesbian therapy community, and the consequences can be devastating to involved clients. I believe that it is within our power as lesbian therapists to curb abuse in our community. Establishing clear boundaries in our psychotherapeutic practices is an essential first step in that process.

Notes

1. The current offender-victim distribution is 80% male therapist-female client, 13% female-female, 5% male-male, and 2% female-male. As in other forms of victimization, sexual exploitation of clients by therapists is predominantly a heterosexual crime.

2. An extensive discussion of these concepts is beyond the scope of this chapter. However, the reader may refer to de Monteflores's (1986) chapter in *Contemporary Perspectives on Psychotherapy With Lesbians and Gay Men* for a more detailed analysis.

3. Lesbians who have sought my services over the years have included Hindu-raised Indians (2%), Christian-raised Latinas and Hispanics (3%), Christian-raised blacks (5%), Jewish-raised whites (33%), and Christian-raised whites (57%). In terms of health status, 100% have been able-bodied and 5% cancer survivors. In terms of education, 95% have been college graduates. Class of origin was poor for 11%, working for 21%, middle for 36%, upper-middle for 25%, and upper for 7%. Their ages have ranged from 19 to 70, with a majority in their 30s and 40s.

4. Also known as DESNOS (disorders of extreme stress not otherwise specified) and formerly called borderline personality disorder. Individuals who have been repeatedly victimized often test the boundaries of subsequent relationships—sometimes quite aggressively. They may also communicate an intense wish for "special" relationships with therapists. The feminist therapy community is especially vulnerable to these requests, because we sometimes share the fantasy that our "special" caring can undo the trauma (J. Herman, personal communication, 1990).

5. All cases in this article have been altered to protect clients' identity.

6. I participate in peer consultation with another psychiatrist and in a consultation group with a social worker, psychologist, and psychiatrist.

7. In the above discussion concerning gift giving, my consultation group acknowledged the important work of Miller et al. at the Stone Center who have encouraged us to incorporate women's relational needs into therapeutic considerations such as this (Kaplan, 1984; Miller, 1986; Surrey, 1985). Miller et al. advocate challenges to traditional patriarchal psychotherapeutic tenets when they are inconsistent with women's experiences (Johnson, 1990).

References

Brodsky, A. M. (1986). *Sex between patient and therapists: Psychology's data and response.* Paper presented at the American Psychological Association annual meeting, Washington, DC.

Brown, L. S. (1985). Power, responsibility, boundaries: Ethical concerns for the lesbian-feminist therapist. *Lesbian Ethics, 1*(3), 30-45.

Brown, L. S. (1989). Beyond thou shalt not: Thinking about ethics in the lesbian therapy community. *Women and Therapy, 8*(1-2), 13-25.

de Monteflores, C. (1986). Notes on the management of difference. In T. S. Stein & C. J. Cohen (Eds.), *Contemporary perspectives on psychotherapy with lesbian and gay men* (pp. 73-101). New York: Plenum.

Gartrell, N. (1984). Combating homophobia in the psychotherapy of lesbians. *Women and Therapy, 3*(1), 13-29.

Gartrell, N., Herman, J., Olarte, S., Feldstein, M., & Localio, R. (1986). Psychiatrist-patient sexual contact: Results of a national survey, I: Prevalence. *American Journal of Psychiatry, 143*(9), 1126-1131.

Gartrell, N., Herman, J., Olarte, S., Feldstein, M., & Localio, R. (1987). Reporting practices of psychiatrists who knew of sexual misconduct by colleagues. *American Journal of Orthopsychiatry, 57*(2), 287-295.

Gartrell, N., Herman, J., Olarte, S., Feldstein, M., & Localio, R. (1988). Management and rehabilitation of sexually exploitive therapists. *Hospital and Community Psychiatry, 39*(10), 1070-1074.

Gartrell, N., Herman, J., Olarte, S., Localio, R., & Feldstein, M. (1988). Psychiatric residents' sexual contact with educators and patients: Results of a national survey. *American Journal of Psychiatry, 145*(6), 690-694.

Herman, J., Gartrell, N., Olarte, S., Feldstein, M., & Localio, R. (1987). Psychiatrist-patient sexual contact: Results of a national survey, II: Psychiatrists' attitudes. *American Journal of Psychiatry, 144*(2), 164-169.

Holroyd, J. C., & Brodsky, A. M. (1977). Psychologists' attitudes and practices regarding erotic and nonerotic physical contact with patients. *American Psychologist, 32*(10), 843-849.

Holroyd, J. C., & Brodsky, A. M. (1980) Does touching patients lead to sexual intercourse? *Professional Psychology, 11*(5), 807-811.

Johnson, K. (1990). *Trusting ourselves.* New York: Atlantic Monthly Press.

Kaplan, A. G. (1984). *The "self-in-relation": Implications for depression in women* (Working Paper No. 14). Wellesley, MA: Wellesley College, The Stone Center.

Lyn, L. (1990). *Life in the fishbowl: Lesbian and gay therapists' social interactions with clients.* Unpublished master's thesis, Southern Illinois University at Carbondale.

Miller, J. B. (1986). *Toward a new psychology of women* (2nd ed.). Boston: Beacon.

Schoener, G., Milgrom, J. H., Gonsiorek, J. C., Luepker, E. T., & Conroe, R. M. (1989). *Psychotherapists' sexual involvement with clients: Intervention and prevention.* Minneapolis, MN: Walk-In Counseling Center.

Subcommittees, Boundary Dilemmas Conference. (1987). *Ethical standards and practice in the lesbian community.* Los Angeles: Ethical Standards Report.

Surrey, J. L. (1985). *Self-in-relation: A theory of women's development* (Working Paper No. 13). Wellesley, MA: Wellesley College, The Stone Center.

7

Lesbian and Gay Male Development

Steps Toward an Analysis of Lesbians' and Gay Men's Lives

ANTHONY R. D'AUGELLI

Much of the theory on the development of sexual orientation has been dominated by perspectives conditioned by heterosexist attitudes about the development of affectional differences. New theoretical perspectives on the development of lesbians and gay men are needed because the conceptual vacuum that currently exists poses serious problems in the understanding of such women's and men's lives. The difficulty in developing theory is a result of the nature of the phenomenon, complex lives changing over time, and the inevitable social and political consequences of models. For example, many gay activists and sympathetic observers prefer biological determinism models of lesbian/gay development, while their conservative heterosexist counterparts argue for a voluntaristic, free-choice "model." Indeed, much argument about inclusion of lesbian or gay status as a legally protected category revolves around this issue of causation. Metatheoretical views are unavoidably grounded in historical time: The "context of discovery" (Kaplan, 1964) must be ideological. In addition to providing the frame, metatheory provides the substrate from which interpretive schemata that guide inquiry emerge.

Both a deterministic view of the development of affectional differences and a perspective assuming that such differences are freely chosen reflect ideology, not empirical neutrality. Unfortunately, there is no empirical database on lesbian and gay male development that can serve as the foundation for a comprehensive formal theory. There are literally no formal longitudinal data on large representative samples of women and men from which reasonable conclusions about development over time can be based. Although social and behavioral scientists know nothing about the normative developmental processes of people who either come to label themselves as lesbian or gay or who self-label at the beginning of a period of observation, efforts at articulating individual, ontogenetic models continue. For example, Ellis and Ames (1987) presented a theory emphasizing prenatal factors that determine sexual orientation. In their model, sexual orientation becomes activated during puberty and may not solidify until early adulthood. Money (1987), in a conceptually similar effort toward a "psychoneuroendocrinology" model, rejected such linear predeterministic thinking and posited a circular causal system whereby social experience and neurochemical processes exert mutual influence, although the pattern of influence changes over time. Friedman (1988) and Isay (1989) endeavored to integrate empirical findings and clinical material on male homosexuals within revisionist psychoanalytic perspectives.

These theories present a common purpose: the objective integration of empirical knowledge (including clinical observation) toward the goal of systematic understanding. However, the lack of normative data reveals the scientism of these efforts. Nor are these views subject to formal disproof, reflecting their prescientific nature. The omission of explicit statements of ideology is another revealing piece of evidence, because without normative longitudinal data meeting routine standards of methodological acceptability to guide theory building, one is left with highly impressionistic (if well-argued and seemingly systematic) viewpoints, not formal scientific theory. These efforts are constructed by rhetorical argument, based on selective use of limited empirical information, and liberally draw from other sources (e.g., hormonal development), as if such information were logically required by the problem at hand.

The assumption of a biological basis for sexual orientation, conceptualized not as a social-historical construct but as an essence, is at the base of these analyses, and this hypothetical assumption is not a central feature of the theories. A detailed critique of these and other efforts is beyond the scope of this chapter. The philosophical, historical, and political nature of these and other efforts at delineating the causes of sexual orientation and homosexuality have been carefully presented by several scholars, including Kinsman (1987), Kitzinger (1988), and Ruse (1988). Ruse (1988) wrote:

> We have far to go before we will properly understand the causes of homosexual orientation. What we can say is that neither of the twin threats, reductionism and determinism, vitiate the work which has been thus far produced. We see through a glass darkly, and this must temper our analysis of normative questions. (p. 175)

Unfortunately, the dark lenses of earlier frameworks, which view lesbians and gay men as psychiatrically impaired and which dictate a focus on etiology, have yet to be replaced with frameworks that effectively suggest different fundamental issues for analysis.

An attempt will be made here to suggest a metatheory that will transcend past approaches and simultaneously enrich future conceptual and empirical investigations. Although it is in principle possible to articulate such a framework without specification of ideology, this seems less useful than a disclosure of guiding values. The discussion that follows is based on the idea that lesbian and gay development represents exceptional developmental processes. Women and men who express their needs for closeness and intimacy more consistently with people of the same gender have evolved within their own life histories and have departed from heterosocial socialization patterns. Continued growth and personal fulfillment as a lesbian or gay man in our culture at this time demands unusual competencies and special strengths. By starting with the assumption of exceptionality, efforts can be made to discover these adaptive coping talents.

The value assumption that lesbians and gay men lead exceptional lives—the affirmation assumption—has considerable heuristic power. Such a view redirects study toward the discovery of creative life solutions to the fundamental dilemmas of lesbian/gay development: the creation of a personal life course, that is, an identity, that affirms one's lesbian or gay male feelings in a heterosocial society. The most common model for lesbian/gay identity "integration" remains social invisibility, in which personal identity is hidden, denied, or distorted. Personal identity is constructed within lesbian and gay social contexts for most people who come to label themselves, and the degree of reintegration into mainstream social life varies considerably from individuals who are fully disclosed to others to those who are totally unknown as lesbian or gay to anyone.

Most analyses of homosexuality focus on the minority who disclose their orientation to researchers, and earlier perspectives were built on the even smaller subgroup who sought long-term professional help. But many other life courses exist: Some lesbians and gay men remain heterosexually married, others care for children from earlier marriages, and some live their lives without admitting their sexual feelings to others. Preconceived notions of the normal development of sexual orientation must incorporate findings of studies of lesbian and gay youth (Herdt, 1989) and of older adults (see Adelman, 1986; Kehoe, 1989; Vacha, 1985) that detail many different patterns of sexual unfolding at different chronological ages. Similar diversity is shown in patterns of family relationships, including disclosure patterns to families of origin (e.g., Cramer & Roach, 1988) and patterns of relating to children from prior marriages, adopted children, or children created via artificial fertilization (see Bozett, 1987, 1989).

The development of close relationships, which until the mid-1980s was hardly mentioned by theorists writing about etiology, is now being charted by empirical studies of increasing sophistication (e.g., Kurdek, 1988). In addition, the nature and expression of socioemotional/sociosexual feelings by people of color, Native Americans (Williams, 1986), and people of varied ethnicity (e.g., Balka & Rose, 1989) continue to complicate assumptions about the development of homosexuality. The complex patterns of lesbian and gay male development over the life span illustrate the remarkable human talent to create an identity under different, yet generally adverse, social conditions. Cultural prescriptions and normlessness (except for denial, suppression, and invisibility) demand distinctive coping. Few groups develop without anticipatory socialization to this degree, and few develop a distinction that results in such intense and relentless social opprobrium. In that exceptions create rules, an appreciation of the richness of lesbian/gay identity development can greatly inform the study of personal development over the life span (Lee, 1987).

The most powerful metatheoretical model for these processes is a life-span human development perspective (Baltes, 1987; Lerner, 1984). This general view, which has many individual variants, involves the explication of patterns of dynamic interaction of multiple factors over time in the development of an individual person. The developing woman or man must be understood in context; simultaneous descriptions of the person's social network, neighborhood and community, institutional settings, and culture are complemented by descriptions of individual physical and psychological change and stability. In contrast with earlier developmental views, the human development model stresses the impact of historical time on processes of development, whether the process is observed during an individual's life, over the lives of family members, within a community, or in a culture. The human development perspective is an effort to discover variations between individuals as they move in time through social situations, community, culture, and history.

One consequence of a human development view for the study of lesbians and gay men is that to talk about the development of their lives without focus on family, social, institutional, cultural, and historical factors is fundamentally distorted. Indeed, to eliminate an appreciation of cultural and historical time is to assume that lesbian and gay lives are unresponsive to social circumstances, history, or culture. Such unidimensional perspectives have been preeminent in this enterprise as scholars, theorists, and researchers have focused on either medical, biological, genetic, hormonal, psychiatric, or psychological factors without explicit inclusion of contextual variables. For example, homosexuality as psychiatric disorder—a view that was held by mental health professions until 1973 and not officially discarded until 1987—embodied a view that dismissed historical, community, social, and family factors. The omission of homosexuality from diagnostic nomenclature resulted from the need to incorporate a set of factors, namely, empirical findings, into traditional biological-deterministic medical thinking. Homosexuality had become a treatable reification, a dysfunctional individual characteristic that existed outside social, cultural, and historical reality.

Most complex human behavioral patterns and characteristics—even such staples of unidimensional science as intelligence—are now seen as multidetermined and must be studied at multiple levels of analysis. To do otherwise is to chance simplistic description and partial explanation and to develop inappropriate change efforts and social policy. The abstraction of affectional/sexual patterns from culture so as to describe, explain, and modify homosexuality was the first step in this oppressive model building. The first part of the process, namely, the emergence of a labeling system, began in the late 1800s, with the rise of "modern" medicine (see Kinsman, 1987, for a review).

The accumulated research on lesbian and gay development shows the flaws that result from a nonhistorical, nondevelopmental point of view. The more recent Kinsey reports (Bell & Weinberg, 1978; Weinberg & Williams, 1974) were both based on a sample of Californians obtained in 1969. Careful reading of the reports finds little sensitivity to the impact of historical time or community setting on the lives tabulated. These are studies of homosexuals, yet the clear implication is that the results are generalizable across developmental history, family history, social and community differences, and cultural and historical time. Even more illustrative, the authors of the 1981 Kinsey report, *Sexual Preference* (Bell, Weinberg, & Hammersmith, 1981), interpreted their findings as reflecting biological determinism, because there was no evidence of simple psychosocial determinism in the retrospective reports of study participants. Mistakenly interpreting a confirmation of the null hypothesis and also ignoring the limits of retrospective self-report data taken cross-sectionally from a self-selected and distinct sample, the authors demonstrate severely flawed unidimensional thinking. Unfortunately, these studies have had powerful consequences on research in this field, because they encouraged a continuance of simplistic thinking and research by appearing to corroborate a biological causal model. The power of simple biological, medical, and psychological models to distort research and social policy is well known; its most destructive consequence is to assume that human characteristics transcend culture and history, that biology is destiny (see, e.g., Kevles, 1985; Lewontin, Rose, & Kamin, 1984).

The Human Development View

Relevant components of a human development model are described below with brief extrapolations to lesbian and gay male development.

1. The first perspective is that individuals develop and change over the entire course of their life span. This means that psychological, cognitive, behavioral, emotional, and physical changes do not stop after the achievement of socially defined adulthood (usually heterosexual marriage and occupational stability), nor do social constructions of development necessarily dictate changes in behavioral development. In the developmental literature, for instance, considerable attention has been

given to both ends of the life span. This shows the unusual complexity of early individual development, once assumed to be directed mostly by organismic processes, and at the other end of the life span, the development processes of older adults, also once assumed to be the consequences of biological aging. Evidence exists, for example, that functioning of infants, adolescents, adults, and the elderly is powerfully influenced by social expectations and reinforcement in interaction with physical and other factors over the life span.

The development of affectional interests should be considered a lifelong developmental process as well. This concept strikes at the heart of a view of sexual orientation as fixed early in life. Such a view is an historical anachronism, although it may be consistent with the men's and women's phenomenological perceptions of their sexual identity. That one's sexual and affectional feelings can change in varying degrees over the course of life must be assumed; efforts to suggest otherwise are disguised social convention. For instance, for an older man or woman to focus his or her emotional life on someone of the same gender late in life does not necessarily imply repression of earlier homosexual feelings. Feelings of physical and emotional closeness for an individual of the same gender can evolve throughout life; they are highly conditioned by social, family, and personal normative expectations. The label *lesbian* or *gay* and the negative connotations to older adults might be a prominent barrier to the expression of intense closeness to same-gendered others. Likewise, individuals who define themselves as lesbian or gay may experience affectional and sexual interests in people of the opposite sex across the span of their lives, although the plasticity of this process is slight given the current process of becoming lesbian or gay in our society. In any event, a human development view allows for multiple changes over time in sexual feelings, attitudes, and behavior and does not assume permanence of sexual developmental status. Stability of personal socioaffective identity is worthy of study itself.

2. The human development model embodies the importance of developmental plasticity. Plasticity suggests that human functioning is responsive to environmental circumstances and changes induced by physical and other biological factors. In essence, the human development model makes few assumptions about the fixed nature of human functioning, but suggests that plasticity is a prime characteristic of human behavior. Plasticity may change over chronological time: At different ages, certain components of human behavioral functioning are

resistant to or responsive to differing circumstances. This view allows that certain historical periods may encourage greater differentiation, whereas others may promote more constriction of behavioral possibilities. The implication for gay and lesbian development is that sexual identity may be fluid during certain parts of the life span, and more crystallized at others. Given the role of hormonal development in sexual identity development, the likelihood is that years temporally proximate to changes in hormonal development in men and women would be periods in which cognitive concepts of sexual orientation become especially salient. Sexual cues may be heightened, and they may have greater impact on the individual because of his or her cognitive development. Yet there is no inevitable process here: Adolescent peer development in our society forces a definition of sexual interests so that expected dating behavior occurs. This dating behavior happens with increasing distance from family monitoring, and thus is increasingly subject to peer and sociocultural influences. The negative consequences of any lesbian or gay feelings are thereby exaggerated.

Still, the emergence of a sense of lesbian/gay identity occurs for many in early adolescence, despite social barriers to expressing this identity. For far more, a sense of consolidated lesbian/gay identity occurs later in life, that is, in late adolescence or early adulthood. This does not suggest delayed development but rather that the psychosocial conditions that led to the consolidation of feelings, thoughts, and actions earlier for some did not occur for those who come out later. The assumption that those who acknowledge their feelings and adopt a lesbian/gay label later have denied this aspect of themselves during earlier life, while true for many, is a misunderstanding of human plasticity. Some individuals do not fully appreciate their feelings, some consciously choose to deny them, and others have learned to accentuate other dimensions of their lives. For many young people, the combination of cues, expectancies, and social circumstances is such that the sociosexual feelings remain diffuse, consciousness of their meaning is not well-developed, and social circumstances, including pervasive homophobia, make the emergence of same-gendered affect extremely difficult. The consequences of early disclosure for those teens whose feelings crystallize are very risky, with family and peer rejection highly probable.

3. The human development model emphasizes interindividual differences in intraindividual behavioral development. In other words, the perspective focuses on behavioral variation; individual women and men

are unique in their own development over the life span. The nature of the interindividual differences in intraindividual functioning varies at different points in life, in different settings, and at different historical periods. For instance, it is generally assumed that behavioral diversity is amplified in adulthood with increasing age, at least until the early older years. This diversity, with its tremendous range of interindividual difference, not only is a biological or psychological event but also is a result of the individual's personal, family, and community social networks. Later in life, such variability may decrease. This decrease in interindividual difference may be partly a function of biological aging as well as changes in social circumstances. Increasing numbers of individuals are no longer in highly varied work settings after retirement and are exposed to more homogeneous social networks. These networks, in becoming more age homogeneous, decrease in time with members' deaths. Changing social networks partly explain decreasing interindividual variation.

In terms of gay and lesbian development, the issue of variability is essential. Indeed, the concept strikes directly at the trichotomization of sexual life in which individuals are assumed to be heterosexual, gay or lesbian, or bisexual. The human development perspective suggests continua of sexual feelings and experience, but would predict less variance in individual sexual self-definitions at certain phases of life, in certain kinds of families, in certain communities, and at certain historical times. That sexual diversity increases during adulthood is the result not only of postadolescent experiential factors but also of exposure to less restrictive expectations and the availability of an increased range of behavioral models for diversity.

4. The human development perspective suggests that the deterministic views of behavior often seen in traditional models of development underestimate the impact that individuals and their families have on their own development. Historically, developmental psychology has been arguing the relative merits of organismic and mechanistic points of view about life-span development (Reese & Overton, 1970). Current integrations of these views suggest that individuals and their families are not passive respondents to social circumstances and that behavioral development at times follows conscious choice and action. Individual acts and the acts of family members (in consort or in varying degrees of coordination) have an impact on the developmental process of the individual person and on the family unit. (This entire discussion could be

recapitulated at the level of individual-family/social structure interface, but will not be done here.) The actions of an individual shape his or her development. If one assumes that development can be conceptualized without ideological distortion as involving increased differentiation, then individuals with refined abilities to behave in diverse ways—whose psychoemotional responsivity allows for behavioral complexity and whose social skills allow for competent performance in a wide range of social settings—are likely to be more highly "developed." Of course, many circumstances are beyond individual control. The learned helplessness occurs to the degree that individuals feel that they cannot shape their circumstances, and this perception is often accurate. Under these conditions, such individuals will develop a cognitive and emotional set that promotes passivity and helplessness. In any event, in contrast to mechanistic views in which individuals are responsive to social circumstances and to organismic views in which internalized developmental processes emerge, this aspect of the human development model demonstrates the power of individuals and their families to promote their own individual development and family change.

Lesbians and gay men shape their own development out of necessity, due to a heterosexist culture that provides no routine socialization for lesbian and gay development. Because of this historical need, there has evolved over a time a series of social institutions for lesbians and gay men that have provided partial socialization experiences. Individuals who enter these social circumstances will have their development promoted, at least within the intrinsic social norms of the settings. The primary structure for urban men has been the gay bar and, to a lesser degree, gay bath houses, which have nearly disappeared in the AIDS era. Lesbian socialization has occurred in the past more often in small, nonpublic informal groups or in women's communities. The nature of these socialization structures has shaped distinct stereotypes: Gay men are sexual machines, whereas lesbians are relationship bound. The increasing number of nonsexual social opportunities for gay men and the larger number of expressive options for lesbians will have a tremendous impact on "normative" development. Women and men in current cohorts will socialize themselves under new circumstances and will have a different developmental history. They will be "different persons." To the degree that emphasis on sexual competence or on relationship processes is a limited template for behavioral development, the increasingly diverse contexts in which individuals can place themselves to explore their affective lives cannot help but promote increased behavioral differentiation.

The tenet that individuals help direct their own development is fundamental to the human development model. It is extraordinarily powerful for understanding lesbian and gay development at different historical times. For an adult in 1950 to decide that he or she had strong lesbian or gay feelings and to become publicly active in the social circumstances available at that time was extremely different from an analogous behavioral sequence in 1990, although the actions may seem similar. Disclosure to family, for example, which remains a universally difficult part of lesbian and gay development, is now facilitated by increased cultural acceptance, more positive imagery in media, and much more gay-affirming resources. In earlier days, families could fear their offspring's arrest, loss of employment, social censure, and isolation. By definition, disclosure of lesbian/gay status was admission of criminal status and mental illness. Currently, fewer fears of this order occur, although realistic worry remains a fundamental dynamic of lesbian/gay development because of the lack of legal protection that lesbians and gay men experience in asserting their rights in housing, adoption of children, employment, military service, and so on. In nearly half of the United States consensual sexual activity between lesbians and between gay men is illegal. Because of these formal social and legal barriers, self-development remains compromised. Identity development and integration must be influenced if such development jeopardizes employment and career, family relationships, and even freedom from arrest and permissible discrimination. In this way, historical, institutional, and cultural practices strongly, and negatively, influence the concept of self-development. Withdrawal and passive aggressiveness can easily be developed as personality traits in response to the pervasive social stigma.

Development occurs on other levels as well: Dyads, groups, and families also evolve and change. A family's actions shape the future of that family's life. For instance, a family that chooses to reject a young person because of affectional status has made a behavioral decision with long-term, often troublesome, consequences. On the other hand, the family that responds affirmatively to a member's disclosure and actively incorporates the person's partners and friends into the family's communal life not only promotes the development of the individual lesbian or gay man in a constructive manner but also shapes the structure and function of the entire family. In this way, families develop in their recognition of their own diversity. The behavioral flexibility of an affirming family can then be transmitted to the younger family members so that younger children will have greater freedom for self-development in the future.

5. The human development model brings along with it a variety of methodological considerations that suggest the kind of empirical research that must be done to make generalizations about development phenomena. The most fundamental consideration is the use of multiple measures linked to each of the major sets of factors that influence development over the life span. Simply studying the person is inadequate.

Another crucial methodological consequence of the life span developmental perspective is the need for longitudinal research designs. Such designs overcome the pervasive problems of cross-sectional research and of the inevitable confusions of retrospective research. The available research on lesbian and gay development is nearly uniformly cross-sectional, retrospective, or a combination of the two. There is no methodologically sound longitudinal research on lesbian/gay development in the social science literature. The more rigorous projects, ranging from the original Kinsey reports through the Blumstein and Schwartz (1983) survey, *American Couples,* include individuals of different ages in their lesbian and gay samples. Yet these projects do not focus on chronological age as an important dimension. Other research projects that were less rigorously designed, such as Spada's (1979) and Saghir and Robins's (1973) reports, aggregate individuals of diverse chronological ages and thus cannot distinguish individuals of different chronological ages or cohorts. Even were they to do this, of course, they would suffer from other flaws endemic to cross-sectional studies.

The other prominent research in the area has been retrospective: Adult men and women are asked to consider their developmental history. This tradition in research on homosexuality goes back as far as the 1950s with the original psychodynamic studies of homosexual patients done by Bieber et al. (1962) and continued up through the publication in 1981 of *Sexual Preference* (Bell et al., 1981), a study of men and women's memories of their childhood. That individuals who were research subjects in 1950 might retrospect and present their earlier histories as those of certain stereotyped dysfunctional patterns is hardly surprising given the professional context of the 1950s in which there was little disagreement that passive fathers and emotionally domineering mothers were the universal causal determinants of adult sexual "inversion." That similar patterns were not found in 1981 in a 1969 San Francisco sample reflects several issues, not the least of which is changes in individuals' understanding of contemporary views of early development. In 1969 individual gay women and men in the sample, who were on the average in their late 20s and early 30s, had been exposed to different ways of thinking about early childhood development, especially a decline in the popularity of the fixed early-determinism model. They were not patients in psychiatric settings and also resided in an area with a large gay community. A strong sense of local community involvement may have helped to deemphasize early historical antecedents. Because individuals in the gay community who had come to San Francisco no doubt varied in their early childhood patterns, they would see little consistency in their histories. Personal variability observed in day-to-day life could affect retrospective accounts of individual development, which is notoriously biased anyway.

Conclusions

Theory building and empirical research on lesbian/gay lives that is consistent with a human development point of view has simply not been done. Normative statements about development must be founded on such a database. To accomplish such research would involve following a large number of individual families from conception through early childhood and into adulthood, and perhaps even through later adulthood, and would attempt to determine various points in time when individuals within different families, different communities, and different contexts would experience varying degrees of affectional interests. Such research would be extraordinarily difficult to accomplish and would involve considerably more methodological precision in assessment of the variability of sexual responsiveness than is currently available.

There is no simple solution to the problem of conducting research in this manner, although some short-term solutions may be possible. The most pragmatic and powerful solution is to incorporate assessment of affectional status in all longitudinal (and developmental) research. Few studies seek information about current affectional status, assuming all participants are heterosexual. Had even simple questions been posed, researchers already would have accumulated rich data about affectional-sexual development. Another possibility is the development of research projects on early adolescence, over a period of time between later childhood and early adulthood. During this period, if data on sexual expression were collected annually, this might demonstrate how sexual feelings evolve over an important phase of development. Finally, additional studies of those phases of family life traditionally ignored would be helpful. Studies of older adults, teens, and grandparents are crucial examples of such work.

The life span human development model offers a strong organizing framework for future scholarship and empirical research. It provides a powerful alternative to earlier perspectives and avoids the damaging ideological commitments of prior models.

References

Adelman, M. (Ed.). (1986). *Long time passing: Lives of older lesbians.* Boston: Alyson.

Balka, C., & Rose, A. (Eds.). (1989). *Twice blessed: On being lesbian, gay, and Jewish.* Boston: Beacon.

Baltes, P. B. (1987). Theoretical propositions of life-span developmental psychology: On the dynamics between growth and decline. *Developmental Psychology, 23,* 611-626.

Bell, A. P., & Weinberg, M. S. (1978). *Homosexualities: A study of diversity among men and women.* New York: Simon & Schuster.

Bell, A. P., Weinberg, M. S., & Hammersmith, S. K. (1981). *Sexual preference: Its development in men and women.* Bloomington: Indiana University Press.

Bieber, I., Dair, H. J., Dince, P. R., Drellich, M. G., Grand, H. G., Gundlach, R. H., Kremer, M. W., Rifkin, A. H., Wilbur, C. B., & Bieber, T. B. (1962). *Homosexuality: A psychoanalytic study of male homosexuals.* New York: Basic Books.

Blumstein, P., & Schwartz, P. (1983). *American couples: Money, work, sex.* New York: William Morrow.

Bozett, F. W. (Ed.). (1987). *Gay and lesbian parents.* New York: Praeger.

Bozett, F. W. (Ed.). (1989). *Homosexuality and the family.* New York: Haworth.

Cramer, D. W., & Roach, A. J. (1988). Coming out to mom and dad: A study of gay males and their relationships with their parents. *Journal of Homosexuality, 15,* 79-92.

Ellis, L., & Ames, M. A. (1987). Neurohormonal functioning and sexual orientation: A theory of homosexuality-heterosexuality. *Psychological Bulletin, 101,* 233-258.

Friedman, R. C. (1988). *Male homosexuality: A contemporary psychoanalytic perspective.* New Haven, CT: Yale University Press.

Herdt, G. (Ed.). (1989). *Gay and lesbian youth.* New York: Harrington Park.

Isay, R. (1989). *Being homosexual: Gay men and their development.* New York: Farrar, Straus and Giroux.

Kaplan, A. (1964). *The conduct of inquiry.* San Francisco: Chandler.

Kehoe, M. (Ed.). (1989). *Lesbians over 60 speak for themselves.* New York: Haworth.

Kevles, D. J. (1985). *In the name of eugenics.* New York: Knopf.

Kinsman, G. (1987). *The regulation of desire: Sexuality in Canada.* Montreal: Black Rose.

Kitzinger, C. (1988). *The social construction of lesbianism.* London: Sage.

Kurdek, L. A. (1988). Relationship quality of gay and lesbian cohabiting couples. *Journal of Homosexuality, 15,* 93-118.

Lee, J. A. (1987). What can homosexual aging studies contribute to theories of aging? *Journal of Homosexuality, 13,* 43-71.

Lerner, R. M. (1984). *On the nature of human plasticity.* Cambridge, UK: Cambridge University Press.

Lewontin, R. C., Rose, S., & Kamin, L. J. (1984). *Not in our genes.* New York: Pantheon.

Money, J. (1987). Sin, sickness, or status? Homosexual gender identity and psychoneuroendocrinology. *American Psychologist, 42,* 384-399.

Reese, H. W., & Overton, W. F. (1970). Models of development and theories of development. In L. R. Goulet & P. B. Baltes (Eds.), *Life-span developmental psychology: Research and theory* (pp. 115-145). New York: Academic Press.

Ruse, M. (1988). *Homosexuality: A philosophical inquiry.* New York: Basil Blackwell.

Saghir, M., & Robins, E. (1973). *Male and female homosexuality: A comprehensive investigation.* Baltimore, MD: Williams & Wilkins.

Spada, J. (1979). *The Spada report: The newest survey of gay male sexuality.* New York: New American Library.

Vacha, K. (1985). *Quiet fire: Memoirs of older gay men.* Trumansburg, NY: Crossing Press.

Weinberg, M. S., & Williams, C. J. (1974). *Male homosexuals: Their problems and adaptations.* New York: Oxford University Press.

Williams, W. L. (1986). *The spirit and the flesh: Sexual diversity in American Indian culture.* Boston: Beacon.

8

The Nature and Correlates of Relationship Quality in Gay, Lesbian, and Heterosexual Cohabiting Couples

A Test of the Individual Difference, Interdependence, and Discrepancy Models

LAWRENCE A. KURDEK

Relationship status is linked to well-being. Compared with persons not in relationships, those in relationships report enhanced positive well-being (Bell & Weinberg, 1978; Wood, Rhodes, & Whelan, 1989). Furthermore, the dissolution of a relationship is perceived as one of the most stressful life events (Dohrenwend, Krasnoff, Askenasy, & Dohrenwend, 1978; Kurdek, 1991a). The documented salience of relationship status for psychological functioning provides one justification for developing models of relationship functioning.

Why Be Interested in Homosexual Couples?

Currently, most of the work on close relationships is based on heterosexual couples. However, there are at least three reasons for a scientific interest in homosexual couples. First, because gender-related socialization is irrelevant to the relationship behavior of lesbians and gay men

AUTHOR'S NOTE: I would like to thank the couples who participated in this study. Thanks also go to David Arnold, Glenna Darnell-Goetschel, and Pete McConnell for their assistance in subject recruitment and data entry.

(Kurdek, 1993a), the study of same-gender relationships provides some insight into how couple roles emerge. Second, because same-gender relationships develop without the support of social institutions and often without the support of members from the family of origin (Kurdek 1988; Kurdek & Schmitt, 1986a), they afford an opportunity to examine how interpersonal dynamics play themselves out without the support typically provided by society at large or by family members in particular. Third, because sexual activity in gay male and lesbian relationships occurs without procreative intent, the study of such relationships provides information on how nontraditional attitudes regarding monogamy and fidelity affect relationship quality.

What Is Known About Lesbian and Gay Male Couples?

Although information about same-gender couples is limited (Kurdek, in press), several findings have been consistently reported. First, and most basic, many gay men and lesbians are involved in relationships. Based on a review of survey data from convenience samples, Peplau and Cochran (1990) estimated that between 40% and 60% of gay men and between 45% and 80% of lesbians are involved in a steady relationship. Furthermore, many gay men and lesbians establish lifelong partnerships (Blumstein & Schwartz,1983; McWhirter & Mattison, 1984).

Second, when the relationship satisfaction of gay men, lesbians, and heterosexuals is compared, few if any differences emerge. In fact, in their review of studies in this area, Peplau and Cochran (1990) concluded that "most gay men and lesbians perceive their close relationships as satisfying and that levels of love and satisfaction are similar for homosexual and heterosexual couples who are matched on age and other relevant characteristics" (p. 333).

Third, the correlates of relationship satisfaction are similar for homosexual and heterosexual couples. In general, relationship satisfaction is positively related to appraisals that the relationship includes high rewards and few costs and to personality characteristics associated with interpersonal competence such as low neuroticism and high expressiveness (Peplau & Cochran, 1990).

Finally, homosexual relationships show normative changes over time that are similar to those observed in heterosexual couples. Generally, the pattern of relationship development begins with a period of *limerence* (absorption with the partner and the relationship and a near-exclusive focus on only the positive characteristics of the partner). As limerence declines, issues of power are confronted, and strategies for dealing with conflict are developed. With time, partners may become independent of one another, yet increase their trust of one another and their feelings of security in the relationship (McWhirter & Mattison, 1984).

What Is Not Known About Lesbian and Gay Male Couples?

Despite the consistency of the above findings, there are many gaps in the knowledge of same-gender couples. Perhaps the most salient limitation is that the bulk of research in this area is atheoretical. Because information on basic relationship issues is still needed, descriptive studies provide useful information. However, if the science of gay and lesbian close relationships is to advance, conceptual frameworks are needed to integrate current findings and to generate testable predictions regarding the nature of such relationships.

Previous Work on Gay Male and Lesbian Couples

The author's work on same-gender couples has involved three projects.

The First Project

The first project compared gay and lesbian cohabiting couples with married and nonmarried heterosexual cohabiting couples. This project was primarily descriptive and indicated that (a) relationship quality and its correlates were similar for gay, lesbian, and married couples (Kurdek & Schmitt, 1986a, 1986b); (b) from a cross-sectional perspective, the second and third years of a relationship were more likely than other years to involve stress and disillusionment (Kurdek & Schmitt, 1986c); (c) married couples perceived more support from family members than did gay and lesbian couples (Kurdek & Schmitt, 1987a); (d) although gay male couples valued fidelity less than did the other couples, sexual satisfaction was positively related to relationship satisfaction for each type of couple (Kurdek, 1991b); (e) gay male couples who were sexually exclusive did not differ from those that were not sexually exclusive on reports of relationship satisfaction (Kurdek & Schmitt, 1986d); and (f) although partners in each type of couple were generally similar to each other, similarity was most marked for lesbian partners (Kurdek & Schmitt, 1987b).

The Second Project

The second project was a 4-year prospective longitudinal study of relationship quality in gay and lesbian couples that had an explicit theoretical focus. This project represents one of the few longitudinal studies of same-gender couples, and it also is one of the few studies to assess how well models of relationship quality derived from research on heterosexual couples predict both relationship stability and changes in relationship satisfaction for same-gender couples. Because findings from the first project suggested that the processes regulating relationship functioning are similar for homosexual and heterosexual couples, models based on work with heterosexual couples seemed like good candidates to integrate information regarding relationship satisfaction and relationship stability in homosexual couples. Three models were of particular interest.

As part of a broader individual difference model, Bradbury and Fincham (1988) proposed that individual difference variables filter relationship information. In support of this model, there is evidence from homosexual and heterosexual couples that individual difference variables (e.g., expressiveness, negative affectivity, and dysfunctional beliefs about relationships) are concurrently related to relationship satisfaction and prospectively predict changes in both marital satisfaction and marital stability (Bentler & Newcomb, 1978; Bradbury & Fincham, 1988; Kelly & Conley, 1987; Kurdek, 1991c, 1992b, 1993b).

In one version of an interdependence model of relationship functioning, Rusbult (1983) proposed that a person satisfied with his or her relationship perceives many rewards from the relationship, perceives few costs to being in the relationship, and evaluates his or her relationship as meeting or exceeding an internal standard of a good relationship. Furthermore, she proposed that relationship stability is related to high satisfaction with the relationship, few attractive alternatives to the relationship, and large investments in the relationship. Supportive evidence for this model comes from studies of concurrent predictors of relationship satisfaction in homosexual and heterosexual couples (Duffy & Rusbult, 1986; Kurdek, 1991d; Kurdek & Schmitt, 1986a) and longitudinal studies of predictors of both relationship satisfaction and relationship stability in homosexual and heterosexual couples (Kurdek, 1992b, 1993b; Rusbult, 1983).

A third model related to relationship satisfaction posits that discrepancies between partners' appraisals of relationship events are negatively related to relationship satisfaction (Cowan et al., 1985). This discrepancy model may be regarded as an extension of the contextual model, because it suggests that relationship distress occurs when partners in the relationship view that relationship from incompatible vantage points. Such viewpoints are likely to lead to the partners' emphasizing different aspects of the relationship, constructing different explanations for negative relationship events, and using different strategies for resolving interpersonal conflict (Baucom & Epstein, 1990). In support of this model, previous studies have found that large discrepancies in married partners' individual difference scores and relationship appraisals predict relationship distress as well as relationship dissolution (Bentler & Newcomb, 1978; Cowan et al., 1985; Kurdek, 1991c, 1993b).

Findings from the second project indicated that (a) demographic variables, individual difference variables, and interdependence variables discriminated between couples who stayed together and those who separated; (b) partner discrepancies on these variables were, surprisingly, generally unrelated to relationship stability; (c) changes in the individual difference and interdependence variables over the 4 years of study were related to changes in relationship satisfaction over this same time period; and (d) variables from the interdependence model mediated the effects of variables from the individual difference model on both relationship stability and changes in relationship satisfaction (i.e., when the effects of the interdependence variables were controlled, the individual difference variables did not predict relationship stability or changes in relationship satisfaction) (Kurdek, 1992b).

The Third Project

The third project is another prospective longitudinal study and has an even stronger theoretical base than the second project in that it relates appraisals of relationship satisfaction to concurrent assessments of variables from problem-solving models of relationship quality as well as those from the individual difference, interdependence, and discrepancy models. In the first wave of the study, although each set of variables was reliably related to relationship satisfaction, the interdependence variables accounted for the lion's share of variability in relationship satisfaction (Kurdek, 1991d). Data from the third annual follow-up have just been collected.

The Current Study

The study of gay and lesbian relationships is of interest in its own right. However, studies that involve a comparison group of heterosexual couples are informative because they provide information about what is different and what is similar about the ways that homosexual and heterosexual couples work. Such data, however, are limited. Fortunately, the second project described above included measures identical to those that were used in a separate ongoing, longitudinal study of relationship satisfaction in newlywed couples (Kurdek, 1991e).

The study reported here added a matched sample of heterosexual married couples from the first wave of data collection in the longitudinal newlywed study to a matched sample of gay and lesbian couples from the first wave of data collection in the longitudinal study of homosexual couples. Unlike some theory-based studies of homosexual relationships that used the individual respondent as the unit of analysis (Duffy & Rusbult, 1986), this study employed the couple as the unit of analysis.

Purposes of the Study

The first purpose of the study was to compare the reported relationship satisfaction of gay, lesbian, and married heterosexual couples. Previous studies using reports of individual partners (Blumstein & Schwartz, 1983; Duffy & Rusbult, 1986; Kurdek & Schmitt, 1986a) have generally found that gay men, lesbians, and married individuals report similar levels of relationship satisfaction. This pattern was expected to be replicated with the couple as the unit of analysis.

The second purpose of the study was to compare gay, lesbian, and heterosexual couples along variables derived from the individual difference and interdependence models as well as by partner discrepancies on these variables. The individual difference variables of interest here included dysfunctional beliefs regarding the relationship, satisfaction with social support, expressiveness, and negative affectivity. The interdependence included rewards derived from the relationship (positive features intrinsic to the relationship), costs to being in the relationship (extent of disagreement), alternatives to the relationship (personal autonomy), and investments in the relationship (pooled finances and emotional investment). Again, based on findings from studies using individual partners as respondents (Duffy & Rusbult, 1986; Kurdek & Schmitt, 1986a), couples were expected to be equivalent on these variables.

The third purpose of the study was to see if variables from the individual difference, interdependence, and discrepancy models were related to relationship satisfaction for each type of couple. In regard to the individual difference variables, dysfunctional beliefs regarding relationships (e.g., that disagreements are destructive to a relationship) have been negatively related to relationship satisfaction (Bradbury & Fincham, 1988), perhaps because such beliefs inhibit the development of constructive, positive problem-solving strategies (Baucom & Epstein, 1990). Satisfaction with social support has been positively related to relationship satisfaction (Kurdek, 1991d), perhaps because persons satisfied with perceived levels of support have the interpersonal resources to handle relationship distress (Sarason, Pierce, & Sarason, 1990). Expressivity (e.g., tenderness, compassion, and warmth) has also been positively related to relationship satisfaction (Kurdek, 1991d), perhaps because persons with these traits focus on the needs of the partner in the course of resolving interpersonal problems (Rusbult, Verette, Whitney, Slovik, & Lipkus, 1991). Finally, persons disposed to report aversive emotional states tend to be dissatisfied with their relationships, perhaps because they experience discomfort even in the absence of overt stress, they dwell on the negative sides of themselves and others, and they exaggerate the significance of negative marital events (Bentler & Newcomb, 1978; Kelly & Conley, 1987; Watson & Clark, 1984).

In regard to the interdependence variables, persons satisfied with their relationships have been found to perceive their relationship as having many rewards and few costs, to minimize the attractiveness of alternatives to the relationship, and to invest heavily in the relationship (Duffy & Rusbult, 1986; Johnson & Rusbult, 1989; Kurdek, 1991d; Kurdek & Schmitt, 1986a).

Based on the above findings, it was expected that for each type of couple, relationship satisfaction would be negatively related to dysfunctional beliefs about relationships and negative affectivity and positively related to satisfaction with social support and expressiveness. In addition, persons who see their relationship as having many rewards and few costs, who have few attractive alternatives to the relationship, and who have made large investments in the relationship were expected to report high relationship satisfaction. Furthermore, couple satisfaction was expected to be negatively related to discrepancies between partners' scores on these variables (Cowan et al., 1985; Kurdek, 1991c, 1992b).

The final purpose of this study was to test whether the interdependence variables mediated the effects of the individual difference variables. This prediction was based on the assumption that the individual difference variables operate at a more distal level than the interdependence variables. Because people bring individual difference characteristics to their relationships, these characteristics were thought to influence how a specific relationship would be appraised (Kurdek, 1991d). Thus the individual difference variables were expected to exert direct effects on the interdependence variables that, in turn, were expected to exert direct effects on relationship satisfaction.

The Design of the Study

Participants

Subjects were selected from larger samples in the first wave of two separate prospective longitudinal studies, one involving same-gender couples and the other involving heterosexual couples. Same-gender couples were recruited through requests for participants published in national gay/lesbian periodicals and newsletters as well as through personal contacts and referrals from couples who had already participated in the study. Heterosexual couples were recruited from marriage licenses published in the *Dayton Daily News.* Because relationship quality varies over time (McWhirter & Mattison, 1984), it was desirable to obtain groups of gay, lesbian, and heterosexual couples who were matched on length of time living together. The pool of homosexual couples involved 80 gay and 53 lesbian couples, whereas the pool of heterosexual couples involved 538 newlywed couples. Because of the large size of the heterosexual pool of subjects, matching on time living together was first done between the gay and lesbian couples.

A total of 39 pairs of gay and lesbian couples were matched within a mean of 1.48 months of cohabitation. These pairs, in turn, were matched with heterosexual couples within 1.01 months of cohabitation. Because each sample was drawn from a larger group of subjects, it was of interest whether the selected samples differed from their respective larger group on reports of relationship satisfaction.

A 2×2 (selected couple versus nonselected couple $\times$ gay male couple versus lesbian couple) analysis of covariance, controlling for months of cohabitation, revealed a significant interaction between selection status and type of couple, $F(1, 128) = 6.39$, $p < .05$. Gay male couples in the selected sample reported lower relationship satisfaction than those not selected, whereas the selected and nonselected lesbian couples did not differ from each other. A one-way (selected couple versus nonselected couple) analysis of covariance, controlling for months of cohabitation, on the heterosexual couples' relationship satisfaction score revealed a nonsignificant effect, $F(1, 535) = 0.08$, $p > .05$. Thus, although the lesbian and heterosexual couples were representative of the larger groups of respective subjects, the selected gay male couples were biased toward lower functioning couples. This bias suggests caution in interpreting findings for the male couples.

Demographic Characteristics of the Participants. More than 87% of the partners in each couple were white. The modal level of education for both gay couples and lesbian couples was college graduation, while that for heterosexual couples was partial college. The modal personal annual income was between $25,000 and $29,999 for the gay couples, between $27,250 and $32,500 for the lesbian couples, and between $20,000 and $24,999 for the heterosexual couples. The mean amount of time living together was approximately 3 years for each type of couple.

Unambiguous comparisons among the three types of couples required that they be comparable on demographic characteristics. Means and standard deviations for the demographic scores are presented by type of couple in Table 8.1. A one-way (type of couple) MANOVA yielded a significant effect, $F(8, 224) = 4.39$, $p < .001$. Subsequent univariate ANOVAs indicated that the multivariate effect was due to educational differences among the three types of couples. As also indicated in Table 8.1, Student Newman-Keuls comparisons ($p < .05$ here and below)

Table 8.1 Means and Standard Deviations for Demographic, Relationship Satisfaction, Individual Difference, and Interdependence Scores by Type of Couple

Variable	*Gay*	*Lesbian*	*Heterosexual*	F
DEMOGRAPHIC				
Age				
Mean	32.64	33.88	30.65	1.97
Standard deviation	4.76	7.12	9.16	
Education				
Mean	6.29[a]	6.33[a]	5.38[b]	13.45**
Standard deviation	0.86	0.96	0.90	
Income				
Mean	6.46	5.67	5.60	1.79
Standard deviation	2.43	1.98	2.20	
Months together				
Mean	36.33	35.24	36.32	0.03
Standard deviation	21.39	20.97	21.79	
SATISFACTION				
Mean	24.14[a]	25.93[b]	25.52[b]	4.83**
Standard deviation	2.83	2.16	2.88	
INDIVIDUAL DIFFERENCE				
Dysfunctional relationship beliefs				
Mean	32.60	31.48	31.82	0.15
Standard deviation	9.18	9.28	8.63	
Social support				
Mean	31.02	31.19	30.85	0.06
Standard deviation	3.25	4.58	3.64	
Expressiveness				
Mean	67.57	68.03	66.18	0.93
Standard deviation	5.02	5.94	6.04	
Negative affectivity				
Mean	19.71	17.11	14.43	1.49
Standard deviation	13.85	11.68	13.72	
INTERDEPENDENCE				
Rewards				
Mean	36.05[a]	40.68[b]	38.85[b]	9.24**
Standard deviation	5.36	4.27	4.69	
Cost				
Mean	22.07[a]	18.57[a,b]	18.62[b]	3.43*
Standard deviation	6.29	6.55	6.99	
Autonomy				
Mean	41.19	41.14	41.30	0.01
Standard deviation	5.79	5.77	6.88	
Joint finances				
Mean	0.34	0.31	0.49	1.69
Standard deviation	0.39	0.40	0.44	
Emotional investment				
Mean	31.33	32.98	32.64	0.99

Table 8.1 (Continued)

Variable	*Gay*	*Lesbian*	*Heterosexual*	F
Standard deviation	5.61	5.41	5.32	
DISCREPANCY (Absolute Value)				
Age				
Mean	6.97[a]	5.15[a,b]	3.35[b]	5.19**
Standard deviation	6.06	4.83	3.66	
Education				
Mean	1.30[a]	0.87[b]	0.61[b]	5.92**
Standard deviation	1.17	0.76	0.67	
Income				
Mean	3.17	2.59	2.48	1.08
Standard deviation	2.43	2.26	1.98	
Satisfaction				
Mean	2.30	1.71	2.02	0.73
Standard deviation	2.74	1.31	2.13	
Dysfunctional relationship beliefs				
Mean	9.87	7.97	8.79	0.81
Standard deviation	6.98	5.71	6.94	
Social support				
Mean	5.12	3.38	4.41	1.73
Standard deviation	4.04	4.07	4.33	
Expressiveness				
Mean	8.20	7.82	10.07	1.03
Standard deviation	8.06	7.68	6.33	
Negative affectivity				
Mean	14.02	11.56	14.25	0.45
Standard deviation	15.24	9.56	15.75	
Rewards				
Mean	5.71	5.12	5.20	0.21
Standard deviation	4.71	4.51	3.75	
Cost				
Mean	4.82	4.23	5.59	0.86
Standard deviation	4.08	4.69	4.87	
Autonomy				
Mean	6.05	5.82	7.15	0.60
Standard deviation	5.78	5.44	5.98	
Emotional investment				
Mean	5.28	5.79	5.30	0.13
Standard deviation	5.13	5.33	4.00	

NOTE: The *n* for each type of couple is 39. Maximum value for education and income score is 8 and 12, respectively. Joint finances is a dichotomous variable, 0 = *no*, 1 = *yes*. For demographic and discrepancy scores, means are observed means and *F* is based on 2 and 114 *df*. For all other scores, means are adjusted for education and *F* is based on 2 and 113 *df*.

a, b Means with different superscripts differ from each other, $p < .05$.

*$p < .05$.

**$p < .01$.

revealed that the gay male and lesbian couples had mean higher levels of education than the heterosexual couples. To ensure that differences between couples were not due to differences in educational level, analyses comparing the couples included education as a covariate.

Data Collection

Each couple was mailed two identical surveys along with a letter of informed consent, measures of demographic variables, a measure of relationship satisfaction, measures of the individual difference variables, and measures of the interdependence variables. A more detailed description of these measures follows. Completed surveys were returned in postage-paid envelopes. Respondents were asked not to discuss their responses with each other until after the surveys were completed, but no checks were made to assess whether this suggestion was followed. In all instances, couple scores were derived by averaging both partners' scores.

Demographic Variables. Participants provided information regarding age, race, education (represented by eight intervals ranging from completion of less than seventh grade to the award of a doctorate), and annual personal income (represented by 12 intervals ranging from $5,000 or less to $50,000 or more).

Relationship Satisfaction. Relationship satisfaction was assessed by the satisfaction subscale of Spanier's (1976) Dyadic Adjustment Scale. This 10-item scale has prospectively predicted relationship dissolution in both homosexual and heterosexual couples (Kurdek, 1992a). A total of 6 of the 10 items were used in this study. These concerned the frequency of considering terminating the relationship, leaving the house after a fight, thinking that things are not going well in the relationship, and regretting that the respondent and his or her spouse live together as well as general assessments of both the degree of unhappiness in the relationship and the lack of success of the relationship. The 4 items were excluded to avoid overlap between this score and the rewards and cost predictors (Fincham & Bradbury, 1987). The deleted items concerned confiding in the partner, kissing the partner, quarreling, and getting on each other's nerves. Information regarding response format and psychometric data for this and all subsequent measures can be found in the cited references. Cronbach α for all summed composite scores used in this study were calculated for each partner/spouse in each couple of the present sample and were found to be acceptable. Collapsed over type of couple, the mean α for partner 1/husband was .79, whereas that for partner 2/wife was .81.

Variables From the Individual Difference Model

Dysfunctional Relationship Beliefs. Dysfunctional beliefs regarding relationships were assessed by the 32-item Relationship Beliefs Inventory (Eidelson & Epstein, 1982). These items required subjects to indicate how strongly they endorsed beliefs regarding the destructiveness of disagreements, mind-reading, partner change, and sexual perfection.

Self-Perceived Expressiveness. Self-ratings of expressiveness were obtained by 12 items (e.g., tender, compassionate, warm, and sympathetic) from the Bem Sex Role Inventory (Bem, 1974). These items defined an orthogonal expressiveness factor in a previous factor analysis of the inventory (Kurdek, 1987).

Satisfaction With Social Support. The short form of the Social Support Scale (Sarason, Sarason, Shearin, & Pierce, 1987) requires subjects to rate their satisfaction with the support they receive in six areas.

Negative Affectivity. Negative affectivity was assessed by the anxiety, depression, and interpersonal sensitivity (i.e., social anxiety) scores from the Symptom Checklist 90-R (Derogatis, 1983). Subjects indicated how much discomfort each of the 32 items caused during the past 7 days.

Variables From the Interdependence Model

Rewards From the Relationship. Perceived rewards from the relationship were assessed by the six-item intrinsic score derived from Rempel, Holmes, and Zanna's (1985) Motivation Scale. For each item, respondents indicated how much the item played a role in the relationship (e.g., "We are close and intimate. We have special ways of demonstrating affection and letting each other know how we feel.").

Costs to the Relationship. Perceived costs to the relationship were assessed by the 15-item consensus score from Spanier's (1976) Dyadic Adjustment Scale, which tapped how much disagreement existed between the respondent and his or her partner on each item.

Investment Size. Investment size was assessed by two variables. These were whether finances were pooled (i.e., couples had a joint savings or a joint checking account) and degree of emotional investment in the relationship. The latter variable was assessed by the six-item faith score derived from Rempel et al.'s (1985) Trust Scale. Subjects indicated the level of agreement with each item (e.g., "I occasionally find myself feeling uncomfortable with the emotional investment I have made in our relationship because I find it hard to completely set aside doubts about what lies ahead."; a reverse-scored item).

Alternatives. Alternatives to the relationship were assessed by the six-item autonomy score derived from Peplau and Cochran's (1981) Survey of Relationship Values. Subjects indicated how important each item was in their relationship (e.g., "Having major interests of my own outside of the relationship.").

Variables From the Discrepancy Model

The discrepancy model was represented by the absolute value of the difference between partners' demographic scores, between partners' individual difference scores, and between partners' interdependence scores. However, because partners were not expected to differ in their report of pooled finances, this interdependence variable was not included in the set of discrepancy variables.

The Findings

Differences Among the Couples

Of interest here was whether the three types of couples differed on relationship satisfaction, scores from the individual difference model, scores from the interdependence model, and scores from the discrepancy model. The means and standard deviations for each set of scores are presented by type of couple in the remainder of Table 8.1. Univariate *F*s and the results of Student Newman-Keuls comparisons of the means adjusted for education level are also shown.

A one-way (type of couple) ANCOVA, with education as the covariate, indicated that gay male couples reported lower relationship satisfaction than either lesbian or heterosexual couples; the latter did not differ from each other. A one-way (type of couple) MANCOVA with education as the covariate on the set of individual difference scores yielded a nonsignificant effect, $F(8, 222) = 0.79$, $p > .05$. However, a one-way (type of couple) MANCOVA on the set of interdependence scores did yield a significant effect, $F(10, 220) = 2.44$, $p < .01$. As shown in Table 8.1, this effect was due to gay couples perceiving fewer rewards to their relationships than either lesbian or heterosexual couples and perceiving greater costs than heterosexual couples. Finally, a one-way (type of couple) MANCOVA indicated that the three types of couples did not differ on the set of discrepancy scores, $F(24, 208) = 1.27$, $p > .05$.

Husbands Compared With the Average Gay Partner and Wives Compared With the Average Lesbian Partner

Because the heterosexual couple score combined information for husbands and for wives, it was of interest to compare information from husbands to that of the average gay partner (i.e., the gay couple score) and to compare information from wives to that of the average lesbian partner (i.e., the lesbian couple score). Separate analyses were performed for the satisfaction score, the set of individual difference scores, and the set of interdependence scores. Education was again used as a covariate.

Husbands' level of relationship satisfaction did not differ from that of the average gay male partner, $F(1, 75) = 3.04$, $p > .05$. However, husbands did differ from the average gay partner on the set of individual difference scores, $F(4, 72) = 4.15$, $p < .01$. Univariate comparisons were significant only for the expressiveness score, $F(1, 75) = 8.15$, $p < .01$. Gay male partners were more expressive than husbands; the adjusted means were 67.88 and 63.16, respectively. Finally, husbands and the average gay male partner did not differ from each other on the set of interdependence scores, $F(5, 71) = 0.96$, $p > .05$.

Wives' level of relationship satisfaction did not differ from that of the average lesbian partner, $F(1, 75) = 0.43$, $p > .05$. In addition, wives and the average lesbian partner did not differ on the set of individual difference scores, $F(4, 72) = 0.21$, $p > .05$, or on the set of interdependence scores, $F(5, 71) = 1.59$, $p > .05$.

Relationship Satisfaction

Pearson correlations between relationship satisfaction and the demographic, individual difference, interdependence, and discrepancy scores are presented for each of the three types of couples in Table 8.2. To test whether the pattern of correlations differed across the three types of couples, structural equation modeling was used to test the equality of three independent correlation matrices for the demographic, individual difference, interdependence, and discrepancy sets of scores (see Green, 1992). For each of the four sets of scores, a chi-square goodness-of-fit test derived from LISREL VII (Jöreskog & Sörbom, 1989) indicated that correlations with relationship satisfaction for each of the three types of couples were equivalent. For the set of demographic scores, $\chi^2 (6) = 5.20$; for the set of individual difference scores, $\chi^2 (8) = 14.28$; for the set of interdependence scores, $\chi^2 (10) = 13.02$; and for the set of discrepancy scores, $\chi^2 (20) = 15.97$. In each case, $p > .05$.

Given evidence of group equivalence, correlations based on the total sample are presented in the last column of Table 8.2. As can be seen, relationship satisfaction was (a) unrelated to each of the demographic scores, (b) negatively related to dysfunctional relationship beliefs and to negative affectivity and positively related to satisfaction with social support and expressiveness (the individual difference scores), (c) positively

Table 8.2 Pearson Correlations Between Relationship Satisfaction and Demographic, Individual Difference, Interdependence, and Discrepancy Scores by Type of Couple and Total Sample

Variable	*Gay*	*Lesbian*	*Heterosexual*	*Total*
DEMOGRAPHIC				
Age	.02	–.01	.23	.09
Education	.09	–.23	–.13	–.12
Income	.03	.04	–.07	–.05
INDIVIDUAL DIFFERENCE				
Dysfunctional relationship beliefs	–.36**	–.45**	–.46**	–.42**
Social support	.17	.57**	.50**	.40**
Expressiveness	.05	.34*	.56**	.32**
Negative affectivity	–.21	–.28*	–.47**	–.33**
INTERDEPENDENCE				
Rewards	.42**	.34*	.56**	.49**
Costs	–.49**	–.67**	–.74**	–.65**
Alternatives	–.18	–.17	.01	–.11
Pooled finances	.00	.04	–.06	.00
Emotional investment	.48**	.80**	.65**	.63**
DISCREPANCY				
Age	.06	–.20	.12	–.06
Education	.19	–.23	–.14	–.08
Income	–.17	–.22	–.30*	–.25**
Dysfunctional relationship beliefs	.07	–.12	–.10	–.07
Social support	–.08	–.45**	–.36**	–.32**
Expressiveness	–.28*	–.20	–.26*	–.22**
Negative affectivity	–.21	–.32*	–.26*	–.25**
Rewards	–.05	–.14	–.17	–.13
Costs	.09	–.35**	–.21	–.14
Alternatives	–.11	–.02	–.05	–.05
Emotional investment	–.19	–.39**	–.21	–.23**

NOTE: The *n* for each type of couple is 39 and for the total group is 119. Pooled finances is a dichotomous score, 0 = *no*, 1 = *yes*.
*$p < .05$.
**$p < .01$.

related to rewards and emotional investment and negatively related to costs (the interdependence scores), and (d) negatively related to the size of differences between partners' personal income, satisfaction with social support, expressiveness, negative affectivity, and emotional investment (the discrepancy scores).

Table 8.3 Pearson Correlations Between the Individual Difference Scores and the Interdependence Scores for the Total Sample

	Interdependence				
Individual Differences	*Rewards*	*Cost*	*Alternatives*	*Pooled Finances*	*Emotional Investment*
Dysfunctional relationship beliefs	−.25**	.45**	.14	−.08	−.50**
Social support	.35**	−.39**	−.08	.04	.53**
Expressiveness	.23**	−.41**	−.10	−.01	.41**
Negative affectivity	−.25**	.28**	.12	−.09	−.31**

NOTE: The *n* is 117.
**$p < .01$.

Test of Mediational Effects

Because the correlational findings were so similar across couples, the mediational hypothesis was tested using the total sample of couples. To see if the interdependence scores mediated the effects of the individual difference scores, three lines of evidence were needed (Baron & Kenny, 1986). First, the individual difference scores and the interdependence scores each had to be related to relationship satisfaction. The data in Table 8.2 satisfy this requirement. Second, the set of individual difference and interdependence scores had to be related to each other. This requirement was satisfied as indexed by the canonical correlation of .68, $p < .01$, between the two sets of variables and the Pearson correlations between scores from the two variable sets (Table 8.3). Finally, the set of individual difference scores should not account for additional unique variance in relationship satisfaction beyond that already accounted for by the interdependence scores.

This final requirement was tested by a four-step hierarchical multiple regression, the results of which are summarized in Table 8.4. Relationship satisfaction was the dependent variable. At step one, three background variables (age, education, and income) were entered. At step two, two contrast variables (gay and lesbian versus heterosexual and gay versus lesbian) were entered, which carried information from the type of couple effect. The set of interdependence scores was entered at step three, followed by the set of individual difference scores at step four. As shown in Table 8.4, significant increases in variance were obtained after

Table 8.4 Summary of Hierarchical Multiple Regression

Step	*Variable(s)*	R^2	R^2 *Change*	F *Change*	*Final* β
1	Age				.00
	Education				–.03
	Income	.03	.03	1.28	–.03
2	Gay & lesbian vs. heterosexual				.00
	Gay vs. lesbian	.11*	.08	4.68**	–.07
3	Rewards				.12
	Costs				–.39**
	Autonomy				.02
	Joint finances				–.05
	Emotional investment	.60**	.49	25.50**	.41**
4	Dysfunctional relationship beliefs				.01
	Social support				–.02
	Expressiveness				–.04
	Negative affectivity	.60**	.00	0.59	–.11

NOTE: The *n* is 117. Final βs are derived from the full four-step model.
*$p < .05$.
**$p < .01$.

steps two and three. Most important, the addition of the individual difference scores did not result in an increase in explained variance. Thus the mediational hypothesis was supported.

The β weights associated with the final equation are presented in the last column of Table 8.4. Two findings are of note. First, given all the other variables, the type of couple variables were not significant. Second, given the set of predictors of interest, only the interdependence variables of cost and emotional investment provided significant unique information.

Discussion

When couples were compared, gay male couples reported lower relationship satisfaction, fewer rewards from the relationship, and more costs to the relationship than either lesbian or heterosexual couples. Because the gay male couples selected for study were less satisfied with their relationship than were gay male couples in the larger sample who were not selected, this finding may be a sampling artifact. An alternative explanation is a social role interpretation (Eagly, 1987), which suggests that women are socialized to value social relationships more than men. Consequently, rather than focus on the low scores of gay couples, which are averages of two men's scores, this interpretation would focus on the high scores of couples in which one (heterosexual) or both (lesbian) partners are women. Support for this interpretation is provided by the finding that the average gay partner did not differ from heterosexual men in reports of relationship satisfaction, rewards from the relationship, and costs to the relationship. Furthermore, the average lesbian partner did not differ from heterosexual women on these same variables. Although this finding provides yet further evidence that appraisals of relationships do not vary between homosexual and heterosexual respondents of the same gender (Duffy & Rusbult, 1986; Kurdek & Schmitt, 1986a), more direct evidence is needed that a social role interpretation accounts for the type of couple effect. Because the average gay male partner was more expressive than the average husband, in accord with previous findings (Kurdek, 1987), one might have expected gay male partners to report greater satisfaction with their relationship than husbands. This did not occur. Future studies could obtain independent assessments of the specific importance of the relationship rather than tap a global trait of expressiveness. Because Rusbult (1983) notes that relationship satisfaction is linked to a comparison between one's current satisfaction with the relationship and one's expected level of satisfaction, future studies could also assess comparison levels.

Correlational analyses provided strong support for the prediction that relationship satisfaction would be related to the individual difference, interdependence, and partner discrepancy variables. The finding that the strength of the correlates of relationship satisfaction was equivalent for each type of couple adds further evidence that individual difference and interdependence variables—as well as partner discrepancies on them—are robust predictors of relationship satisfaction for both homosexual and heterosexual couples (Duffy & Rusbult, 1986; Kurdek, 1991c, 1991d; Kurdek & Schmitt, 1986a).

The finding of greatest theoretical significance involves evidence that the interdependence variables mediate the effect of the individual difference variables on relationship satisfaction. As noted above, each set of variables was related to relationship satisfaction. However, when the effects of the interdependence variables were controlled, the individual difference variables failed to explain additional variance in relationship satisfaction. This finding suggests that personality traits act as filters through which relationship information is processed (Baucom & Epstein,

1990). In fact, reliable linkages were found between each of the four individual difference variables of interest as well as rewards, cost, and emotional investment (see Table 8.3). Longitudinal data and structural modeling analyses would indicate more clearly the causal relations between the two sets of variables.

Conclusion

Despite the fact that gay male, lesbian, and heterosexual couples differ on important dimensions, this study indicates that they also are quite similar. Gay male couples do not differ from heterosexual men on appraisals of their relationships, nor do lesbian couples differ from heterosexual women. Furthermore, individual difference, interdependence, and partner discrepancy variables do a good job of predicting the level of relationship satisfaction in each type of couple, lending support for the position that the processes that regulate relationship satisfaction across homosexual and heterosexual couples are quite similar.

References

Baron, R. M., & Kenny, D. A. (1986). The moderator-mediator variables distinction in social psychological research: Conceptual, strategic, and statistical considerations. *Journal of Personality and Social Psychology, 51,* 1173-1182.

Baucom, D. H., & Epstein, N. (1990). *Cognitive-behavioral marital therapy.* New York: Brunner/Mazel.

Bell, A. P., & Weinberg, M. S. (1978). *Homosexualities: A study of diversity among men and women.* New York: Simon & Schuster.

Bem, S. L. (1974). The measurement of psychological androgyny. *Journal of Consulting and Clinical Psychology, 47,* 155-162.

Bentler, P. M., & Newcomb, M. D. (1978). Longitudinal study of marital success and failure. *Journal of Consulting and Clinical Psychology, 46,* 1053-1070.

Blumstein, P., & Schwartz, P. (1983). *American couples: Money, work, sex.* New York: William Morrow.

Bradbury, T. N., & Fincham, F. D. (1988). Individual difference variables in close relationships: A contextual model of marriage as an integrative framework. *Journal of Personality and Social Psychology, 54,* 713-721.

Cowan, C. P., Cowan, P. A., Heming, G., Garrett, E., Coysh, W. S., Curtis-Boles, H., & Boles, A. J. (1985). Transitions to parenthood. *Journal of Family Issues, 6,* 451-481.

Derogatis, L. (1983). *SCL 90-R: Administration, scoring, and procedures manual.* Towson, MD: Clinical Psychometric Research.

Dohrenwend, B. S., Krasnoff, L., Askenasy, A. R., & Dohrenwend, B. P. (1978). Exemplification of a method for scaling life events: The PERI Life Events Scale. *Journal of Health and Social Behavior, 19,* 205-229.

Duffy, S. M., & Rusbult, C. E. (1986). Satisfaction and commitment in homosexual and heterosexual relationships. *Journal of Homosexuality, 12,* 1-23.

Eagly, A. (1987). *Sex differences in social behavior: A social-role interpretation.* Hillsdale, NJ: Lawrence Erlbaum.

Eidelson, R. J., & Epstein, N. (1982). Cognition and relationship maladjustment: Development of a measure of relationship beliefs. *Journal of Consulting and Clinical Psychology, 50,* 715-720.

Fincham, F. D., & Bradbury, T. N. (1987). The assessment of marital quality: A reevaluation. *Journal of Marriage and the Family, 49,* 797-809.

Green, J. A. (1992). Testing whether correlation matrices are different from each other. *Developmental Psychology, 28,* 215-224.

Johnson, D. J., & Rusbult, C. E. (1989). Resisting temptation: Devaluation of alternative partners as a means of maintaining commitment in close relationships. *Journal of Personality and Social Psychology, 57,* 967-980.

Joreskog, K. G., & Sorbom, D. (1989). *LISREL VII: User's guide.* Mooresville, IN: Scientific Software.

Kelly, E. L., & Conley, J. J. (1987). Personality and compatibility: A prospective analysis of marital stability and marital satisfaction. *Journal of Personality and Social Psychology, 52,* 27-40.

Kurdek, L. A. (1987). Sex role self schema and psychological adjustment in coupled homosexual and heterosexual men and women. *Sex Roles, 17,* 549-562.

Kurdek, L. A. (1988). Perceived social support in gays and lesbians in cohabiting relationships. *Journal of Personality and Social Psychology, 54,* 504-509.

Kurdek, L. A. (1991a). The dissolution of gay and lesbian couples. *Journal of Personal and Social Relationships, 8,* 265-278.

Kurdek, L. A. (1991b). Sexuality in homosexual and heterosexual couples. In K. McKinney & S. Sprecher (Eds.), *Sexuality in close relationships* (pp. 177-191). Hillsdale, NJ: Lawrence Erlbaum.

Kurdek, L. A. (1991c). Marital stability and changes in marital quality in newlywed couples: A test of the contextual model. *Journal of Social and Personal Relationships, 8,* 27-48.

Kurdek, L. A. (1991d). Correlates of relationship satisfaction in cohabiting gay and lesbian couples: Integration of contextual, investment, and problem-solving models. *Journal of Personality and Social Psychology, 61,* 910-922.

Kurdek, L. A. (1991e). Predictors of increases in marital distress in newlywed couples: A 3-year prospective longitudinal study. *Developmental Psychology, 27,* 627-636.

Kurdek, L. A. (1992a). Dimensionality of the Dyadic Adjustment Scale. *Journal of Family Psychology, 6,* 22-35.

Kurdek, L. A. (1992b). Relationship stability and relationship satisfaction in cohabiting gay and lesbian couples: A prospective longitudinal test of the contextual and interdependence models. *Journal of Social and Personal Relationships, 9,* 125-142.

Kurdek, L. A. (1993a). The allocation of household labor in gay, lesbian, and heterosexual married couples. *Journal of Social Issues, 49*(3), 127-140.

Kurdek, L. A. (1993b). Predicting marital dissolution: A 5-year prospective longitudinal study of newlywed couples. *Journal of Personality and Social Psychology, 64,* 221-242.

Kurdek, L. A. (in press). Lesbian and gay male close relationships. In A. R. D'Augelli & C. J. Patterson (Eds.), *Lesbian and gay identities over the lifespan: Psychological perspectives on personal, relational, and community processes.* New York: Oxford University Press.

Kurdek, L. A., & Schmitt, J. P. (1986a). Relationship quality of partners in heterosexual married, heterosexual cohabiting, and gay and lesbian relationships. *Journal of Personality and Social Psychology, 51,* 711-720.

Kurdek, L. A., & Schmitt, J. P. (1986b). Interaction of sex role self-concept with relationship quality and relationship beliefs in married, heterosexual cohabiting, gay, and lesbian couples. *Journal of Personality and Social Psychology, 51,* 365-370.

Kurdek, L. A., & Schmitt, J. P. (1986c). Early development of relationship quality in heterosexual married, heterosexual cohabiting, gay, and lesbian couples. *Developmental Psychology, 22,* 305-309.

Kurdek, L. A., & Schmitt, J. P. (1986d). Relationship quality of gay men in closed or open relationships. *Journal of Homosexuality, 12,* 85-99.

Kurdek, L. A., & Schmitt, J. P. (1987a). Perceived emotional support from family and friends in members of homosexual, married, and heterosexual cohabiting couples. *Journal of Homosexuality, 14,* 57-68.

Kurdek, L. A., & Schmitt, J. P. (1987b). Partner homogamy in married, heterosexual cohabiting, gay, and lesbian couples. *Journal of Sex Research, 23,* 212-232.

McWhirter, D. P., & Mattison, A. M. (1984). *The male couple: How relationships develop.* Englewood Cliffs, NJ: Prentice-Hall.

Peplau, L. A., & Cochran, S. D. (1981). Value orientations in intimate relationships of gay men. *Journal of Homosexuality, 6,* 1-9.

Peplau, L. A., & Cochran, S. D. (1990). A relational perspective on homosexuality. In D. P. McWhirter, S. A. Sanders, & J. M. Reinisch (Eds.), *Homosexuality/heterosexuality: Concepts of sexual orientation* (pp. 321-349). New York: Oxford University Press.

Rempel, J. K., Holmes, J. G., & Zanna, M. (1985). Trust in close relationships. *Journal of Personality and Social Psychology, 49,* 95-112.

Rusbult, C. E. (1983). A longitudinal test of the investment model: The development (and deterioration) of satisfaction and commitment in heterosexual involvements. *Journal of Personality and Social Psychology, 45,* 101-117.

Rusbult, C. E., Verette, J., Whitney, G. A., Slovik, L. F., & Lipkus, I. (1991). Accommodation processes in close relationships: Theory and preliminary empirical evidence. *Journal of Personality and Social Psychology, 60,* 53-78.

Sarason, I. G., Pierce, G. R., & Sarason, B. R. (1990). Social support and interactional processes: A triadic hypothesis. *Journal of Social and Personal Relationships, 7,* 495-506.

Sarason, I. G., Sarason, B. R., Shearin, E. N., & Pierce, G. R. (1987). A brief measure of social support: Practical and theoretical implications. *Journal of Social and Personal Relationships, 4,* 497-510.

Spanier, G. B. (1976). Measuring dyadic adjustment. *Journal of Marriage and the Family, 38,* 15-28.

Watson, D., & Clark, L. A. (1984). Negative affectivity: The disposition to experience aversive emotional states. *Psychological Bulletin, 96,* 465-490.

Wood, W., Rhodes, N., & Whelan, M. (1989). Sex differences in positive well-being: A consideration of emotional style and marital status. *Psychological Bulletin, 106,* 249-264.

9

Children of the Lesbian Baby Boom

Behavioral Adjustment, Self-Concepts, and Sex Role Identity

CHARLOTTE J. PATTERSON

More than 40 years ago, as families were reunited after World War II, the United States was in the throes of a baby boom. This widely acknowledged increase in births during the 1950s has had many social and economic consequences. Today, the rise in births among openly lesbian women in the United States has been so dramatic that many observers have labeled it a lesbian baby boom, which may have consequences that are at least as significant as the postwar baby boom (Patterson, 1992; Weston, 1991). In this chapter, some implications for children growing up in lesbian homes are examined.

Lesbians have, of course, always been mothers (Golombok, Spencer, & Rutter, 1983; Green, 1978; Hoeffer, 1981; Huggins, 1989; Kirkpatrick, Smith, & Roy, 1981). Parents in the "old" lesbian mother families bore children in the context of heterosexual relationships, then came out as lesbians, often in the context of a divorce. Although some were denied

AUTHOR'S NOTE: Support from the Society for Psychological Study of Social Issues for this work is gratefully acknowledged. Portions of this chapter were presented at the annual meetings of the American Psychological Association in San Francisco, 1991. Special thanks to Mitch Chyette, Deborah Cohn, Carolyn Cowan, Philip Cowan, Charlene Depner, Ellie Schindelman, and all of the participating families for their invaluable support and assistance. I also wish to thank Alicia Eddy, David Koppelman, Meg Michel, and Scott Spence for their efficient work in coding the data.

child custody by the courts after separation from their male partners, other lesbians retained custody of their children (Falk, 1989; Hitchens, 1979-1980; Ricketts & Achtenberg, 1990). Despite psychological, judicial, and popular assumptions to the contrary, a substantial research literature attests to the normal development of sexual identity, other personal characteristics, and social relationships among children in these families (Gibbs, 1989; Patterson, 1992).

Parents in the "new" lesbian families with children, in contrast, came out as lesbians first and only later bore or adopted children in the context of their lives as lesbians. Seligmann (1990) estimated that there are 5,000 to 10,000 new lesbian mother families with children in the United States today, but most observers comment on the difficulty of making such estimates (Polikoff, 1990; Pollack & Vaughn, 1987; Weston, 1991; Wilson, 1991). Although the numbers are consistently described as growing (Cade, 1988; Edwards, 1991; Kahn, 1991; Martin, 1989; Patterson, 1992; Pollack & Vaughn, 1987; Weston, 1991; Wilson, 1991), precise estimates are not available.

Little is known as yet about psychosocial development among the children of the lesbian baby boom. Two studies are available in the published literature. On the basis of extensive family interviews, McCandlish (1987) described psychosocial development among seven young children born to five lesbian mother families. It was reported that the children's development appeared normal in all respects.

In the first systematic study to compare psychosocial development of children born to lesbian mothers with those born to heterosexual mothers, Steckel (1985, 1987) studied the progress of separation-individuation among 3-year-old offspring of 11 lesbian and 11 heterosexual couples. Using parent interviews, parent and teacher Q sorts, and structured doll play techniques, Steckel compared independence, ego functions, and object relations among children in the two types of families.

The principal results of Steckel's (1985, 1987) study documented an impressive similarity in the development of children in the two groups, but some provocative differences also were reported. Children of heterosexual parents saw themselves as somewhat more aggressive than did children of lesbians, and they were seen by parents and teachers as more bossy, domineering, and negative. Children of lesbian parents, on the other hand, saw themselves as more lovable and were seen by parents and teachers as more affectionate, more responsive, and more protective toward younger children. In view of the small sample size and the large number of statistical tests performed, these results must be considered suggestive rather than definitive. Steckel's study is, however, worthy of special attention because it was the first to make systematic comparisons of development among children born to lesbian and to heterosexual couples.

The study described here was designed to enhance the understanding of child development in the families of the lesbian baby boom. First, demographic and other characteristics of the families who participated in this research were described. In addition, the behavioral adjustment, self-concepts, and sex role behavior of children in these families were explored. The principal aims of the work were thus twofold: to describe some characteristics of this particular family form and to explore the development of children who grow up in this environment.

To allow comparisons between children with lesbian and heterosexual parents, a group of children in "new" lesbian mother families was studied, and the children's scores on standardized measures were compared with national or other available norms. This procedure allowed for the collection of data from a wide variety of new lesbian mother families and yet also left open the possibility of comparing development among these children with average levels for normative groups of children of their age.

Method

Participants

Eligibility and Recruitment of Families

Families were considered eligible to participate if they met all the following three criteria: (a) at least one child between 4 and 9 years of age had to be present in the home, (b) the child had to be born to or adopted by a lesbian mother or mothers, (c) the family had to live within the greater San Francisco Bay Area.

Recruitment began by contacting friends, acquaintances, and colleagues who might be likely to know eligible lesbian mother families. The proposed research was described and help was solicited in locating families. Each family located in this way was then contacted by telephone. The potential participants were told how their name had been obtained, were given a description of the study, and were encouraged to ask questions about the researcher or the study. Families meeting the three criteria for participation were asked if they would be willing to take part. If a family agreed to participate, an appointment was arranged for a visit to the family's home. The process of discussion, decision making, and appointment setting required between 2 and 10 telephone conversations per family; in some cases, letters also were exchanged before an appointment was made.

In all, contact was made with 39 eligible families, of which 37 (95%) agreed to participate in the study. This high level of participation among eligible families enhances the likelihood that the results are representative of the group of families located by these methods.

Participating Families

Of the 37 participating families, 26 (70%) were headed by a lesbian couple and 7 (19%) were headed by a single mother living with her child. In the remaining 4 (11%) families, the child had been born to a lesbian couple who had since separated, and the child was in de facto joint custody (i.e., living part of the time with one mother and part of the time with the other mother). In this last group of families, one mother was out of town during the period of testing and so was not included in the study.

A total of 66 women took part in the study. Of these, 61 (92%) identified themselves as predominantly lesbian, and 5 (8%) identified themselves as predominantly bisexual. Their ages ranged from 28 to 53 years, with a mean age of 39.6. There were 61 (92%) self-described white or non-Hispanic Caucasian women, 2 (3%) African-American or black women, and 3 (4%) who described themselves as coming from other racial or ethnic backgrounds. Most were well educated; 74% had received college degrees and 48% had received graduate degrees.

The great majority of mothers (94%) had regular employment outside the home, and 54% said that they worked 40 hours or more per week. A total of 41 (62%) of the women were in professional occupations (e.g., law and nursing), 6 (9%) were in technical or mechanical occupations (e.g., car repair), 6 (9%) were in business or sales (e.g., real estate), and 9 (14%) worked in other occupations (e.g., artist). Only four mothers (6%) were not employed outside the home. There were 34 (92%) families with incomes greater than $30,000 per year, and 17 (46%) families with incomes more than $60,000 per year.

For the statistical analyses of this study, the biological or legal adoptive mother of the focal child was designated "Mother 1." If, as in most families, there was another mother, she was designated "Mother 2." No statement about the relative importance or behavior of either woman was intended by these labels; they were employed solely as a statistical convenience. In one family headed by a lesbian couple, the women did not wish to identify one as the biological and the other as the nonbiological parent of the focal child; in this case, one was identified as Mother 1 and one as Mother 2 by a coin toss.

In each family, the focal child was between 4 and 9 years of age (mean age: 6 years, 2 months); there were 19 girls and 18 boys. A total of 34 (92%) of the children were born to lesbian mothers, and 3 (8%) had been adopted by lesbian mothers. There were 30 (81%) children who were described by their mothers as white or non-Hispanic Caucasian, 3 (8%) as Hispanic, and 4 (11%) as another racial or ethnic heritage.

Procedure

The three principal assessments of children's adjustment were the Achenbach and Edelbrock Child Behavior Checklist, the Eder Children's Self-View Questionnaire, and a standard interview relating to sex role identity.

Social Competence and Behavior Problems

To assess both levels of child competence and child behavior problems, the Child Behavior Checklist (CBCL) (Achenbach & Edelbrock, 1983) was administered. The CBCL was selected because of its ability to discriminate among children in the clinical versus normative range of functioning for both internalizing (e.g., inhibited or overcontrolled behavior) and externalizing (e.g., aggressive, antisocial, or undercontrolled behavior) problems as well as in social competence. It is designed to be completed by parents. In this study, all participating mothers completed this instrument.

The CBCL is designed to record in a standardized format the competencies and behavioral problems of children from 4 to 16 years of age (Achenbach & Edelbrock, 1983). There are 118 behavior problem items, and each one is scored on a three-step scale (not true, somewhat or sometimes true, very true or often true). Answers are tabulated to create subscales for internalizing, externalizing, and total behavior problems. The 20 social competence items "obtain parents' reports of the amount and quality of their child's participation in sports, hobbies, games, activities, organizations, jobs and chores, and friendships; how well the child gets along with others and plays/works by himself/herself; and school functioning" (Achenbach & Edelbrock, 1983, p. 7). Extensive information on the reliability and validity of the CBCL scales is available in Achenbach and Edelbrock (1983).

Norms were obtained from heterogeneous normal samples of 200 children aged 4 to 5 years and 600 children aged 6 to 11 years as well as from equivalent numbers of children at each age who were drawn from clinical populations (e.g., those receiving services from community mental health centers, private psychological and psychiatric clinics or practices, and child guidance clinics). For purposes of this research, mean scores reported by Achenbach and Edelbrock (1983, pp. 210-214) were averaged across the 4- to 5- and 6- to 11-year age levels to provide estimates of average scores for social competence, internalizing, externalizing, and total behavior problems among normative and clinical populations at the ages studied. The scores for children in the current sample were compared with these figures.

Self-Concepts

Assessment of children's self-concepts was accomplished using five scales from Eder's (1990) Children's Self-View Questionnaire. These scales, designed especially to assess psychological concepts of self among children aged 3 to 8 years, assessed five different dimensions of children's views of themselves. The Aggression scale assessed the degree to which children saw themselves as likely to hurt or frighten others. The Social Closeness scale assessed the degree to which children enjoy being with people and prefer to be around others. The Social Potency scale assessed the degree to which children like to stand out and/or to be the center of attention. The Stress Reaction scale assessed the extent to which children said they often felt scared, upset, and/or angry. Finally, the Well-Being scale assessed the degree to which children felt joyful, content, and comfortable with themselves. Information on validity and test-retest reliability of these scales is provided by Eder (1990). Using hand puppets (rather than the large puppets and puppet stage described by

Eder, 1990), the CSVQ was administered individually to participating children, and their answers were tape-recorded for later scoring.

Sexual Identity

Following Money and Ehrhardt (1972), three aspects of sexual identity were distinguished. The first, gender identity, concerns a person's self-identification as male or female. For children tested here, appropriate gender identity was so clearly in place that the procedure of asking each child directly about gender identity was deemed unnecessary. A second aspect of sexual identity, sexual orientation, refers to a person's choice of sexual partners: heterosexual, homosexual, or bisexual. Because the youngsters tested here were prepubertal, this issue was judged premature. Thus assessments of sexual identity focused on the third aspect of sexual identity: Sex role behavior, which concerns the extent to which a person's activities, occupations, and the like are regarded by the culture as masculine, feminine, or both.

Sex role behavior preferences were assessed in a standard, open-ended interview format, such as that employed in earlier research on children of divorced lesbian mothers (e.g., Golombok et al., 1983; Green, 1978; Green, Mandel, Hotvedt, Gray, & Smith, 1986). Each child was told that the interviewer was interested in learning more about his or her friends, favorite toys, and other things. Each child was asked to name the friends and other children he or she liked to play with. Following this, each child was asked to name his or her favorite toys; games; and characters from television, movies, or books. The children's responses were recorded by hand and on audiotape, and the interviewer's notes were later checked for accuracy against the tapes.

After the interview had been completed, the children's answers for each of the four topics (peer friendships, favorite toys, favorite games, and favorite characters) were coded into one of four categories in regard to their sex role relevant qualities: (a) mainly same sex (e.g., a boy reports having mostly or entirely male friends), (b) mixed sexes (e.g., an even or almost even mix of sexes in the friends mentioned by the child), (c) opposite sex (e.g., a girl reports having mostly or entirely male friends), and (d) can't tell (i.e., an answer was unscorable or not clearly sex typed, e.g., when a reported favorite game is Chutes and Ladders). Because children's play groups are known to be highly sex segregated at the ages studied, children were expected to give mainly same-sex answers to these questions.

Interviews

As noted above, an appointment was arranged for a visit to the family's home. When the researcher arrived at the family's home, she explained the study, answered questions about it, and asked for written consent from the mother or mothers who were present; oral assent was also obtained from children. The visit began with a semistructured family interview, which involved a number of questions about family background (e.g., education and occupation) and family history (e.g., circumstances surrounding focal child's birth or adoption). This was followed by an individual interview with the focal child, during which the sex role identity interview was given, followed by the CSVQ. During the time that the interviewer was with the focal child (usually in his or her room), mothers were asked to fill out a number of questionnaires, among which was the Achenbach and Edelbrock CBCL. In families headed by a lesbian couple, both women were asked to complete the questionnaires without consulting one another. When both mothers and children had completed these materials, they were thanked for their assistance and given an opportunity to ask any questions about the study. Each visit lasted between 90 and 150 minutes.

Results

Results are presented in four parts, corresponding to the four main categories of information collected: characteristics of participating families, children's social competence and behavior problems, children's self-concepts, and children's sexual identity. The principal questions for the latter three areas concern the degree to which children with lesbian mothers differ from other children, if at all.

Characteristics of Participating Families

A variety of descriptive information was collected. Mothers were asked to explain the circumstances surrounding the child's conception and birth and/or adoption. Mothers were also asked about the child's biological father or sperm donor, about the degree to which they had knowledge of or contact with the father, and about the degree to which the focal child had knowledge of the father's identity and/or contact with him. Mothers also were asked to give the child's last name and to explain how the child had received that name.

The mothers' accounts of the conception and birth and/or adoption of their children made clear that the focal children were, in general, children who had been very much wanted. The average amount of time that it took for the biological mother to conceive the focal child after she began to attempt to become pregnant was 10 months. The range in this regard was from a few women who became pregnant on their first try to another for whom 8 years and numerous miscarriages preceded her child's conception. Adoptive mothers reported that, on average, the adoption process took approximately 12 months. In the great majority of cases, then, these lesbian mothers had made considerable efforts to bear or adopt their children.

There was tremendous variability in the amount of information that families had about the donor or biological father of the focal child. In 17 families (46%), the child had been conceived via donor insemination (DI) with sperm from an anonymous donor (e.g., sperm that was provided by a sperm bank or clinic). In these cases, families had only very limited information (e.g., race, height, weight, and hair color) about the donor, and none knew the donor's name. In 10 families (27%), the child was conceived via DI with sperm provided by a known donor (e.g., a family friend). In 4 families (11%), children were conceived when the biological mother had intercourse with a man. In 3 families (8%), the child was adopted. In the 3 remaining families, some other set of circumstances applied or the parents acknowledged that the child had been born to one of the mothers, but preferred not to disclose any further information about their child's conception.

Mothers reported relatively little contact with biological fathers or donors. A total of 23 (62%) of the families reported no contact with the biological father or donor during the previous year. Only 10 families (27%) had had two or more contacts with the father during the previous year. Given that many families did not know the identity of the child's biological father and that most currently had little or no contact with him, it is not surprising that the father's role with the child was seen by the mothers as being quite limited. In 22 families (60%), mothers reported that the donor or biological father had no special role vis-à-vis the child; this figure includes the families in which the sperm donor had been anonymous. In 13 families (35%), the biological father's identity was known to parents and children, but he took the role of a family friend rather than that of a father. There were only two families (5%) in which the biological father was acknowledged as such and in which he was described as taking on the role of a father with the child.

In the families of the lesbian baby boom, questions about selection of the child's last name are of particular interest. In this sample, the largest number of children (26, or 70%) bore the surnames of their biological or adoptive mothers; this figure includes children in 4 families in which *all* family members (i.e., both mothers and all children) shared the same last name. In 7 (19%) families, children had been given hyphenated last names, created from the two mothers' surnames. Finally, in 4 (11%) families, the children had some other last name (e.g., the surname of the nonbiological mother).

Children's Social Competence and Behavior Problems

Scores for the Social Competence, Internalizing Behavior Problems, Externalizing Behavior Problems, and Total Behavior Problems scales of the CBCL were computed for each mother's reports about each child (Table 9.1). To assess adaptation among children of lesbian mothers, their scores were compared with the mean scores for the large normal and clinical samples studied by Achenbach and Edelbrock (1983). As noted, an average of the mean scores for 4- to 5-year-olds and for 6- to 11-year-olds was taken for each scale.

In many cases, data like these can be studied using analysis of variance techniques. This avenue was not open for this study, however, because the raw data on which Achenbach and Edelbrock's (1983) means were based were not available. Because of this and in view of the very large and representative nature of samples studied by Achenbach and Edelbrock, the scores for children in their normal and clinical samples were treated as population means in a series of t tests for comparison with the scores of children of lesbian mothers. To correct for the potential inflation of α levels that would otherwise be inherent in the use of this procedure, a Bonferroni correction was applied. Because there were 16 comparisons, the protected .05 α level was effectively $.05 \div 16 = .003$ (Table 9.1).

Table 9.1 Children's Social Competence and Behavior Problems

	Achenbach and Edelbrock		*Study Sample*		*Mean* t *Scores*			
	Normal Population	*Clinical Population*	*Mother 1 Report*	*Mother 2 Report*	*Mother 1 Versus Normal* (t[36])	*Mother 2 Versus Normal* (t[28])	*Mother 1 Versus Clinical* (t[36])	*Mother 2 Versus Clinical* (t[28])
Social Competence	51.2	37.7	51.3 (10.8)	51.6 (10.4)	< 1	< 1	7.68*	7.15*
Behavior Problems								
Internalizing	51.3	66.3	52.4 (8.1)	48.9 (7.9)	< 1	1.64	10.38*	11.86*
Externalizing	50.8	66.4	50.6 (9.6)	49.7 (10.5)	< 1	< 1	10.03*	8.56*
Total Problems	50.1	68.3	52.4 (10.1)	49.9 (10.2)	1.37	< 1	9.54*	9.73*

NOTE: Standard deviations for study sample means are given in parentheses. All *t* tests are two-tailed. To protect α levels against inflation caused by multiple comparisons, the Bonferroni correction was applied to all *t* tests. Data for normal and clinical populations are from Achenbach and Edelbrock (1983).
*$p < .01$ (protected).

As expected, social competence among children with lesbian mothers was rated as normal. Scores for children of lesbian mothers were significantly higher than those for the clinical sample, but were not different from those for the normal sample. This was true for reports given by both mothers in the lesbian mother families.

Results for behavior problems revealed the same pattern. For internalizing, externalizing, and total behavior problems, scores for children of lesbian mothers were significantly lower than those for children in the clinical sample, but did not differ from those in the normal sample. This was true of reports given by both mothers in the lesbian mother families. Overall, then, the behavior problems of lesbian mothers' children were rated as significantly smaller in magnitude than those of children in the clinical sample and as no greater than those of children in the normal sample.

Children's Self-Concepts

Scores for each of the five subscales of the CSVQ were computed for each child, and the mean scores are shown in Table 9.2. To assess self-concepts among children of lesbian mothers, their scores were compared with those for Eder's (1990) sample of 5.5-year-old children growing up in middle-class heterosexual families (Table 9.2).

As for social competence and behavior problems, a series of *t* tests was performed, comparing scores for the children of lesbian mothers with those for children in Eder's (1990) sample. Because the size of Eder's sample was of the same order of magnitude as the study sample, two-sample *t* tests were employed. To correct for the potential inflation of α levels that would otherwise be inherent in multiple *t* tests, a Bonferroni correction was again applied. Because there were 5 comparisons, the protected .05 α level was effectively $.05 \div 5 = .01$ (Table 9.2).

There were no significant differences between children of lesbian and of heterosexual mothers on self-concepts relevant to Aggression, Social Closeness, and Social Potency. Children of lesbian mothers in the study sample did not see themselves as either more or less aggressive, sociable, or likely to enjoy being the center of attention than did children of heterosexual mothers in Eder's sample. Steckel's (1985, 1987) finding that children of lesbian parents saw themselves as less aggressive but more sociable than did children of heterosexual parents was not confirmed here.

Table 9.2 Children's Self-Concepts

	Eder Sample (n = 60)	*Study Sample* (n = 35)	t(93)
Aggression	1.19 (1.15)	1.89 (1.53)	2.35
Social Closeness	3.48 (1.31)	3.77 (1.14)	1.13
Social Potency	2.71 (1.44)	3.29 (1.53)	1.82
Stress Reaction	1.19 (1.35)	2.80 (1.80)	4.57*
Well-Being	3.59 (1.53)	5.80 (1.30)	7.49*

NOTE: Standard deviations are given in parentheses. All *t* tests are two-tailed. To protect α levels against inflation caused by multiple comparisons, the Bonferronni correction was applied to all *t* tests. Data for the comparison sample are from Eder (1990).
*$p < .01$ (protected).

Children of lesbian mothers, however, reported greater stress reactions than did children of heterosexual mothers, but they also reported a greater overall sense of well-being than did children of heterosexual mothers (Table 9.2). In other words, children of lesbian mothers said that they more often felt angry, scared, or upset but also said that they more often felt joyful, content, and comfortable with themselves than did children of heterosexual mothers.

Children's Sexual Identity

The aspect of children's sexual identity studied here was that of preferences for sex role behavior. Results from the interviews with children about their peer friendships, favorite toys, favorite games, and favorite characters were tabulated to assess how many children's preferences could be categorized as mainly same sex, mainly opposite sex, or mixed sexes (Table 9.3).

As expected, most children reported preferences for sex role behaviors that are considered to be normative at this age (Green, 1978). Also as expected, every child reported that his or her group of friends was mainly or entirely made up of same-sex children. The great majority of children also reported favorite toys and favorite characters (from books, movies, and television) that were of the same sex. In the case of favorite games, many children mentioned games that can not be clearly sex typed (e.g., board games) and hence were not categorizable. For games that can be sex typed, however, the great majority mentioned games that are generally associated with their own rather than with the opposite sex. In

Table 9.3 Children's Sex Role Behavior

	Peer Friendships	*Favorite Toys*	*Favorite Games*	*Favorite Characters*
Mainly same sex	35	31	12	24
Mixed sexes	1	0	1	9
Mainly opposite sex	0	1	1	2
Not clearly sex typed	0	4	22	1

short, preferences for sex role behavior among the children of lesbian mothers studied appeared to be quite normal.

Discussion

The study described here represents the first systematic empirical research on 4- to 9-year-old children born to or adopted by lesbian mothers. Consistent with the results of research on children of divorced lesbian mothers (Gibbs, 1989; Patterson, 1992) and on younger children born to lesbian couples (McCandlish, 1987; Steckel, 1985, 1987), the present findings reveal that social and personal development among children born to lesbian mothers proceeds in a manner very similar to that expected among children of heterosexual mothers.

Although psychosocial development among children of lesbian versus heterosexual parents was generally quite similar, there were nevertheless also some differences among children in the two groups. The most notable differences emerged in the area of children's self-concepts. In particular, children of lesbians reported that they experienced more reactions to stress (e.g., feeling angry, scared, or upset), and also a greater sense of well- being (e.g., feeling joyful, content, and comfortable with themselves) than did the children of heterosexual parents studied by Eder (1990).

What is the best interpretation of this difference? One possibility is that the children of lesbian mothers report greater reactivity to stress because, in fact, they experience greater stress in their daily lives than do other children. As a result of heterosexist, homophobic, and/or other aspects of their environment, children with lesbian mothers may actually encounter more stressful events and conditions than do children with heterosexual mothers. If children with lesbian mothers experience greater stress in their day-to-day lives than do other children, then their more frequent reports of emotional responses to such stress might simply reflect the more stressful nature of their experience.

Another possibility is that, regardless of actual stress levels, children of lesbian mothers may be more willing to report their experiences of negative emotional states. If, as some writers suggest (Pollack & Vaughn, 1987; Rafkin, 1990), children in lesbian homes have more experience with the verbal discussion of feelings in general, then they might exhibit increased openness to the expression of negative as well as positive feelings. In this view, the greater tendency of lesbian mothers' children to admit feeling angry, upset, or scared might be attributed not as much to any differences in objective levels of stress as to a greater openness to emotional experience of all kinds.

Consistent with this latter interpretation, another difference between the self-concepts of children with lesbian versus heterosexual mothers was in the overall sense of well-being. Children of lesbian mothers reported greater feelings of joy, contentedness, and comfort with themselves than did children of heterosexual mothers in Eder's (1990) sample. Although they do not rule out the possibility that children of lesbian women do indeed experience greater stress, the results suggest that these children may be more willing than other children to report a variety of intense emotional experiences, whether positive or negative. Because this study was not designed to evaluate alternative interpretations of these differences, clarification of these issues must await the results of future research.

A considerable amount of descriptive information about the characteristics of lesbian mother families was also collected. Although there was some diversity, the lesbian mothers in this sample were primarily white, well-educated, and relatively affluent. Because only two mothers who were contacted refused to take part in the study, sample characteristics cannot be attributed to differential refusal rates among families with characteristics other than those that were most common in this sample. The predominantly white, middle-class character of the sample may be attributable to biases introduced by the white, middle-class status of the researcher and by the nature of her contacts in Bay Area lesbian communities. If so, this represents an important limitation on the representativeness of the sample, and hence of the findings reported here.

An alternative interpretation of the predominantly white, middle-class character of the sample is also available. Indeed, the fact that the sample recruited for this study had just these particular characteristics points to what may be a significant fact about the lesbian baby boom: Perhaps, at least in its earliest phases, lesbians in relatively privileged social and economic positions have been more likely to participate in it. Whether or not this is the case, it will be important for future research to identify conditions that make lesbian childbearing more or less likely to occur (Patterson, in press).

One such condition might be the nature of the community in which women live. It is almost certainly not incidental that the San Francisco Bay Area, with its large and well-organized lesbian and gay communities, has supported the growth of lesbian parenting long before organized groups appeared in most other parts of the country. The presence of supportive, openly lesbian communities is almost certainly an important factor in the emergence of the lesbian baby boom. As one lesbian mother has remarked, "As soon as there was a public movement that allowed us to increase our sense of security and self-esteem, we added more children to our lives" (Cade, 1988, p. 13). It would be valuable to learn more about sources of diversity among lesbian families with children (Martin, 1989; Patterson, 1992; Pollack & Vaughn, 1987; Rafkin, 1990) and also to identify conditions that make childbearing appear to be a realistic choice for lesbians (Patterson, in press; Pies, 1985, 1990).

The results of this study have significant implications for a number of influential psychological theories of human development. In particular, the fact that children born to lesbian mothers showed normal personal and social development represents an important challenge to developmental theories that emphasize the importance of structural aspects of home environments (see Patterson, 1992). Only two of the children studied here lived in homes that also contained a male adult, and in neither case was this man either the biological father of the child or living in the child's home on a full-time basis. For all practical purposes, then, children in the sample grew up in homes that contained either one or two female parents. The psychological health of these children suggests that structural properties of family environments such as father presence versus absence and parental sexual orientation cannot be crucial for successful developmental outcomes to occur.

In this way, the results are consistent with those of research on other nontraditional families (e.g., Eiduson & Weisner, 1978; Emery, 1982; O'Leary

& Emery, 1984; Weisner & Wilson-Mitchell, 1990). It may well prove to be the case with lesbian mother families—as it has in research with other kinds of nontraditional families—that family process variables are of greater significance than structural ones in predicting child outcomes. If so, another important task for future research in this area will be to identify those conditions of life in lesbian mother families that support and encourage positive outcomes among children growing up in them.

The present findings also have implications for a number of legislative and judicial issues in the area of family law. First, the normal psychosocial development of children born to or adopted by lesbian mothers is relevant to legal issues surrounding foster care and adoption (Ricketts & Achtenberg, 1990). When the normal development of children born to or adopted by lesbian mothers is considered, there would seem to be no empirical cause for concern about the welfare of children who might be in foster care with lesbian parents or who might be adopted by lesbian parents and hence no cause for excluding lesbians from roles as adoptive or foster parents solely on the basis of sexual orientation.

Another area of family law to which the current results might be applied is that of child custody and visitation rights for lesbian mothers (Falk, 1989; Polikoff, 1990). Of the children growing up in lesbian couple families studied here, most could be regarded as having two psychological parents (Goldstein, Freud, & Solnit, 1973). In law, however, only the biological (or adoptive) mother generally has parental rights and responsibilities toward the child; the nonbiological mother is usually treated as a legal stranger to the child. Thus, if the lesbian mothers separate, the nonbiological mother would have little or no legal recourse in custody or visitation disputes. By the same token, if the biological mother were to die or to become incapacitated, the nonbiological mother would be vulnerable to custody suits brought by the biological mother's blood relatives. In such circumstances, the child's best interest would seem to lie in the preservation of his or her relationship with the surviving psychological parent, but this interest is often left unprotected by the law. As a result, courts experience tremendous difficulties and indeed often fail to serve the child's best interests when making decisions about custody and visitation in such circumstances. Legal reform that recognizes the realities of life in nontraditional families could ameliorate these difficulties (Polikoff, 1990).

It is important to acknowledge that there are some limitations of the results of this study. As discussed above, sampling issues include the predominantly white, middle-class character of the sample and its recruitment from a single geographical region. In addition, the study did not involve collection of observational data on children's or parents' behavior, nor did it involve collection of information from friends, teachers, or others outside the immediate family. As research on the lesbian baby boom expands, many of these and other limitations may be addressed in future studies.

In summary, this study was conducted in an effort to examine psychosocial development among preschool and school-aged children of the lesbian baby boom. Compared with available norms, children of lesbian mothers showed normal social competence, behavior, and sexual identity. Their self-concepts did not differ from those of children with heterosexual parents, except that they reported more negative emotional reactions to stress (such as anger and fear) and more positive emotional feelings (such as joy and contentment) about themselves. One interpretation of this result is that children of lesbians do actually experience more stress in their day-to-day lives than other children; another is that, regardless of actual stress levels, children of lesbians are more able to acknowledge both positive and negative aspects of their emotional experience. Overall, the most important result was that normal psychosocial development had occurred among the present sample of children born to or adopted by lesbian parents. If confirmed by future research, this result will have far-reaching psychological and legal implications.

References

Achenbach, T. M., & Edelbrock, C. (1983). *Manual for the Child Behavior Checklist and Revised Child Behavior Profile.* Burlington: University of Vermont, Department of Psychiatry.

Cade, C. (1988, November). Lesbian mothers' nitty gritty anthologies. *Off Our Backs*, pp. 12-13.

Eder, R. A. (1990). Uncovering young children's psychological selves: Individual and developmental differences. *Child Development, 61*, 849-863.

Edwards, J. N. (1991). New conceptions: Biosocial innovations and the family. *Journal of Marriage and the Family, 53*, 349-360.

Eiduson, B. T., & Weisner, T. S. (1978). Alternative family styles: Effects on young children. In J. H. Stevens & M. Mathews (Eds.), *Mother/child father/child relationships* (pp. 197-221). Washington, DC: National Association for the Education of Young Children.

Emery, R. E. (1982). Interparental conflict and the children of discord and divorce. *Psychological Bulletin, 92*, 310-330.

Falk, P. J. (1989). Lesbian mothers: Psychosocial assumptions in family law. *American Psychologist, 44*, 941-947.

Gibbs, E. D. (1989). Psychosocial development of children raised by lesbian mothers: A review of research. *Women and Therapy, 8,* 55-75.

Goldstein, J., Freud, A., & Solnit, A. J. (1973). *Beyond the best interests of the child.* New York: Free Press.

Golombok, S., Spencer, A., & Rutter, M. (1983). Children in lesbian and single-parent households: Psychosexual and psychiatric appraisal. *Journal of Child Psychology and Psychiatry, 24,* 551-572.

Green, R. (1978). Sexual identity of 37 children raised by homosexual or transsexual parents. *American Journal of Psychiatry, 135,* 692-697.

Green, R., Mandel, J. B., Hotvedt, M. E., Gray, J., & Smith, L. (1986). Lesbian mothers and their children: A comparison with solo parent heterosexual mothers and their children. *Archives of Sexual Behavior, 7,* 175-181.

Hitchens, D. (1979-1980). Social attitudes, legal standards, and personal trauma in child custody cases. *Journal of Homosexuality, 5,* 1-20, 89-95.

Hoeffer, B. (1981). Children's acquisition of sex-role behavior in lesbian-mother families. *American Journal of Orthopsychiatry, 5,* 536-544.

Huggins, S. L. (1989). A comparative study of self-esteem of adolescent children of divorced lesbian mothers and divorced heterosexual mothers. In F. W. Bozett (Ed.), *Homosexuality and the family* (pp. 123-135). New York: Harrington Park.

Kahn, Y. H. (1991). Hannah, must you have a child? *Outlook, 3*(3), 39-43.

Kirkpatrick, M., Smith, C., & Roy, R. (1981). Lesbian mothers and their children: A comparative survey. *American Journal of Orthopsychiatry, 51,* 545-551.

Martin, A. (1989). The planned lesbian and gay family: Parenthood and children. *Newsletter of the Society for the Psychological Study of Lesbian and Gay Issues, 5,* 6, 16-17.

McCandlish, B. (1987). Against all odds: Lesbian mother family dynamics. In F. Bozett (Ed.), *Gay and lesbian parents* (pp. 23-38). New York: Praeger.

Money, J., & Ehrhardt, A. A. (1972). *Man and woman, boy and girl: The differentiation and dimorphism of gender identity from conception to maturity.* Baltimore, MD: Johns Hopkins University Press.

O'Leary, K. D., & Emery, R. E. (1984). Marital discord and child behavior problems. In M. D. Levine & P. Satz (Eds.), *Middle childhood: Development and dysfunction* (pp. 345-364). Baltimore, MD: University Park Press.

Patterson, C. J. (1992). Children of lesbian and gay parents. *Child Development, 63,* 1025-1042.

Patterson, C. J. (in press). Lesbian and gay couples considering parenthood: An agenda for research, service and advocacy. *Journal of Lesbian and Gay Social Services.*

Pies, C. (1985). *Considering parenthood.* San Francisco: Spinsters/Aunt Lute.

Pies, C. (1990). Lesbians and the choice to parent. In F. W. Bozett & M. B. Sussman (Eds.), *Homosexuality and family relations* (pp. 137-154). New York: Harrington Park.

Polikoff, N. (1990). This child does have two mothers: Redefining parenthood to meet the needs of children in lesbian mother and other nontraditional families. *Georgetown Law Journal, 78,* 459-575.

Pollack, S., & Vaughn, J. (1987). *Politics of the heart: A lesbian parenting anthology.* Ithaca, NY: Firebrand.

Rafkin, L. (1990). *Different mothers: Sons and daughters of lesbians talk about their lives.* Pittsburgh: Cleis.

Ricketts, W., & Achtenberg, R. (1990). Adoption and foster parenting for lesbians and gay men: Creating new traditions in family. In F. W. Bozett & M. B. Sussman (Eds.), *Homosexuality and family relations* (pp. 83-118). New York: Harrington Park.

Riley, C. (1988). American kinship: A lesbian account. *Feminist Issues, 8,* 75-94.

Seligmann, J. (1990, Winter-Spring). Variations on a theme. *Newsweek* [Special edition], pp. 38-46.

Steckel, A. (1985). *Separation-individuation in children of lesbian and heterosexual couples.* Unpublished doctoral dissertation, Wright Institute Graduate School, Berkeley, CA.

Steckel, A. (1987). Psychosocial development of children of lesbian mothers. In F. W. Bozett (Ed.), *Gay and lesbian parents* (pp. 75-85). New York: Praeger.

Weisner, T. S., & Wilson-Mitchell, J. E. (1990). Nonconventional family lifestyles and sex-typing in six year olds. *Child Development, 61,* 1915-1933.

Weston, K. (1991). *Families we choose: lesbians, gays, kinship.* New York: Columbia University Press.

Wilson, S. (1991, March 15). The lesbian baby boom. *Hampshire Life,* pp. 8-12.

10

Internalized Homophobia

Conceptual and Empirical Issues in Measurement

ARIEL SHIDLO

The construct of internalized homophobia can serve as a central organizing concept for a gay and lesbian affirmative psychology. There are several reasons why this construct is significant. First, the internalization of homophobia is a developmental event experienced to varying degrees by almost all lesbians and gay men raised in a heterosexist and antigay society (Forstein, 1988; George & Behrendt, 1988; Gonsiorek, 1988; Sophie, 1988).

Second, internalized homophobia is often an important cause of psychological distress in lesbians and gay men (American Psychological Association, 1991; Gonsiorek, 1982; Malyon, 1982). Third, reduction of internalized homophobia can be considered an important measure of the success of therapies and prevention efforts with lesbians and gay men (Malyon, 1982; Martin, 1982; Sophie, 1988). Similarly, conversion therapies that increase internalized homophobia can be viewed as psychologically damaging to gay persons (Martin, 1984). Finally, internalized

AUTHOR'S NOTE: I wish to thank Gregory M. Herek, April Martin, and James Rogula for their encouragement, advice, and help with this chapter. Some of the results in this chapter were presented at the 1987 meeting of the American Psychological Association in New York.

homophobia can be a heuristic construct that organizes factors unique to lesbians and gay men in the areas of development, psychopathology, psychotherapy, and prevention. It can account for a portion of the variance not accounted for by other social and personological variables that affect nongay persons (Gonsiorek, 1982; Malyon, 1982).

The task of this chapter is to assess the status of theory and empirical data on internalized homophobia. A framework adopted from Brewer and Hunter (1989) is used to evaluate the status of internalized homophobia as a construct. These writers suggest that "for measurements to be useful in building and testing theories, the measures must provide good empirical estimates of the social phenomena about which we theorize" (p. 127). An important question is how the simplification involved in operationalizing and measuring a phenomenon affects the realism of the resulting theory. It is the author's observation that efforts at assessing internalized homophobia often have had limited validity because insufficient attention was paid to the process of operationalization. The review begins, therefore, with an examination of the conceptual issues involved in the definition, operationalization, and assessment of internalized homophobia. This is followed by a review of the empirical work in this area. Finally, data on the construct validity of internalized homophobia are presented.

Conceptual Framework

Homophobia and Homonegativity

The term *homophobia* was coined by Weinberg (1972) to describe the phenomenon in heterosexuals of "the dread of being in close quarters with homosexuals" and its counterpart in gay persons, "self-loathing" (p. 4). The introduction of this term played a pioneering role in social-science discourse about lesbians and gay men in the 1970s (Herek, this volume). However, *homophobia* is an unsatisfactory term because of its etiological and functional bias in favor of a phobic or defensive basis for negative attitudes toward homosexuality (Herek, 1984). It discourages recognition that attitudes toward homosexuality can serve other, nondefensive functions. For example, prejudicial attitudes toward gay persons can be a vehicle for expressing cultural or religious values. Other terms such as *homonegativism* (Hudson & Ricketts, 1980) provide a more neutral and inclusive designation for the total universe of negative attitudes toward homosexuality. The terms *internalized homonegativism* and *internalized homonegativity* may be preferable to internalized homophobia for these reasons and are used interchangeably with it in this chapter.

Evidence for the pervasiveness of homonegative attitudes in our society is plentiful. In a review of stigma, prejudice, and violence against lesbians and gay men, Herek (1991) reported that surveys suggest that roughly 66% of Americans condemn homosexuality or homosexual behavior as morally wrong or as sinful. Furthermore, a variety of institutional policies stigmatize and discriminate against lesbians and gay men. This systemic mistreatment includes the absence of legal recognition of lesbian and gay relationships and the outlawing of private sexual contact between same-sex partners in nearly one-half of the states. Finally, gay people experience considerable violence. In one national survey conducted by the *San Francisco Examiner,* 10% of lesbians and 5% of gay men reported physical abuse or assault in the previous year because of their sexual orientation (quoted in Herek, 1991).

Internalized Homophobia

Internalized homophobia is defined here as a set of negative attitudes and affects toward homosexuality in other persons and toward homosexual features in oneself. These features include same-gender sexual and affectional feelings; same-gender sexual behavior; same-gender intimate relationships; and self-labeling as lesbian, gay, or homosexual. Homonegativity is so widespread in our society that the internalization of homophobia is viewed by many writers as a normative developmental event, whereby almost all gay men and lesbians adopt negative attitudes toward homosexuality early in their developmental history (Forstein, 1988; Gonsiorek, 1988; Loulan, 1984; Malyon, 1982; Pharr, 1987; Sophie, 1988). Malyon (1982) proposed that this set of negative attitudes is incorporated into one's self-image, and causes a fragmentation of sexual and affectional facets that interferes with the developmental process. Models of lesbian and gay identity development view the process of coming out as including the (varyingly successful) neutralization of internalized homophobia and a consequent adoption of a positive and integrated lesbian or gay identity (Cass, 1979; Stein & Cohen, 1984; Troiden, 1979).

Prevalence

Although much has been written on internalized homophobia, there is a dearth of empirical data on how widespread it actually is. The prevalence data that exist are limited by lack of methodological sophistication, most notably in the use of single items to assess internalized homophobia. In addition, existing data were collected in the early 1970s and thus predate important events in the emancipation of the gay community in the United States. Consequently, they may not reflect possible historical changes in rates of internalized homophobia. Nonetheless, these data bear reporting because they comprise the best descriptive information available.

In a large-scale study of more than 1,000 gay men and lesbians in the San Francisco Bay Area (Bell & Weinberg, 1978), about 28% of the white gay men and almost 50% of the black gay men reported "some guilt" over their sexual activities with men, and about 25% of the white and black gay men reported viewing homosexuality as an "emotional disorder." The figures were somewhat lower for lesbians, with 20% of the white lesbians and 33% of the black lesbians reporting some degree of guilt over their sexual activities with women, and less than 25% of both white and black lesbians viewing homosexuality as an emotional disorder.

Similar results were obtained in a mail survey by Jay and Young (1977) with a convenience sample of more than 5,000 gay men and lesbians. In response to the question, "Do you ever or have you ever experienced . . . shame [or] guilt . . . in connection with your homosexuality?," 37% of the gay men and 30% of the lesbians answered "quite a lot" or "some." On the other hand, almost 38% of the gay men and 50% of the lesbians responded "not at all." (The meaningfulness of Jay and Young's [1977] data is limited by many methodological problems, including the confounding of present and past negative feelings toward homosexuality in the way the question was presented to respondents.) In sum, the studies suggest that between 33% and 25% of lesbians and gay men (and possibly a larger proportion of black gay men) may have negative attitudes or feelings about their homosexuality at some point in their lives.

The impact of developmental events on lesbians' and gay men's levels of internalized homophobia has not been studied. Consequently, it is not known (a) what percentage of lesbian and gay teens hold internalized homophobia, (b) how prevalence rates change through the years as lesbians and gay teens enter adulthood, (c) how consistent internalized homophobia levels are throughout adulthood in any given individual, (d) what gender and ethnic differences might exist, and (e) what generational differences might exist as a result of the dramatic cultural and social changes that have occurred in the post-Stonewall era of the gay community.

It is likely that there is wide variability in internalized homonegativity in lesbians and gay men. Societal factors such as region of residence, ethnicity, and social class may be differentially associated with homonegativity. Familial factors, such as level of homophobia held by parental figures and significant others (Nungesser, 1983), and personological variables, such as the special vulnerabilities, needs, and defensive strategies of each individual (Malyon, 1982), are also likely to affect levels of internalized homonegativity. Thus any attempt to measure internalized homophobia should use an instrument that assesses subtle expressions as well as more extreme ones.

Impact on Psychological Adjustment

An important advance in the conceptualization of internalized homophobia was the recognition that the significance of this construct lies in its deleterious and pathogenic impact on developmental events in gay people and their psychological functioning. As Malyon (1982) wrote, gay-affirmative psychology "regards homophobia . . . as a major pathological variable in the development of certain symptomatic conditions among gay [persons]" (p. 69). He hypothesized that internalized homophobia causes depression, influences identity formation, self-esteem, the elaboration of defenses, patterns of cognition, psychological integrity, object relations, and superego functioning. He viewed the pathogenic effects of internalized homophobia as a (usually temporary) suppression of homosexual feelings, an elaboration of a heterosexual persona, and an interruption of the process of identity formation.

Other writers have suggested that internalized homophobia causes distrust and loneliness (Finnegan & Cook, 1984), difficulties in intimate/affectional relationships (Friedman, 1991; George & Behrendt, 1988), under- and overachievement (Gonsiorek, 1988; Pharr, 1988), impaired sexual functioning (Brown, 1986; Reece, 1988), unsafe sex (Shidlo, 1992), domestic violence (Pharr, 1988), avoidant coping with AIDS in HIV seropositive gay men (Nicholson & Long, 1990), alcoholism (Finnegan & Cook, 1984), substance abuse (Glaus, 1988), eating disorders (Brown, 1987), fragmentation and borderline-like features (Gonsiorek, 1982; Malyon, 1982), and suicide (Rofes, 1983). Because internalized homophobia may be one important determinant of psychopathological conditions in lesbians and gay men, psychotherapy with this population should routinely include the assessment and treatment of internalized homophobia (cf. Gonsiorek, 1982; Malyon, 1982; Stein & Cohen, 1984).

Unconscious Internalized Homophobia

Several theorists have described internalized homonegativity as including not only conscious negative attitudes toward homosexuality but also unconscious homonegativity (Brown, 1986; Friedman, 1991; Gonsiorek, 1988; Loulan, 1984; Malyon, 1982; Margolies, Becker, & Jackson-Brewer, 1987). Margolies et al. (1987) described internalized homophobia as consisting of a series of defense mechanisms including rationalization, denial, projection, and identification with the aggressor. Other unconscious features of internalized homophobia include internalization of distorted images of lesbian sexuality, both as deviant and as overidealized (Brown, 1986; Loulan, 1984); tolerance of discriminatory or abusive treatment from others; sabotaging of career goals by blaming external bigotry (Gonsiorek, 1988); a sensed lack of entitlement to give and receive love; irrational efforts to undermine intimate relationships; and the projection of the devalued self-image to one's partner (Friedman, 1991).

What has been termed unconscious internalized homophobia can be considered what Malyon (1982) has referred to variously as "abstractions," "secondary and tertiary adaptations," "derivatives," and "elaborations" of internalized homophobia. In other words, the internalization of homophobia can have deleterious effects on many facets of intra- and interpersonal functioning. These secondary and tertiary manifestations of internalized homophobia can be regarded as unconscious in the sense that their original connection with conscious internalized homophobia has been lost to the individual. Thus some of what has been termed unconscious homophobia may be considered as diffuse, intrapsychic *consequences* of conscious internalized homophobia.

Whereas theorists have described unconscious internalized homophobia, its operationalization and assessment have received limited attention and still pose great challenges. A brief example will illustrate the elusive nature of the concept of unconscious internalized homophobia. As an indicator of the defensive expression of internalized homophobia, Margolies et al. (1987) provided the item "feeling superior to heterosexuals" or "heterophobia." In their framework, a lesbian who reports feeling that lesbians are better than heterosexuals can be inferred to be suffering from a defensive, unconscious internalized homophobia. On examination, however, feelings of superiority can be related to internalized homophobia only if one views heterophobia as the expression of a defense mechanism against internalized homophobia. An alternate view is that heterophobia (or "heteronegativity") is a useful coping mechanism for persons who feel under siege and oppressed by a dominant or oppressive heterosexual society. It also can be a biased expression of pride in the accomplishments of and characteristics of the lesbian and gay communities. Thus the relationship between observable manifestations of purported unconscious homophobia and actual homonegative content may be difficult to evaluate. Additional theoretical work around unconscious internalized homophobia and its empirical characteristics is greatly needed. Empirical data obtained with projective tests (Herek, 1987) and physiological measures (Shields & Harriman, 1984) may be helpful in this process.

Operationalizing Internalized Homophobia

Face Validity and Content Validity

The task of operationalizing a construct is to provide a measurable means of the focal concept (Brewer & Hunter, 1989), or the concept to be measured. Thus there are two initial steps in operationalizing internalized homonegativity: (a) determining which observable behaviors are to be included to maximize face validity and (b) ensuring that an adequate sampling of these social behaviors is obtained to get good content validity.

Using the criteria of adequate face and content validity, most of the research in the area of internalized homophobia has not been very satisfactory (the notable exceptions are Nungesser, 1983, and Alexander, 1986). Internalized homophobia has been assessed using a single-item or a very small pool of items with limited content validity and the absence of an explicit theoretically based direction in selecting items. Furthermore, almost all of this research has been restricted to gay men, excluding lesbians. One possible reason for the limited quality of this research is that it preceded the publication of seminal papers in gay-affirmative psychology (e.g., Gonsiorek, 1982; Malyon, 1982) that would have provided the theoretical framework necessary for successful operationalization. Another reason for the limited interpretability of this research is that most of it appears to have studied internalized homophobia only incidentally in the context of larger projects on homosexuality. The following section examines the face validity of measures of internalized homophobia, followed by consideration of their content validity.

The Threat to Face Validity

An item contributes to face validity if it is obviously more pertinent to the meaning of the focal concept than it is to the meaning of other concepts. An extreme example of poor face validity would be an attempt to measure air temperature with a ruler (Brewer & Hunter, 1989). The main difficulty of obtaining good face validity stems from the challenging process of deciding which behaviors actually reflect negative attitudes toward homosexuality. For example, how are researchers to determine whether an item such as "I do not think I will be able to have a long-term relationship with another man" (Nungesser, 1983) belongs in a measure of internalized homophobia? A helpful guide is to ask whether the item in question is closer to the focal concept being studied than to other related but distinct focal concepts (Brewer & Hunter, 1989). Is Nungesser's item closer to the focal concept of internalized homophobia than to another focal concept, such as personal "difficulty with intimacy"? Although difficulties with intimacy in gay men may or may not be empirically associated with internalized homonegativity, this is an example of an item that is best viewed as a correlate. As a correlate, it may *antecede* internalized homonegativity as a preexisting trait (e.g., gay men with intimacy difficulties may have only troubled short-term relationships with other men and conclude that all gay relationships are inherently short-lived) or may be a *consequence* of homonegativity (e.g., high-homonegative men may date men less than low-homonegative men and develop difficulties with intimacy). A rephrasing of Nungesser's (1983) item that would avoid confounding homophobia with difficulty in intimacy is "Relationships between gay men cannot last."

In sum, an item that is part of a focal concept that is either an antecedent or consequence of internalized homonegativity may best remain outside the boundaries of a tightly defined construct of homonegativity rather than be adopted in an overfluid, overinclusive view of internalized homonegativity. In subsequent stages of research, it is the role of construct validation (Anastasi, 1982) to evaluate the network of relationships between internalized homonegativity and antecedent and consequent constructs, such as fear of intimacy.

Another illustration of a conceptualization of internalized homophobia that overlaps with other constructs in an equivocal way is provided in the work of Margolies et al. (1987). One item describes lesbians who restrict their attraction to unavailable women, heterosexual partners, or those already in other relationships. On the one hand, as the authors argue, this behavior could be seen as a manifestation of internalized homophobia (e.g., "only straight women are worth being attracted to") or some acting-out of impossible attempts at intimacy because of a belief that gay relationships cannot work. One could argue, however, that a lesbian can restrict attraction to unavailable women (just as a heterosexual woman could restrict attraction to unavailable men) as a reflection of characterological issues that have less to do with internalized homophobia than with personal fear of intimacy. A related item provided by these authors categorizes short-term relationships as an expression of internalized homophobia because they can be used to pass as heterosexual with family and coworkers. Once again, this behavior may also be an expression of characterological issues of fear of commitment or rejection.

Another example of an item that is related to internalized homonegativity in a complex way is "My life would be much easier if I were heterosexual" (Savin-Williams, 1990). Although this item is described by Savin-Williams as providing a measure of "comfort with homosexuality," it confounds internalized homophobia with a realistic perception of the societal challenges of being gay in a homophobic society. This brings up the general question: When is distress over being gay not a reflection of internalized homophobia but rather a realistic reaction to societal oppression? For example, an isolated but publicly identified lesbian in a small town who suffers ongoing physical abuse, rejection, and isolation because of extreme societal homophobia may have ample reality-based reasons to view her homosexuality as a negative feature in her life. She may even wish she were not gay. Does this woman suffer from internalized homonegativity? One yardstick that can be used to distinguish maladaptive internalized homonegativity from a reality-based perception of homosexuality as having a negative impact on one's life is to assess the locus of the blame one places for the difficulties in one's life. When gay people blame themselves rather than a homophobic society for difficulties they experience as a gay person or when they are ashamed of their homosexuality, it is likely a reflection of internalized homonegativity (Sophie, 1988). This is in contrast to individuals who are able to separate the fact of their homosexuality from the realities of social oppression.

A related view has been put forth by Crocker and Major (1989) in a review of self-esteem in stigmatized minority groups. They found that members of stigmatized minority groups who blame themselves for the difficulties they experience tend to have lower self-esteem than those who blame society. Crocker and Major (1989) described the self-protective function of externally attributing personal difficulties to forces such as racism and prejudice. It would be interesting to see whether this relationship extends to lesbians and gay men. In other words, do lesbians and gay men display higher self-esteem to the extent that they attribute gay-related difficulties in their lives to an oppressive society rather than to their sexual orientation? Would it be helpful to view the operationalization of internalized homophobia as including the maladaptive blaming of gay-related difficulties on sexual orientation, ignoring the impact of a heterosexist society? An example of this type of operationalization is included in Nungesser's (1983) item "Most problems that homosexuals have come from their status as an oppressed minority, not from their homosexuality per se." In sum, let me articulate one of the major challenges of the successful operationalization of internalized homophobia. Although it is necessary to have a sufficiently inclusive face validity to capture with realism the social manifestations of homonegativity in lesbians and gay men, it is important not to have an overinclusive operationalization that overlaps with related constructs, such as difficulty in intimate relationships and self-esteem. An overinclusive operationalization of internalized homophobia dilutes its distinctiveness as an explanatory construct for understanding lesbians and gay men as contrasted with psychological factors that affect all people, gay and nongay.

Content Validity

Content validity requires that a measure include a sufficient range of social behaviors and situations to capture the actual diversity of experiences that lesbians and gay men have regarding negative attitudes toward homosexuality. Thus a scale of internalized homophobia should include mildly negative items such as "Gay persons' lives are not as fulfilling as heterosexuals' lives" (Nungesser, 1983) and extreme items such as "I have tried killing myself because I couldn't accept my homosexuality" (Shidlo, 1992). It should also include (with reverse scoring) positive items such as "It's important for me to feel part of the gay community" (Shidlo, 1992). A good measure of internalized homophobia must be useful for gay persons with only incidental negative attitudes and affect about their homosexuality as well as for persons for whom homosexuality is a central cause of extreme psychological distress.

Empirical Studies

An early empirical study of gay men that examined attitudes toward homosexuality was conducted by Weinberg and Williams (1975). Four sets of one- and two-item scales were used: (1) anxiety regarding homosexuality, (2) homosexual commitment ("I wish I were not homosexual"), (3) conception of homosexuality as an illness, and (4) conception of choice over homosexuality ("Homosexuality is beyond's one's control"). In regard to face validity, the first three items (anxiety, commitment, and illness) fall reasonably within the focal concept of internalized homophobia. The fourth item of perceived choice over homosexuality may or may not reflect a negative attitude toward homosexuality. In other words, whether one regards homosexuality as a matter of choice or genetics is not necessarily correlated with homonegativity. A later project by the same research group (Bell & Weinberg, 1978) showed improvement in the scope of content assessed by including the following areas: regret versus acceptance of homosexuality, thinking about and trying to discontinue homosexual behavior, viewing homosexuality as an emotional disorder, perceived distress if respondent's child were to be gay, and wanting a "magic heterosexuality pill."

Martin and Dean (1987) introduced a nine-item scale for gay males termed internalized homophobia (IHP). The operationalization was based on criteria of the DSM-III (American Psychiatric Association, 1980) for ego-dystonic homosexuality. Items were similar to those used by Bell and Weinberg (1978). The content centered around wanting to avoid homosexual sexual behavior and gay relationships and trying to experience heterosexual behavior and feelings. Internal consistency was good, with a Cronbach α of .79 (Meyer cited in Sbordone, 1993). However, this scale has limited content validity, because its items tap rather extreme internalized homophobia associated with the desire to change a homosexual orientation. Thus it may be helpful with very homophobic gay men, but may underestimate moderate and subtle internalized homophobia.

The publication of Nungesser's (1983) work was a qualitative advance in the empirical study of internalized homonegativity in gay men. His items include both moderate and extreme homophobic content. The Nungesser Homosexuality Attitudes Inventory (NHAI) consists of a three-subscale, 34-item instrument (see Appendix A of this chapter). Of particular importance, the operationalization of each subscale was made explicit. Nungesser conceived of internalized homonegativity as falling into three factors: (1) attitudes toward the fact of one's own homosexuality (Self), (2) attitudes toward homosexuality in general and toward other gay persons (Other), and (3) reaction toward others knowing about one's homosexuality (Disclosure). Nungesser (1983) obtained moderate to good measures of internal consistency of the total NHAI ($\alpha = .94$) with the figures for the subscales ranging between .68 and .93. Item-subscale correlation coefficients ranged between .42 and .82, with the exception of one item ("Marriage between two homosexuals should be legalized," for which the correlation was .14).

Nungesser's tripartite system permits differentiation between global attitudes toward homosexuality and attitudes toward one's own homosexual feelings and behavior. Previously, internalized homonegativity was conceptualized and measured in such a way that it was not possible to distinguish between gay individuals who might have global positive attitudes toward homosexuality but negative attitudes toward their own sexuality (e.g., "Homosexuality is not an illness, but I hate myself for not being heterosexual") and persons who have globally negative attitudes but positive attitudes toward their own homosexuality (e.g., "Gay persons generally flaunt their homosexuality too much and are too promiscuous, but I carry my homosexuality discreetly and with dignity"). Unknown significant differences in the psychological and interpersonal adaptations of these two kinds of persons may be assessed by an instrument that permits this distinction. Interrelationships among the NHAI subscales obtained by Shidlo (1987) were moderate, ranging between .62 and .67 ($p < .01$). Somewhat lower interrelationships were obtained by Sbordone (1993) with the range between .42 and .51. These data provide preliminary evidence for the distinctiveness of the subscales. However, factor analysis and replication are necessary to explore this issue further.

In regard to the comfort with Disclosure subscale, some may object to viewing discomfort with disclosure as an example of internalized homophobia. Perhaps the degree to which one feels comfortable disclosing one's homosexuality overlaps with factors such as a realistic perception of the benefits and dangers of disclosure in a homophobic society. Gonsiorek (1988) suggested that an adaptive development of a decision-making process about disclosure takes prejudice and ostracism into account through a complex cost-benefit analysis. Over the range of feelings about disclosure, those who never disclose to anyone, *not even to other gay persons,* are likely experiencing internalized homonegative shame (Sophie, 1988). In the middle of the range may lie persons who accurately judge when it is safe and functional to disclose their homosexuality. Finally, on the other extreme are those fortunate enough to live in a nonoppressive environment who usually can be open about their gayness. In sum, comfort over disclosure is probably related not only to internalized homonegativity but also to the external realities of societal homophobia, lack of civil rights protection, differential penalties in different professions, ability to withstand rejection by homophobic others, and risk-taking personality characteristics.

The second instrument that provides adequate face and content validity is the Internalized Homophobia Inventory (IHI) (Alexander, 1986). Alexander asked experts in gay psychology to select items that provided high face validity for internalized homophobia. The result was a measure of 25 items, with an internal consistency of .85. Face and content validity appears high, with items covering a broad range of areas, including desire to affiliate with other lesbians and gay men (reverse scoring) and pleasure at being perceived by others as heterosexual.

Construct Validity

The extent to which instruments of internalized homophobia actually measure the trait of internalized homophobia is termed *construct validity* (Anastasi, 1982). There are preliminary empirical data to support theoretical predictions made about internalized homophobia, most notably in the area of psychological distress and self-esteem. As almost all this research has involved attempts to obtain convergent validity for the NHAI measure (Nungesser, 1983), this section will be limited to studies that have assessed its relationship with other variables (see Table 10.1). It is noted here that this work has been limited to gay men, to the exclusion of lesbians, and has not explored ethnic differences. (To improve interpretability, in the reporting of results the author has reversed the original direction of scores in the NHAI, so that high scores signify high internalized homophobia.)

Seeking concurrent validity for the NHAI (Nungesser, 1983), Alexander (1986) found a strong positive correlation between the NHAI and his own IHI. In a study of gay fathers, Sbordone (1993) found a moderate positive association between the NHAI and Martin and Dean's (1987) Internalized Homophobia (IHP) scale (Table 10.1). These three measures of internalized homonegativity (the NHAI, IHI, and IHP) appear to measure a similar concept.

Shifting to behavioral indicators, Nungesser (1983) found significant negative correlations between level of internalized homophobia (NHAI) and number of persons to whom the respondent was out as gay, frequency of socializing with gay men, and level of positive reaction of significant others to homosexuality (as perceived by the respondent). He also found a positive correlation between internalized homophobia and reported frequency of passing as heterosexual (Table 10.1).

Evidence for the negative correlation of internalized homophobia with self-esteem (as measured by Rosenberg, 1965) was obtained by Alexander (1986). Similar results were obtained by Sbordone (1993) in a sample of gay men who chose to be fathers and gay nonfathers. Conversely, depression as assessed by the Multiscore Depression Inventory (MDI) (Berndt, Petzel, & Berndt, 1980) was positively associated with homophobia: Homophobic men were more highly depressed (Alexander, 1986; see Table 10.1). Similar results were obtained by Nicholson and Long (1990), who found that HIV seropositive gay men who were highly

Table 10.1 Relationships Between NHAI (Internalized Homophobia) and Other Measures

	NHAI Total					
Other Measures	*Alexander (1986)*	*Nicholson and Long (1990)*	*Nungesser (1983)*	*Sbordone (1993)*	*Study 1 (Shidlo, 1987)*	*Study 2 (Shidlo, 1992)*
ARIH						.68 (60)***
IHI (Alexander, 1986)	.70 (92)***					
IHP (Martin & Dean, 1987)				.59 (159)**		
Psychological distress (SCL-90-R)						.43 (60)***
Depression	.41*** (MDI)	.44 (89) (POMS)			.37 (59)** (Rosenberg)	
Somatic symptoms					.49 (59)***	
Stability of self					–.35 (59)**	
Distrust					.62 (59)***	
Loneliness					.62 (59)***	
Self-esteem	–.28* (Rosenberg)	–.52 (89) (Rosenberg)		–.20 (161)**	–.59** (Shrauger; self-worth)	–.56 (60)*** (Rosenberg); –.42 (61)*** (Shrauger; self-confidence)
SRS (MacDonald, 1974)	–.34 (95)***					
Overall social support		–.45 (89) (Kaplan)			–.41 (34)** (Sarason)	–.25 (56)*

Satisfaction with social support					−.33 (34)* (Sarason)	
Relative gay social support			−.50 (50)*** (Nungesser)		−.42 (34)** (Shidlo)	
Overlap of gay and nongay supports					−.32 (59)**	
Number of persons out to as gay			−.61 (50)***			
Positive reaction by others to disclosure			−.23 (50)***			
Frequency pass as heterosexual			.66 (50)***			
Coping with AIDS		−.24 (89) (proactive); .42 (89) (avoidant)				
Social desirability					.02 (54)	−.35 (59)* (with NHAI Self)
High-risk sex (anal or vaginal without condom)						t = −.12; report: M = 1.63, SD = .41 deny: M = 1.64, SD = .43
Indeterminate risk sex (oral sex without condom)						t = 2.65*; report: M = 1.59, SD = .40 deny: M = 2.06, SD = .38

NOTE: All tests are two-tailed except Sbordone (1993). High scores on NHAI, IHI, and IHP indicate high internalized homophobia. M = mean; SD = standard deviation.
*$p < .05$; **$p < .01$; ***$p < .001$.

homophobic (NHAI) tended to have lower self-esteem and higher depression scores, as assessed by the Profile of Mood States (McNair, Lorr, & Droppleman, 1971). These results support the predicted association of internalized homophobia with lowered self-esteem and increased depression (Malyon, 1982).

Other results include a moderate negative association between internalized homophobia and support for equality for women and men (Alexander, 1986) as measured by the Sex Appropriate Behavior subscale of the Sex-Role Survey (MacDonald, 1974). This is similar to the relationship found between homonegativity in heterosexuals and other kinds of prejudice (Herek, 1984). An intriguing finding was that of Sbordone (1993), who found that gay men who choose to be fathers (through adoption or in arrangement with a surrogate) were significantly less homophobic on the NHAI (mean = 55.5, standard deviation = 12.3) than gay men who were not fathers (mean = 61.5, standard deviation = 14.2), $t(159) = -2.84$, $p < .005$. Sbordone suggested that gay men who are less homonegative may also be less likely to accept the homophobic attitude that gay men should not become parents.

Nicholson and Long (1990) found a positive association between homophobia (NHAI) in HIV seropositive gay men and self-blame with respect to HIV. Homophobia was also associated with avoidant coping (Folkman, Lazarus, Dunkel-Schetter, DeLongis, & Gruen, 1986). In contrast, lower levels of homophobia were associated with greater use of problem-solving and support-seeking coping. They also found that HIV seropositive gay men who reported higher levels of social support tended to be less homophobic.

In conclusion, there is a growing body of empirical evidence that provides support for the construct validity of the NHAI as a valid instrument in assessing internalized homophobia in gay men. Specifically, the NHAI appears to share a significant portion of the variance with self-esteem and depression in gay men as well as coping with AIDS in HIV seropositive gay men. Replication, cross-validation with other samples, and factor analysis are necessary.

Two Studies of Internalized Homophobia

The relationship of internalized homonegativity with psychological distress, self-esteem, social support, and safer sex in gay men has been of particular interest to the author. Two studies were conducted to investigate the construct validity of the NHAI in which eight relationships between internalized homonegativity and other constructs were explored: (1) level of psychological distress, (2) level of self-esteem, (3) level of loneliness, (4) level of social support and satisfaction with social support, (5) level of gay relative to nongay social support, (6) level of overlap among gay and nongay networks, (7) AIDS-related high-risk sexual behavior, and (8) level of social desirability response bias. It was expected that high-homonegative gay men, compared with low-homonegative gay men, would show the following characteristics: (a) high level of psychological distress, (b) low level of self-esteem, (c) high level of loneliness, (d) low level of satisfaction with support and low gay relative to nongay social support, (e) low overlap among gay and nongay networks, and (f) high-risk sexual behavior.

The studies also assessed the degree to which responses to the NHAI are colored by social desirability bias. Specifically, it might be difficult for gay persons to acknowledge and admit homonegative beliefs in the face of a general tendency to discourage such verbal behavior within the lesbian and gay community. As Martin (personal communication, December 1992) pointed out, there is "shame about shame" in many of her psychotherapy patients to admit homophobic feelings about themselves. It was hypothesized that reported levels of internalized homonegativity would show a low or moderate correlation with social desirability.

Another goal was to improve the content validity of the assessment of internalized homophobia by developing a new scale that would account for AIDS-related changes that the gay community has experienced since Nungesser's original instrument was published in the early 1980s. The new scale is called AIDS-Related Internalized Homonegativity (ARIH) and was introduced to describe the subset of internalized homonegative beliefs that are AIDS related. ARIH includes the following beliefs: (a) AIDS is caused by homosexuality, (b) AIDS is just retribution or punishment for homosexuality, (c) gay persons who have had multiple sexual partners are immoral and self-destructive and therefore deserve to get sick, and (d) because homosexuality causes AIDS, "I will try to become heterosexual." Items were derived from the author's clinical work with HIV seronegative and seropositive gay men in psychotherapy (see Appendix B of this chapter).

A particular focus of this work was the impact of AIDS-related internalized homonegativity on the adoption of safer-sex practices by gay men. Although a variety of factors are likely associated with high-risk behavior, AIDS-related internalized homonegativity beliefs so saliently contradict the messages of gay safer sex that it appears important to explore the relationship of ARIH to high-risk behavior. Thus gay men who believe that "homosexual behavior causes AIDS" may have difficulty adopting the schema inherent in safer-sex guidelines, which discriminate between high- and low-risk homosexual sexual behavior. High ARIH individuals were expected to be more likely to engage in high-risk behavior than were low ARIH persons.

Study 1: Method

Measures

The independent variable was internalized homophobia as assessed by the NHAI (Nungesser, 1983). Total scores were divided by number of items. Psychological distress was assessed by scales adopted from Rosenberg (1965). These scales included depression (α = .88), somatic symptoms (α = .85), and stability of self-concept (α = .79). Distrust was assessed using a measure devised by Raulin (unpublished data, 1987). Loneliness was assessed by a four-item measure (α = .75) of Russel, Peplau, and Cutrona (1980). Self-esteem was assessed by the self-worth subscale of the Personal Evaluation Inventory (Shrauger, unpublished data, 1992). Three measures of social support were used. First was the 27-item Social Support Questionnaire (SSQ) (Sarason, Levine, Basham, & Sarason, 1983), which provides a quantitative index of supports (α = .97) and an index of perceived satisfaction with social support (α = .94). A second measure (Shidlo, 1987) was based on a set of 6 items asking respondents to indicate on a four-point scale the frequency with which they socialize with male and female gay, bisexual, and heterosexual individuals. A ratio was obtained by dividing the frequency of socializing with male and female gay supports by frequency of socializing with all other supports. The third measure (Shidlo, 1987) consisted of an item asking respondents to indicate the degree to which nongay supports socialize with and/or know about gay supports. Social desirability was assessed with the Marlowe-Crowne measure (Crowne & Marlowe, 1960).

Procedure

A total of 125 questionnaires were distributed in 1986 to volunteer male members of gay community groups in several cities in the northeastern United States. Subjects were asked to return the completed questionnaires by mail. A total of 60 questionnaires were returned, 54 of which were used for the analysis. Subjects were predominantly white (82%) with only 18% representation of ethnic minorities. The average age was 32, with a range of 17 to 64. Average annual income was approximately $20,000. Approximately 60% of subjects had a college-graduate-level education or above.

Study 2: Method

Measures

Internalized homophobia was assessed using the modified NHAI (see Appendix A of this chapter). Psychological distress was measured by the SCL-90-R (Derogatis, 1977). Self-esteem was assessed using the Rosenberg (1965) measure. High-risk sexual behavior was assessed by asking subjects to estimate their frequency of anal and vaginal intercourse without condoms over the period of 12 months before the interview. Indeterminate-risk sexual behavior was assessed by asking subjects to estimate their frequency of oral sex without condoms. AIDS-Related Internalized Homonegativity (ARIH) was assessed by a newly introduced 15-item subscale (see Appendix B of this chapter). Items were rated on a four-point scale. The options were 1, strongly disagree; 2, mainly disagree; 3, mainly agree; and 4, strongly agree. Total scores were divided by number of items. The α coefficient was .82, with a mean of 1.56 (standard deviation = .40). Social desirability was assessed with the Marlowe-Crowne measure (Crowne & Marlowe, 1960).

Procedure

Study 2 was conducted in 1990. A total of 180 questionnaires were distributed in New York City. Subjects were handed a questionnaire with a self-addressed, stamped envelope and asked to complete it, mail it, and then phone the investigator for a follow-up telephone interview or, if they preferred, a face-to-face interview. Subjects were recruited at a gay community center, in the waiting area of a local health clinic with a large gay practice, a gay pride march, and in black gay bars. A total of 71 completed questionnaires were obtained. The final usable sample included 62 gay and bisexual males. Exclusionary criteria included a diagnosis of AIDS and heterosexuality. Approximately 68% of the subjects were white; 21%, black or African-American; 7%, Hispanic or Latino; 3%, Asian American; and 1%, Native American or American Indian. The average age was 32.27 (standard deviation = 9.59). The range of age was 18 to 68 years. Average annual income was between $20,000 and $30,000, with 56% reporting being at least college graduates.

Studies 1 and 2: Results

No consistent differential pattern of association among the NHAI subscales and other measures was noted. Therefore, only analyses using the total NHAI score are reported here. Internal reliability for the NHAI was .90. The reliability for the ARIH was .81. The positive correlation between NHAI and ARIH was significant (see Table 10.1).

It was expected that internalized homonegativity (NHAI) would be predictive of psychological distress. This hypothesis was supported by moderate positive correlations between NHAI and measures of overall distress (SCL-90-R), depression, somatic complaints, sense of stability of self, distrust, and loneliness (Table 10.1). This finding suggests that internalized homonegativity shares a significant portion of its variance with psychological distress in gay men. The variance shared by NHAI scores ranged from 16% for the overall index of distress, to 25% for the somatic complaints subscale, to 36% for the distrust subscale.

Studies 1 and 2 both found a strong negative correlation between level of homonegativity and self-esteem (Table 10.1). Just under 35% of the variance in self-esteem was accounted for by the NHAI. This suggests that internalized homonegativity and self-esteem are interconnected but not identical constructs.

In Study 1, the general social-support measure (SSQ) showed a negative correlation with internalized homophobia scores. Subjects with high levels of social support and low ratios of gay supports demonstrated higher homonegativity than those with high levels of gay supports. Persons who estimated most of their social supports as being lesbian or gay were less likely than those who reported them as mostly heterosexual to show internalized homophobia. A third measure of social-support consisted of the degree to which nongay supports know and/or interact with gay supports. Persons who avoided telling their heterosexual supports that they had gay friends or who kept their gay supports socially apart from their heterosexual friends tended to be more homonegative. (Unfortunately, because a single item was used, the data do not permit the distinction between the two discrete factors: heterosexual supports knowing about gay supports versus socializing with them).

In Study 2, both NHAI and ARIH failed to serve as useful predictors of high-risk sexual behavior (Table 10.1). Persons who reported anal or vaginal intercourse without condoms over the previous 12 months were no more likely to be homonegative than those who denied high-risk behavior.

An unexpected finding was the strong negative correlation between NHAI scores and indeterminate-risk sexual behavior (Table 10.1). Persons who reported oral sex without condoms were characterized by lower levels of homonegativity than were those who did not report oral sex. (Only one respondent reported oral sex with a condom and was excluded from this analysis.)

In Study 1, no significant correlations were obtained between the Marlowe-Crowne (M-C) measure and the three subscales of the NHAI. However, in Study 2 the Self subscale of NHAI showed a significant negative association with M-C scores (Table 10.1). Subjects who minimized homophobia about their own homosexuality were more likely to be concerned about appearing socially desirable. Because of these inconsistent results it remains unclear whether social desirability is a source of response bias to the NHAI.

Studies 1 and 2: Conclusions

The results of these studies on the construct validity of the NHAI are consistent with research by other investigators. High internalized homophobia appeared significantly associated with overall psychological distress and other measures of adjustment. High-homonegative gay men were also characterized by lower self-esteem, lower social support and satisfaction with support, less gay relative to nongay supports, less overlap between gay and nongay networks, and greater loneliness. Homonegativity was not associated with high-risk sexual behavior (i.e., anal or vaginal sex without condoms). However, gay men who reported oral sex without a condom were more likely to be low on homophobia than those who did not have oral sex at all.

Conclusions

This chapter has argued that the construct of internalized homophobia can serve as a central organizing concept for a gay and lesbian affirmative psychology. The term *internalized homonegativity* carries a more neutral and inclusive meaning than *internalized homophobia*. Constructs that are either antecedents or consequences of IH (such as difficulty with intimacy) are best not included as part of its operationalization. These related constructs need to be explored as part of the construct validation of IH. The following are conceptual and empirical characteristics of internalized homonegativity (IH) examined in this chapter that support this contention:

a. IH is a distinctive factor that can account for important developmental and intrapsychic events in lesbians and gay men.
b. The data (restricted at this time to gay men) suggest that IH shares a significant portion of the variance with overall psychological distress, depression, somatic symptoms, self-esteem, loneliness, and distrust. Thus highly homonegative gay men are more distressed, have poorer self-esteem, complain of greater loneliness, and are more distrustful.
c. IH is associated with a relative paucity of general social support. Furthermore, highly homonegative men are more likely to have a lower proportion of gay supports in their network and to keep them apart from their heterosexual network.
d. IH does not appear to be related to high-risk sexual behavior but is related to sexual behavior of ambiguous risk, i.e., oral sex without condoms.
e. Low levels of IH appear associated with proactive coping styles and decreased avoidant coping in gay men who are HIV seropositive.
f. Gay men who choose to be fathers through adoption or the help of a surrogate appear less homonegative than gay nonfathers.
g. The data are contradictory regarding the presence of social desirability bias in the assessment of IH.
h. At this time, the instrument for measuring IH with the most construct validity is the NHAI. It is available in a version for gay men (Nungesser, 1983) and an unpublished version for lesbians (D. Malmud, personal communication, August 1992). Content validity of the NHAI may be improved

by adding extreme-distress items such as suicidal ideation and behavior related to homonegativity, reverse-coded gay affirmative items such as feelings of pride in gay community, and AIDS-related items (see Appendixes A and B of this chapter).

There are a variety of neglected areas in which empirical data would be of great use. These include:

a. differences in IH between lesbians and gay men;
b. ethnic and cultural differences in IH;
c. the developmental relationship between internalized homonegativity, the coming-out process, and the development of symptomatic conditions in lesbians and gay men;
d. whether IH varies over time in some people, while remaining stable in others;
e. the role of internalized homonegativity in suicidal behavior in lesbian and gay teenagers and adults;
f. the impact of IH on lesbian and gay couples;
g. the impact of IH on domestic violence;
h. the relationship of IH to substance abuse;
i. the relationship of therapeutic efficacy with lesbians and gay men to the reduction of internalized homonegativity;
j. the relationship of homophobia levels in the psychotherapist and therapeutic change in the patient as well as differential impact of gay and nongay therapists and gay therapists who are out to their patients versus those who are not;
k. the danger and damage of "sexual orientation conversion therapies" and their impact on IH;
l. the role of gay-specific school programs like the Hetrick-Martin Institute on IH in gay teens;
m. the impact of secondary prevention programs in the school system, such as Project 10 and the Rainbow Curriculum, aimed at reducing homophobia in students and teachers, on the IH levels of gay students;
n. the relationship of homophobia to AIDS-related sexual risk behavior; and
o. the impact of IH on the physical health or illness of gay persons, as measured by immune function indicators.

Answers to these questions may be helpful to understand why some lesbians and gay men have dysfunctional high levels of internalized homonegativity, whereas others appear to negotiate a homophobic society with minimal or moderate internalization of these beliefs.

Appendix A
Revised (Shidlo) NHAI: Item Total Correlations

Subscale Self (Personal Homonegativity)

1. When I am in conversation with a gay man [homosexual] and he touches me, it does not make me uncomfortable. (R; .33)
2. Whenever I think a lot about being gay [a homosexual], I feel depressed. (.67)
3. I am glad to be gay. (R)
4. When I am sexually attracted to another gay man [close male friend], I feel uncomfortable. (.55)
5. I am proud to be a part of the gay community. (R; .54)
6. My homosexuality does not make me unhappy. (R; .50)
7. Whenever I think a lot about being gay, I feel critical about myself. (.59)
8. I wish I were heterosexual. (.37)
9. [I do not think I will be able to have a long-term relationship with another man.] (.58)

New Items

10. I have been in counseling because I wanted to stop having sexual feelings for other men. (.21)
11. I have tried killing myself because I couldn't accept my homosexuality. (.39)
12. There have been times when I've felt so rotten about being gay that I wanted to be dead. (.45)
13. I have tried killing myself because it seemed that my life as a gay person was too miserable to bear. (.26)
14. I find it important that I read gay books or newspapers. (R; .00)
15. It's important to me to feel part of the gay community. (R; .38)

NOTE: R signifies reverse scoring. Omissions from Nungesser (1983) are indicated by brackets. Item total correlations were obtained by Shidlo (1992). Items 3, 23, 25, 27, and 39 were omitted in that survey. Several revisions are proposed by the author for the NHAI, including (a) improving content validity by adding more extreme items such as suicidal items, (b) improving grammatically awkward or unclear items, and (c) omitting items that conceptually confound with other constructs too much (e.g., whether or not adults should be penalized for having sex with minors: see Item 25).

Subscale Other (Global Homonegativity)

16. Homosexuality is not as satisfying [good] as heterosexuality. (.53)
17. [Male] homosexuality is a natural expression of sexuality in humans [human males]. (R; .39)
18. Gay men [male homosexuals] do not dislike women any more than heterosexual men dislike women. (R; .27)
19. Marriage between gay people [two homosexuals] should be legalized. (R; .18)
20. Gay men [male homosexuals] are overly promiscuous. (.39)
21. Most problems that gay persons [homosexuals] have come from their status as an oppressed minority, not from their homosexuality per se. (R; .17)
22. Gay persons' lives [homosexual lifestyles] are not as fulfilling as heterosexuals' lives [heterosexual lifestyles]. (.47)
23. Children should be taught that being gay is a normal and healthy way for people to be. (R) [Choosing an adult gay lifestyle should be an option for children].
24. Homosexuality is a sexual perversion. (.37)
25. [Adult homosexual males who have sex with boys under eighteen years of age should be punished by law].

Subscale Disclosure

26. I wouldn't mind if my boss knew that I was gay. (R; .58)
27. When I tell my *nongay* friends about my homosexuality, I do not worry that they will try to remember things about me that would make me appear to fit the stereotype of a homosexual. (R)
28. When I am sexually attracted to another gay man, I do not mind if someone else knows how I feel. (R; .55)
29. When women know of my homosexuality, I am afraid they will not relate to me as a man. (.46)
30. I would not mind if my neighbors knew that I am gay. (R; .39)
31. It is important for me to conceal the fact that I am gay from most people. (.66)
32. If my straight friends knew of my homosexuality, I would be uncomfortable. (.59)
33. If men knew of my homosexuality, I'm afraid they would begin to avoid me. (.58)
34. If It were made public that I am gay [homosexual], I would be extremely unhappy. (.67)
35. If my peers knew of my homosexuality, I am afraid that many would not want to be friends with me. (.57)

36. If others knew of my homosexuality, I wouldn't worry particularly [would not be afraid] that they would think of [see] me as [being] effeminate. (R; .35)
37. When I think about coming out to peers, I am afraid they will pay more attention to my body movements and voice inflections. (.47)
38. I am afraid that people will harass me if I come out more publicly. (.43)
39. [When I think about coming out to a heterosexual male friend, I do not worry that he might watch me to see if I do things that are stereotypically homosexual.]

Appendix B
ARIH: Item Total Correlations

1. Occasionally, when I am thinking about AIDS, I start wishing that I weren't gay. (.41)
2. I'm proud of the way the gay community has dealt with the AIDS crisis. (R; .27)
3. Sometimes I can't help but wonder whether AIDS is caused by homosexuality. (.58)
4. Since the AIDS crisis began, I find myself reaching out more to other gay people. (R; .35)
5. Sometimes it almost seems like AIDS is a punishment for being gay. (.60)
6. The AIDS crisis has sometimes made me wonder whether homosexuality is an illness. (.46)
7. The AIDS crisis has made me feel stronger about my identity as a gay person. (R; .60)
8. There have been times when I couldn't help but feel that gay people with AIDS are at least partially to blame for getting sick. (.60)
9. AIDS has brought out the best in the gay community. (R; .38)
10. Since the AIDS crisis began, I find myself wishing sometimes that I were heterosexual. (.50)
11. Sometimes I feel like AIDS is a gay disease. (.55)
12. AIDS is just another one of those risks that are part of the life of gay persons. (.17)
13. The AIDS scare has made me try to stop being homosexual. (.40)
14. The AIDS crisis has made me feel like I have to count more on the gay community than ever before. (R; .13)

References

Alexander, R. A. (1986). *The relationship between internalized homophobia and depression and low self-esteem in gay men.* Unpublished doctoral dissertation, University of California at Santa Barbara.

American Psychiatric Association. (1980). *Diagnostic and statistical manual of mental disorders* (3rd ed.). Washington, DC: Author.

Anastasi, A. (1982). *Psychological testing* (5th ed.). New York: Macmillan.

Bell, A. P., & Weinberg, M. S. (1978). *Homosexualities: A study of diversity among men and women.* New York: Simon & Schuster.

Berndt, D. J., Petzel, T. P., & Berndt, S. M. (1980). Development and initial evaluation of a multiscore depression inventory. *Journal of Personality Assessment, 44,* 396-404.

Brewer, J., & Hunter, A. (1989). *Multimethod research.* Newbury Park, CA: Sage.

Brown, L. S. (1986). Confronting internalized oppression in sex therapy with lesbians. *Journal of Homosexuality, 12,* 99-107.

Brown, L. S. (1987). Lesbians, weight, and eating: New analyses and perspectives. In The Boston Lesbian Psychologies Collective (Ed.), *Lesbian psychologies: Explorations and challenges.* Urbana: University of Illinois.

Cass, V. (1979). Homosexual identity formation: A theoretical model. *Journal of Homosexuality, 4,* 219-235.

Committee on Lesbian and Gay Concerns. (1991). *Bias in psychotherapy with lesbians and gay men.* Washington, DC: American Psychiatric Association.

Crocker, J., & Major, B. (1989). Social stigma and self-esteem: The self-protective properties of stigma. *Psychological Review, 96,* 608-630.

Crowne, D. P., & Marlowe, D. (1960). A new scale of social desirability independent of psychopathology. *Journal of Consulting Psychology, 24,* 349-354.

Derogates, L. R. (1977). *SCL-90-R administration, scoring, and procedure manual* (Vol. 1). Baltimore, MD: Clinical Psychometric Research.

Finnegan, D. G., & Cook, D. (1984). Special issues affecting the treatment of male and lesbian alcoholics. *Alcoholism Treatment Quarterly, 1,* 85-98.

Folkman, S., Lazarus, R. S., Dunkel-Schetter, C., DeLongis, A., & Gruen, R. J. (1986). Dynamics of a stressful encounter: Cognitive appraisal, coping, and encounter outcomes. *Journal of Personality and Social Psychology, 50,* 992-1003.

Forstein, M. (1988). Homophobia: An overview. *Psychiatric Annals, 18,* 33-36.

Friedman, R. C. (1991). Couple therapy with gay couples. *Psychiatric Annals, 21,* 485-490.

George, K. D., & Behrendt, A. E. (1988). Therapy for male couples experiencing relationship problems and sexual problems. *Journal of Homosexuality, 14,* 77-88.

Glaus, O. K. (1988). Alcoholism, chemical dependency and the lesbian client. *Women and Therapy, 8,* 131-144.

Gonsiorek, J. C. (1982). The use of diagnostic concepts in working with gay and lesbian populations. *Journal of Homosexuality, 7,* 9-20.

Gonsiorek, J. C. (1988). Mental health issues of gay and lesbian adolescents. *Journal of Adolescent Health Care, 9,* 114-122.

Herek, G. M. (1984). Beyond "Homophobia": A social psychological perspective on attitudes toward lesbians and gay men. *Journal of Homosexuality, 10,* 1-21.

Herek, G. M. (1987). Can functions be measured? A new perspective on the functional approach to attitudes. *Social Psychology Quarterly, 50,* 285-303.

Herek, G. M. (1991). Stigma, prejudice, and violence against lesbians and gay men. In J. C. Gonsiorek & J. D. Weinrich (Eds.), *Homosexuality: Research implications for public policy* (pp. 60-80). Newbury Park, CA: Sage.

Hudson, W., & Ricketts, W. A. (1980). A strategy for measurement of homophobia. *Journal of Homosexuality, 5,* 357-371.

Jay, K., & Young, A. (1977). *The gay report.* New York: Summit.

Isensee, R. (1990). *Love between men.* New York: Prentice-Hall.

Loulan, J. (1984). *Lesbian sex.* San Francisco: Spinsters.

MacDonald, A. P. (1974). The importance of sex-role to gay liberation. *Homosexual Counseling Journal, 1*(4), 169-180.

Malyon, A. K. (1982). Psychotherapeutic implications of internalized homophobia in gay men. *Journal of Homosexuality, 7,* 59-70.

Margolies, L., Becker, M., & Jackson-Brewer, K. (1987). Internalized homophobia: Identifying and treating the oppressor within. In Boston Lesbian Psychologies Collective (Ed.), *Lesbian psychologies: Explorations and challenges* (pp. 229-241). Urbana: University of Illinois.

Martin, A. (1982). Some issues in the treatment of gay and lesbian patients. *Psychotherapy: Theory, Research and Practice, 19,* 341-348.

Martin, A. D. (1984). The emperor's new clothes: Modern attempts to change sexual orientation. In E. S. Hetrick & T. S. Stein (Eds.), *Innovations in psychotherapy with homosexuals* (pp. 23-58). Washington, DC: American Psychiatric Press.

Martin, J. L., & Dean, L. L. (1987). *Ego-dystonic homosexuality scale.* Available from School of Public Health, Columbia University.

McNair, D. M., Lorr, M., & Droppleman, L. F. (1971). *Profile of mood states.* San Diego: Educational & Industrial Testing Service.

Meyer, I. (1989, August). *The effects of internalized homophobia on mental health and coping among gay men.* Paper presented at the 97th Annual Convention of the American Psychological Association, New Orleans, LA.

Nicholson, W. D., & Long, B. C. (1990). Self-esteem, social support, internalized homophobia, and coping strategies of HIV+ gay men. *Journal of Consulting and Clinical Psychology, 58,* 873-876.

Nungesser, L. G. (1983). *Homosexual acts, actors, and identities.* New York: Praeger.

Pharr, S. (1988). *Homophobia: A weapon of sexism.* Little Rock: Chardon.

Reece, R. (1988). Causes and treatments of sexual desire discrepancies in male couples. *Journal of Homosexuality, 14,* 157-172.

Rofes, E. E. (1983). *I thought people like that killed themselves: Lesbians, gay men and suicide.* San Francisco: Grey Fox.

Rosenberg, M. (1965). *Society and the adolescent self-image.* Princeton, NJ: Princeton University Press.

Russel, D., Peplau, L. A., & Cutrona, C. E. (1980). The Revised UCLA Loneliness Scale: Concurrent and discriminant validity evidence. *Journal of Personality and Social Psychology, 39,* 472-480.

Sarason, I. G., Levine, H. M., Basham, R. B., & Sarason, B. R. (1983). Assessing social support: The Social Support Questionnaire. *Journal of Personality and Social Psychology, 44,* 127-139.

Savin-Williams, R. C. (1990). *Gay and lesbian youth: Expressions of identity.* New York: Hemisphere.

Sbordone, A. J. (1993). *Gay men choosing fatherhood.* Unpublished dissertation, City University of New York.

Shidlo, A. (1987, August). *Homonegativity and gay enmeshment: An investigation of adjustment in gay males.* Paper presented at 95th Annual Convention of the American Psychological Association, New York.

Shidlo, A. (1992). *AIDS related health behavior: Psychosocial correlates in gay men.* Unpublished doctoral dissertation, SUNY at Buffalo.

Shields, S. A., & Harriman, R. E. (1984). Fear of male homosexuality: Cardiac responses of low and high homonegative males. *Journal of Homosexuality, 10,* 53-67.

Sophie, J. (1988). Internalized homophobia and lesbian identity. *Journal of Homosexuality, 14,* 53-66.

Stein, T. S., & Cohen, C. J. (1984). Psychotherapy with gay men and lesbians: An examination of homophobia, coming out, and identity. In E. S. Hetrick & T. S. Stein (Eds.), *Innovations in psychotherapy with homosexuals* (pp. 59-74). Washington, DC: American Psychiatric Press.

Troiden, R. (1979). Becoming homosexual: A model of gay identity acquisition. *Psychiatry, 42,* 362-373.

Weinberg, G. (1972). *Society and the healthy homosexual.* Boston: Alyson.

Weinberg, M. S., & Williams, C. J. (1975). *Male homosexuals: Their problems and adaptations* (rev. ed.). New York: Penguin.

11

Assessing Heterosexuals' Attitudes Toward Lesbians and Gay Men

A Review of Empirical Research With the ATLG Scale

GREGORY M. HEREK

In the early 1970s, two related events paved the way for modern research on heterosexuals' attitudes toward lesbians and gay men. In 1972 Weinberg published his highly influential book, *Society and the Healthy Homosexual,* in which he introduced the concept of homophobia. In 1973 the American Psychiatric Association's board of trustees voted to remove homosexuality from the *Diagnostic and Statistical Manual* (*DSM*), a decision subsequently upheld in a referendum of the general membership (Bayer, 1987).

Weinberg's book and the *DSM* revision both were elements of a zeitgeist in which gay men and lesbians were vigorously challenging the stigma historically imposed on them by a heterosexist society. Both events reflected a new recognition by mental health practitioners and researchers that sexual orientation was not correlated with psychopathology (see Gonsiorek, 1991, for a review of relevant literature). Both raised a new question for society and science: If homosexuality is not a mental illness, why has it been regarded as one for most of the 20th century?

Perhaps it was inevitable that the question would be raised whether the real sickness might be some heterosexuals' hatred for homosexuals (and some homosexuals' hatred for themselves). Indeed, Weinberg (1972) began his first chapter with the statement, "I would never consider a patient healthy unless he had overcome his prejudice against homosexuality" (p. 1). A few pages later, he characterized such prejudice as a phobia, and briefly defined homophobia (among heterosexuals) as "the dread of being in close quarters with homosexuals" (p. 4).[1]

Some implications of framing prejudice against homosexuality in this way will be discussed later. It is sufficient here to note that Weinberg's terminology caught on and remains in use today. The 1992 edition of the *American Heritage Dictionary,* for example, included an entry for *homophobia* (p. 867). Of even greater importance for the present discussion, the phenomenon described by Weinberg became an object of scientific study by researchers from a wide variety of perspectives. Beginning with a brief article by Smith (1971; see also Weinberg, 1972, pp. 132-136), the literature on homophobia now comprises hundreds of published papers.[2]

My own work in this area began in 1976 when I was an undergraduate student at the University of Nebraska. I was just deciding to pursue a career in social psychology, a field whose tradition of scientifically studying society's problems appealed to me strongly. As earlier social psychologists had studied majority group attitudes toward racial, religious, and ethnic minorities, so I hoped to study heterosexuals' attitudes toward homosexuality.

I quickly realized, however, that an empirical approach to homophobia required a valid way of operationalizing the construct, and the few recently developed scales in this area all had problems associated with them. Most lacked reliability and validity data beyond a single study (sometimes conducted with the same sample with which the scale had been initially constructed). Most had not been factor analyzed. Most were excessively long and, therefore, impractical in many research settings.

A particularly serious problem was that existing scales did not assess attitudes toward lesbians separately from attitudes toward gay men. Most were worded to refer to homosexuals in general (Dunbar, Brown, & Amoroso, 1973; Hansen, 1982; Henley & Pincus, 1978; Hood, 1973; Larsen, Reed, & Hoffman, 1980; Levitt & Klassen, 1974; Lumby, 1976; Smith, 1971). This was an unfortunate practice, because an unknown proportion of respondents was likely to equate *homosexuality* with *male* homosexuality (Black & Stevenson, 1984). Some scales included separate items concerning lesbians and gay men but did not have scoring procedures for distinguishing attitudes between the two groups (e.g., Hudson & Ricketts, 1980).

I set out, therefore, to construct a relatively short scale that would reliably and validly measure attitudes toward lesbians and attitudes toward gay men. The effort ultimately spanned several years, including much of my graduate school career, and resulted in the Attitudes Toward Lesbians and Gay Men (ATLG) scale. This chapter is a brief review of my own empirical studies with the ATLG. The first section describes how the scale was developed. Then substantive findings that have been obtained with it are summarized. Finally, the construct assessed by the scale is briefly considered and its use is discussed.

Development of the ATLG Scale

Factor Analysis of Item Pool

I began in the late 1970s by conducting a series of factor-analytic studies, using statements about homosexuality from published attitude studies (e.g., Levitt & Klassen, 1974; MacDonald & Games, 1974; Millham, San Miguel, & Kellogg, 1976; Smith, 1971) as well as newly constructed items. During this phase of the research program, I administered four different item sets to a total of 1,212 undergraduates at five campuses in three different states (see Herek, 1984b, for a detailed discussion of the methodology).

Throughout the analyses, a stable general factor consistently emerged that accounted for most of the explained variance in responses. The factor loadings of the various items did not differ significantly between male and female respondents or for statements targeting gay men or lesbians. This finding indicated that although heterosexual men and women might differ in the intensity of their attitudes (see the discussion of gender differences below), they appeared to evaluate lesbians and gay men alike along one cognitive dimension. I labeled this the *condemnation-tolerance* factor and argued that the items constituting it corresponded to the personal and cultural attitudes popularly termed homophobia. I argued further that, for most purposes, a scale assessing heterosexuals' attitudes toward lesbians and gay men should restrict its content to items loading highly on this general factor.

Construction of the ATLG

I next undertook the development of such a scale. In addition to creating a psychometrically sound instrument, I sought to develop one that was short enough to be used easily in a variety of research settings, and that would assess heterosexuals' attitudes toward lesbians separately from their attitudes toward gay men.

I developed two versions of a Likert-format questionnaire consisting of the 37 items with high loadings on the condemnation-tolerance factor (Herek, 1984b). In one version, all of the items were worded to refer to lesbians; 133 undergraduate volunteers at the University of California at Davis completed this questionnaire (94 females, 39 males). A second version, in which the items referred to gay men, was completed by 147 students (89 females, 58 males).

Item-total correlations were computed for all items on both versions of the questionnaire, and the 20 items correlating highest with the total score were selected for the ATLG scale. The ATLG consists of two 10-item subscales, one for attitudes toward gay men (ATG) and the other for attitudes toward lesbians (ATL). The items are listed in Table 11.1.

The 20 statements are presented to respondents in Likert format, usually with a 9-point scale ranging from "strongly disagree" to "strongly agree." Scoring is accomplished by summing scores across items for each subscale. Reverse scoring is used for some items as indicated in Table 11.1. With a 9-point response scale, total scale scores can range from 20 (extremely positive attitudes) to 180 (extremely negative attitudes); ATL and ATG subscale scores can range from 10 to 90.

Preliminary Assessment of Reliability and Validity

The reliability and construct validity of the ATLG were first assessed with a sample of 368 undergraduate volunteers at the University of California at Davis (249 females, 119 males), who completed the scale during a lecture period in introductory psychology courses.[3] As a check for item order effects, the 20 items were presented in reverse order to one-half of the sample. No significant differences in mean scores were noted between the two versions.

Mean scores on the ATL were 43.67 for females and 40.83 for males; for the ATG, means were 51.54 for females and 57.96 for males. Alpha

Table 11.1 The ATLG Scale

Attitudes Toward Lesbians (ATL) Subscale
1. Lesbians just can't fit into our society. (S)
2. A woman's homosexuality should *not* be a cause for job discrimination in any situation. (R)
3. Female homosexuality is detrimental to society because it breaks down the natural divisions between the sexes.
4. State laws regulating private, consenting lesbian behavior should be loosened. (R; S)
5. Female homosexuality is a sin. (S)
6. The growing number of lesbians indicates a decline in American morals.
7. Female homosexuality in itself is no problem, but what society makes of it can be a problem. (R; S)
8. Female homosexuality is a threat to many of our basic social institutions.
9. Female homosexuality is an inferior form of sexuality.
10. Lesbians are sick. (S)
Attitudes Toward Gay Men (ATG) Subscale
11. Male homosexual couples should be allowed to adopt children the same as heterosexual couples. (R)
12. I think male homosexuals are disgusting. (S)
13. Male homosexuals should *not* be allowed to teach school.
14. Male homosexuality is a perversion. (S)
15. Just as in other species, male homosexuality is a natural expression of sexuality in human men. (S)
16. If a man has homosexual feelings, he should do everything he can to overcome them.
17. I would *not* be too upset if I learned that my son were a homosexual. (R)
18. Homosexual behavior between two men is just plain wrong. (S)
19. The idea of male homosexual marriages seems ridiculous to me.
20. Male homosexuality is merely a different kind of lifestyle that should *not* be condemned. (R; S)

NOTE: Based on respondents' comments, Items 1 and 4 were reworded slightly from their form in Herek (1984b) to clarify their meaning. R means the item was reverse scored and S means that the item appears on the short form.

coefficients indicated satisfactory levels of internal consistency for the ATLG scale (α = .90) and the subscales (αs = .89 for the ATG and .77 for the ATL).

Construct validity analyses were completed with 110 heterosexual students (73 females, 37 males) who volunteered to participate in additional research for extra credit points. Most of the respondents were unmarried freshmen or sophomores. The group's mean age was 18.7 years. Three weeks after the ATLG's initial administration, they completed a battery of paper-and-pencil measures that included several conceptually related scales as well as alternate versions of the ATL and ATG subscales.

As expected, ATL and ATG scores were significantly ($ps < .05$) correlated with the construct validity measures. For males, higher ATG and ATL scores (more negative attitudes) were significantly correlated with (1) traditional sex role attitudes, (2) belief in a traditional family ideology, (3) high levels of dogmatism, (4) the perception that one's friends agreed with one's own attitudes toward homosexuality, and (5) the absence of positive past interactions with lesbians or gay men. For female respondents, the same pattern was observed, with additional significant correlations between higher ATL and ATG scores and (6) frequent attendance at religious services, (7) membership in a conservative religious denomination, (8) endorsement of Christian fundamentalist beliefs, and (9) having few or no gay male friends.

In addition to the construct validity measures, the students also completed alternate forms of the ATL and ATG. (Because they consist of different items, raw mean scores from the ATL and ATG scales are not directly comparable. Parallel forms are necessary, therefore, to compare directly attitudes toward lesbians with attitudes toward gay men.) The parallel versions were created by rewriting the ATG items so that they referred to lesbians and rewriting the ATL items to refer to gay men. The alternate versions of the ATLG, ATG, and ATL all yielded satisfactory α coefficients (.96, .92, and .92, respectively). They also showed acceptably high correlations with their corresponding version, which had been administered 3 weeks earlier (correlations were $r = .90$ for the ATLG and its alternate, .83 for the ATG and its alternate, and .84 for the ATL and its alternate).

Additional Validity and Reliability Studies With Student Samples

In addition to the initial construct validity study described above, several other studies were conducted with the ATLG to assess its reliability and validity.

Discriminant Validity

The ATLG was administered to members of local lesbian and gay organizations ($n = 13$ females, 16 males). As expected, their scores were at the positive end of the range. The mean ATLG score for lesbian respondents was 28.08 (14.54 on the ATG and 13.54 on the ATL). For gay men, the mean ATLG score was 37.71 (16.59 on the ATG and 21.12 on the ATL) (Herek, 1988).

Reliability and Validity With a Multicampus Sample

The ATLG and supplementary measures were administered during class sessions to 405 student volunteers (226 females, 179 males) at six different universities. The multicampus sample was made up of undergraduates at state universities in Nebraska and Indiana, an East Coast Ivy League College, a New England state university, the University of California at Davis, and another northern California State university.

Calculation of coefficient α for the ATLG, ATG, and ATL yielded values of .95, .91, and .90, respectively, indicating once again a high degree of internal consistency. For male and female respondents alike, higher ATL and ATG scores (more negative attitudes) were significantly correlated with (1) traditional sex role attitudes, (2) adherence to a fundamentalist religious ideology, (3) frequent attendance at religious services, (4) membership in a conservative religious denomination, (5) having few or no gay or lesbian friends, (6) negative past experiences with gay men or lesbians, and (7) the absence of positive past experiences with gay men or lesbians (Herek, 1988).

Development of a Short Form of the ATLG With a Community Sample

Social psychological studies of attitudes frequently are criticized for relying entirely on student samples and paper-and-pencil (rather than behavioral) measures of attitudes. To avoid these shortcomings, I administered the ATLG to an adult (nonstudent) sample whose attitudes toward lesbians and gay men had been behaviorally manifested through their involvement with a municipal political campaign.

In 1980 an initiative appeared on the ballot in a small northern California town (population approximately 40,000) that would have directed the city council to draft an ordinance to protect residents from discrimination on the basis of sexual orientation. Before its eventual defeat by a two-to-one margin, numerous public meetings were held to discuss the initiative. People displayed yard signs, wore campaign buttons, and distributed literature about the initiative. Some residents wrote letters or signed endorsements that subsequently were published in local newspapers. These individuals constituted the population from which the sample was drawn.

In 1983 I collected the names of supporters and opponents of the initiative from past editions of local newspapers. I was able to contact 48 persons, of whom 38 agreed to be interviewed. Two of them were subsequently dropped from the analysis because of incomplete data, leaving a final sample of 36 participants. One-half of them (9 males, 9 females) had written letters or signed endorsements sympathetic to the ordinance (they will be referred to as the pro-ordinance group). The remainder (9 males, 9 females) had written letters or signed endorsements opposing the ordinance (referred to here as the antiordinance group). Although numerous reasons probably existed for supporting or opposing the ordinance, members of the pro-ordinance group were assumed to have generally favorable attitudes toward lesbians and gay men and members of the antiordinance group were assumed to have generally unfavorable attitudes.

The pro-ordinance and antiordinance groups did not differ substantially in age (mean age was 43 years), marital status (all were currently married or had been married previously), or income (two-thirds of all respondents reported household incomes greater than $30,000 per year). The pro-ordinance sample, however, reported higher levels of formal education: 16 had earned at least a baccalaureate degree (89%) and 11 had earned a postgraduate degree (61%), whereas 8 of the antiordinance respondents held a bachelor's degree (50%) and only 2 had a postgraduate degree (11%). This difference is consistent with previous findings that highly educated individuals are more likely than others to express favorable attitudes toward lesbians and gay men (Herek & Glunt, 1993a; Irwin & Thompson, 1977; Nyberg & Alston, 1976).

Because of time limitations, a briefer version of the ATLG was needed for administration to the community sample. A short-form ATLG was created by selecting five ATG items and five ATL items that were highly correlated with total ATLG scores in previous samples. Four items with reverse scoring were included to avoid response sets. In a reanalysis of data from the multicampus sample described above, coefficients α were .87 for the short form of the ATG (hereafter ATG-S); .85 for the ATL-S; and .92 for the ATLG-S. Each short version correlated highly with its longer counterpart (ATG with ATG-S, $r = .96$; ATL with ATL-S, $r = .95$; ATLG with ATLG-S, $r = .97$). When members of the community sample completed the ATLG-S, acceptably high levels of internal consistency were observed: α was .87 for the ATL-S and .91 for the ATG-S. As expected, pro-ordinance respondents scored significantly lower on the ATLG than antiordinance respondents.

As in previous studies, the construct validity of the ATLG-S was supported by its significant correlations with the other measures. Higher scores on both the ATL and ATG (more negative attitudes) were associated with (1) more traditional sex role attitudes, (2) adherence to a traditional family ideology, (3) higher levels of authoritarianism, (4) frequent attendance at religious services, (5) membership in a conservative religious denomination, and (6) adherence to fundamentalist religious beliefs.

Other Administrations of the ATLG to Nonstudent Samples

The community study described above represented an attempt to broaden the ATLG database beyond the college campus. As another step in this direction, the ATG-S was administered in 1988 to 155 adult focus group participants (most of whom were not students) in five U.S. cities as part of a study of AIDS-related attitudes (Herek & Glunt, 1991, 1993a). Internal consistency was acceptably high (α = .83). Higher ATG-S scores were significantly correlated with AIDS-related stigma: Respondents with more negative attitudes toward gay men were generally more willing to stigmatize people with AIDS and to impose punitive policies on them (e.g., quarantine).

Also in 1988 the ATG-S items were included in a national telephone survey with a probability sample of adults (n = 960).[4] Respondents indicated whether they disagreed, were in the middle, or agreed with each item (with responses scored 0, 1, and 2, respectively). Item responses were reversed as necessary and then summed, so that higher scale scores indicate stronger antigay attitudes. The ATG-S displayed acceptable internal consistency in this, its first administration by telephone (α = .85). When the five ATG-S items were combined into a scale, scores ranged from 0 (extremely favorable attitudes) to 10 (extremely hostile attitudes). The overall mean score was 5.97 (standard deviation = 3.65). As with the focus groups, higher ATG-S scores predicted greater willingness to stigmatize people with AIDS. Responses to the individual ATG-S items are reported in Table 11.2 (see Herek & Glunt, 1991, 1993a, 1993b, for a more detailed discussion).

Table 11.2 Attitudes Toward Gay Men (ATG-S) Item Responses, 1988

ATG Item	*Percentage Agree*	*Percentage in Middle*	*Percentage Disagree*
Homosexual behavior between two men is just plain wrong	63.6	3.7	31.7
Male homosexuality is merely a different kind of lifestyle that should not be condemned	44.8	6.8	47.9
I think male homosexuals are disgusting	50.4	6.3	42.4
Male homosexuality is a perversion	55.1	7.5	36.8
Male homosexuality is a natural expression of sexuality in men	29.2	8.3	61.9

NOTE: Response proportions are poststratified by gender, age, and geographic region; $n = 960$.

In 1990-1991 four ATG-S items ("just plain wrong," "disgusting," "perversion," and "natural") were included in another national survey of U.S. adults ($n = 538$). Respondents were provided four response alternatives for each item: *agree strongly, agree somewhat, disagree somewhat,* and *disagree strongly.* As in previous administrations, scale scores were calculated by summing item responses (see Herek & Capitanio, 1993, for a description of the study's methodology). Internal consistency was acceptably high ($\alpha = .80$). Approximately 1 year later, new interviews were conducted with the same sample (for the follow-up, $n = 371$). The follow-up survey protocol included three ATG-S items as well as the same three items reworded to refer to lesbians (following the procedure described above for the alternate forms of the ATG and ATL). Internal consistency was acceptably high for both the ATG-S and ATL-S ($\alpha = .76$ for each) and the combined ATLG-S ($\alpha = .89$). Responses to the items are summarized in Table 11.3.

Substantive Findings With the ATLG Scale

The studies described in the preceding pages demonstrate that the ATLG is a psychometrically sound instrument for assessing heterosexuals' attitudes toward lesbians and gay men. Although data supporting

Table 11.3 Attitudes Toward Gay Men (ATG-S) and Lesbians (ATL-S) Item Responses, 1990-1991 and 1991-1992

Item	*1990-1991*	*1991-1992*
Sex between two men is just plain wrong.		
Percentage agree (somewhat/strongly)	69.8	68.3
Percentage disagree (somewhat/strongly)	28.7	31.4
I think male homosexuals are disgusting.		
Percentage agree (somewhat/strongly)	54.1	59.9
Percentage disagree (somewhat/strongly)	44.8	39.7
Male homosexuality is a natural expression of sexuality in men.		
Percentage agree (somewhat/strongly)	23.6	24.6
Percentage disagree (somewhat/strongly)	74.4	75.4
Male homosexuality is a perversion.		
Percentage agree (somewhat/strongly)	55.3	NA
Percentage disagree (somewhat/strongly)	39.7	NA
Sex between two women is just plain wrong.		
Percentage agree (somewhat/strongly)	NA	64.3
Percentage disagree (somewhat/strongly)	NA	35.3
I think lesbians are disgusting.		
Percentage agree (somewhat/strongly)	NA	59.9
Percentage disagree (somewhat/strongly)	NA	39.7
Female homosexuality is a natural expression of sexuality in women.		
Percentage agree (somewhat/strongly)	NA	26.6
Percentage disagree (somewhat/strongly)	NA	73.2

NOTE: NA = item was not administered in that wave of the study. Only responses from self-identified heterosexuals (*ns* = 506 in 1990-1991 and 363 in 1991-1992) are included in the table. Response proportions are poststratified by gender and race. Some items were slightly reworded for easier oral administration.

the scale's reliability and validity are a necessary prerequisite for it to be used in empirical studies of heterosexuals' attitudes, most readers will be more interested in the substantive results of research employing the ATLG. In the following sections, some of the principal findings are highlighted from studies I have conducted with the ATLG during the past 10 years.

Correlates of Heterosexuals' Attitudes

Using the ATLG, I have attempted to identify the principal correlates of heterosexuals' attitudes. No single variable has emerged as the best predictor of ATLG scores. Rather, attitudes toward lesbians and gay men appear to be influenced by a variety of factors. These include demographic factors, such as gender and education. Respondents to the 1988 national survey (Herek & Glunt, 1991, 1993a, 1993b), for example, were more likely to express hostile attitudes toward gay men if they were male or reported a low educational level.

In addition, ATLG scores are consistently associated with several social psychological variables. These include (1) attitudes about gender and family roles, (2) religiosity, (3) political ideology, and (4) the extent and quality of interpersonal contact with lesbians and gay men (Herek, 1987a, 1988; Herek & Glunt, 1993b). In brief, heterosexuals are more likely to hold positive attitudes toward lesbians and gay men to the extent that they accept nontraditional roles for men and women, are not religious or belong to a liberal religious denomination, describe themselves as politically moderate or liberal, and have had positive interpersonal experiences with gay men or lesbians. In contrast, greater hostility is predicted by acceptance of traditional gender roles, high religiosity or membership in a conservative or fundamentalist denomination, political conservatism, and lack of interpersonal contact. In addition, heterosexuals with negative attitudes may be more likely to perceive that their friends agree with their attitudes; given the findings from national studies (see Tables 11.2 and 11.3), such perceptions may well be accurate. The same variables appear to exert similar effects for male and female heterosexuals, and on attitudes toward gay men and lesbians alike (Herek, 1988).

Religious Influences on Heterosexuals' Attitudes

In the 1950s and 1960s social scientists were puzzled to observe that whites' antiblack racism was positively correlated with their religious commitment. This finding seemed at odds with the teachings of most religious denominations in the United States. Allport proposed a resolution to this seeming paradox by suggesting that there really are two ways of being religious. Some people have a religious orientation that is primarily *extrinsic,* a self-serving, instrumental approach conforming to social conventions. Others, in contrast, have an *intrinsic* religious orientation; religion provides them with a meaning-endowing framework in terms of which all life is understood.

Allport and Ross (1967) summarized this distinction: "The extrinsically motivated person uses his religion, whereas the intrinsically motivated lives his religion" (p. 434). They reported that an extrinsic orientation tends to be positively associated with prejudice, whereas an intrinsic orientation tends to be negatively correlated. In other words, because intrinsics use religious teachings to inform their everyday interactions with others, they love their neighbor; for them "there is no place for rejection, contempt, or condescension" toward other human beings (Allport & Ross, 1967, p. 441). The extrinsically motivated, in contrast, are religious primarily to enjoy social acceptance and integration; religion provides them with "security, comfort, status, or social support" (p. 441). Because prejudice often provides similar benefits, extrinsics are likely to be prejudiced (Allport & Ross, 1967).

As noted above, religiosity is a principal correlate of heterosexuals' antigay prejudice. I wondered, therefore, whether the intrinsic-extrinsic distinction might help to explain this correlation. Perhaps, as Allport and Ross (1967) observed, heterosexuals with an intrinsic religious orientation truly have no place for rejection, contempt, or condescension toward anyone, including gay people. To address this question, I compared white heterosexuals' attitudes toward lesbians and gay men with their racial attitudes, using a sample of 126 undergraduates from four different universities (Herek, 1987a).

I found that, as in past research with racial attitudes, whites were more likely to manifest antiblack prejudice to the extent that their religious beliefs were extrinsically motivated. An intrinsic orientation was not associated with racial prejudice. For attitudes toward gay men and lesbians, however, I observed a different pattern. *Both* types of religious orientation were associated with negative attitudes toward lesbians and gay men. Heterosexuals whose religious orientation was intrinsic, extrinsic, or indiscriminate (i.e., both intrinsic and extrinsic) were more likely than nonreligious respondents to express antigay attitudes. Additional regression analyses indicated that racial attitudes were predicted by religious orientation whereas attitudes toward gay men and lesbians were predicted by religious fundamentalism.

Interpersonal Contact and Heterosexuals' Attitudes

In addition to religious beliefs, interpersonal contact is a significant predictor of heterosexuals' attitudes toward lesbians and gay men. In the 1988 national attitude survey, Eric Glunt and I (Herek & Glunt, 1991, 1993a, 1993b) used the ATG subscale to explore this relationship. We assessed personal contact with the question, "Have any of your female or male friends, relatives, or close acquaintances let you know that they were homosexual?" Responses were coded as "yes," "no," and "no answer." ATG scores were significantly lower for the 321 participants (34.7% of the sample) who indicated that they had a friend, relative, or acquaintance who was homosexual (mean = 4.08, versus 6.96 for the 616 not reporting contact).

Table 11.4 shows that people with contact experiences consistently held more favorable attitudes than those without contact, even when other background variables were taken into account. This observation was confirmed by multiple regression analyses which showed that the contact variable explained a significant proportion of variance in ATG scores even when it was entered into the equation after a large number of other demographic, social, and psychological variables.

It should not be assumed, however, that the relationship between contact and attitudes is unidirectional. Rather, it appears that some heterosexuals are more likely than others to know lesbians or gay men. From a logistic regression analysis, we determined that respondents were more likely to report contact to the extent that they were (1) highly educated, (2) politically liberal, (3) young, and (4) female. Thus not only does contact tend to foster greater acceptance of gay men generally but, in addition, heterosexuals with already positive attitudes (or who belong to groups in which accepting attitudes are common) are more likely than others to experience contact. The latter pattern may result from greater opportunities for contact as a consequence of being in an environment where lesbians and gay men are visible, such as a college campus. It also may result from a tendency among lesbians and gay men for selective disclosure: They may be more likely to take the risk of voluntarily disclosing their sexual orientation to heterosexuals from whom they expect a positive response (Schneider, 1986; Weinberg, 1983; Wells & Kline, 1987).

Table 11.4 Breakdown of ATG Scores by Contact Within Selected Demographic Groups

		Contact				F (ANOVA)
Demographic Group	*Group Mean*	*Yes*	*No*	*Contact*	*Group*	*Contact × Group*
Entire sample	5.97	4.08	6.96	152.89**		
Gender						
Female	5.34	3.33	6.60	137.36**	28.99**	*n.s.*
Male	6.66	5.13	7.30			
Race						
White	5.91	3.76	7.04	42.50**	7.10*	*n.s.*
Black	6.69	5.60	7.19			
Education						
Less than 12 years	7.28	6.23	7.50	33.39**	7.12**	*n.s.*
High school diploma	6.61	5.05	7.09			
Beyond high school	5.58	3.84	6.79			
Age						
18-29	5.93	4.58	6.79	86.54**	*n.s.*	*n.s.*
30-49	5.47	3.63	6.79			
50-64	6.25	3.89	7.17			
65+	6.97	5.38	7.23			
Geographic residence						
Northeast/Mid-Atlantic	5.27	3.43	6.46	115.84**	3.58*	*n.s.*
Pacific Coast	5.35	3.66	6.35			

Mountain/Southwest	5.67	3.75	6.70			
Central/Midwest	6.33	4.18	7.32			
South/Southeast	6.47	4.67	7.31			
Relationship status						
Married/widowed	6.33	4.67	7.04	74.77**	4.47*	*n.s.*
Never married	5.58	3.09	7.25			
Divorced/separated	5.10	3.39	6.43			
Cohabiting	4.91	3.44	5.90			
Religious denomination						
Conservative	4.11	4.57	7.29	94.78**	46.04**	*n.s.*
Nonconservative	6.47	2.72	5.38			
Religious attendance						
Never	4.23	2.07	6.01	126.33**	20.48**	*n.s.*
Monthly	5.38	3.75	6.28			
Several times monthly	6.00	4.45	7.05			
Weekly or more often	7.17	5.53	7.72			
Political ideology						
Liberal	4.13	2.23	5.94	91.00**	40.75**	7.05**
Moderate	5.63	4.23	6.54			
Conservative	7.45	6.52	7.70			
Political party						
Republican	6.60	4.84	7.34	42.58**	5.74*	*n.s.*
Democrat	5.55	3.83	6.55			
Independent	4.82	3.77	5.66			

NOTE: Higher ATG scores indicate more negative attitudes toward gay men; maximum n for any group is 937.
*$p < .01$; **$p < .001$.

The Psychological Functions of Heterosexuals' Attitudes

The research described to this point does not support a single-factor explanation for heterosexuals' attitudes toward lesbians and gay men. Instead, the influence of different variables might best be understood in terms of individual differences. I have proposed a theoretical formulation that explains individual attitudes toward lesbians and gay men in terms of the psychological functions they serve (Herek, 1986a). This functional framework predicts that no single variable will explain most of the variance in attitudes held by a heterogeneous group. Rather, several variables will be significant because of their importance to the social and psychological needs of different subsets of individuals in the group.

In an empirical study with this framework (Herek, 1987b), I used a content analysis technique to identify the principal psychological functions served by heterosexuals' attitudes toward lesbians and gay men. Using original essays written by 205 students, I identified three different functions: (1) descriptions of specific past experiences that provided the basis for a cognitive schema associated with current attitudes toward lesbians and gay men in general (*experiential-schematic* function), (2) statements suggesting personal anxieties and insecurities associated with gender or sexuality that are exacerbated by homosexual persons (*defensive* function), and (3) assertions of attitudes toward lesbians and gay men based on personal values important to self-concept and relations with others (*self-expressive* function).

I found that individuals manifesting each function also displayed other theoretically relevant characteristics. Those whose attitudes served an experiential-schematic function were more likely than others to report previous interactions with a gay man or lesbian and were less likely to hold stereotypical beliefs about gay people. Those with attitudes serving a defensive function tended generally to use externalizing defense mechanisms more than did others and manifested a high level of conformity to gender roles. Those with attitudes serving a self-expressive function exhibited a greater need than others for social approval and tended to have more tightly knit social networks (which could create greater pressure for conformity).[5] Self-expressive individuals with negative attitudes toward gay men and lesbians were more likely than others to attend religious services at least monthly, to belong to a conservative religious denomination, and to endorse an orthodox religious ideology;

this pattern is consistent with the religious content of most negative self-expressive attitudes. Throughout this research, the ATLG was consistently correlated in the predicted direction with the various measures employed in the study.

The Gender Gap in Heterosexuals' Attitudes

A gender gap in heterosexuals' attitudes toward lesbians and gay men has often been observed (see Kite, 1984; this volume). The existence of such a gap has been confirmed with the ATLG. In questionnaire studies with undergraduates, I have observed that heterosexual males routinely score higher (more negative attitudes) than heterosexual females on both the ATL and ATG subscales. In addition, heterosexuals tend to score higher on the ATLG subscale targeting gay people of their own gender. This pattern is stronger among heterosexuals males, that is, their ATG scores tend to be higher than their ATL scores, females' ATL scores, or females' ATG scores (Herek, 1987a, 1987b, 1988).

In the 1988 national survey, males scored significantly higher than females on the five-item ATG (Herek & Glunt, 1993a, 1993b; see also Table 11.4). In the 1990-1991 survey (Herek & Capitanio, 1993), a similar pattern was observed for the four-item ATG. In the 1991-1992 follow-up survey, which included three-item versions of the ATL and ATG, heterosexual males scored higher than heterosexual females on both subscales. The highest (most negative) scores were for heterosexual males' attitudes toward gay men.

Discussion

The studies reviewed here establish the ATLG as a reliable and valid instrument for assessing heterosexuals' attitudes toward lesbians and gay men. Unless a larger number of items is explicitly desired, I encourage researchers to use the short forms of the ATL and ATG as brief but effective measures. If researchers wish to draw direct comparisons between respondents' attitudes toward lesbians and their attitudes toward gay men, they should use one subscale and its parallel version. This procedure yields two-item sets that are identical except that one set refers to gay men and the other to lesbians.[6]

The ATLG appears to measure heterosexuals' personal feelings toward homosexuality and toward lesbians and gay men as a group. These feelings do not constitute the full universe of relevant attitudes in this area. National opinion surveys, for example, indicate that public attitudes concerning civil rights for lesbians and gay men are often independent of moral evaluations of homosexuality. Whereas most Americans disapprove of homosexuality on moral grounds or consider it to be wrong, they also feel that lesbians and gay men should have equal employment opportunities and free speech rights (e.g., Herek, 1991).[7] Nor do ATLG items tap heterosexuals' beliefs and stereotypes about lesbians and gay men.[8] I recommend, therefore, that researchers who wish to assess additional aspects of heterosexuals' attitudes toward lesbians and gay men consider supplementing the ATLG with items from recent public opinion polls (e.g., Hugick, 1992) or other sources.

The conceptualization of heterosexuals' attitudes toward lesbians and gay men that underlies the ATLG (and my research with it) differs considerably from Weinberg's (1972) original notion of homophobia. This difference, I believe, also reflects broader trends in the way that researchers and society as a whole conceptualize heterosexuality and homosexuality.

Since Stonewall, the gay movement's original liberationist agenda has yielded to one dominated by reformist goals such as protection from employment discrimination (D'Emilio, 1983). Liberationists sought to transform society radically by changing or abolishing concepts of gender and sexual orientation; coming out was seen as an intermediate step on the road to releasing the ambisexual potential in everyone. The reformist view, in contrast, adopted a strategy of minority group politics and so fostered the notion of lesbians and gay men as members of a (relatively) well-defined group with its own needs, goals, and interests that deserve legitimation within the larger society.

The liberationist-to-reformist shift has also affected how we conceptualize antigay hostility at the individual level. In a liberationist paradigm, heterosexuals' psychological homophobia inevitably must be understood as a rejection of their own homoerotic desires. It is a conflict within the self; change requires confronting one's own sexuality. Within the reformist paradigm, in contrast, heterosexuals' homophobia is a rejection of members of an outgroup (similar to racism and anti-Semitism). The conflict is interpersonal or intergroup: "me (or us) versus them." Change requires challenging a heterosexual person's reactions to and misconceptions of "them" (homosexuals). The minority-group focus predominates in contemporary theory and research, probably because the reformist paradigm is more popular in the present historical moment.

The ATLG reflects this current worldview. It is designed as an attitude scale along the lines of previous measures for intergroup attitudes. The studies described above in which the ATLG was used indicate that the psychological processes underlying heterosexuals' attitudes toward lesbians and gay men are similar to racial, ethnic, and religious attitudes.

This analysis suggests that the ATLG should always be used with an understanding of its cultural context. Like other attitude scales, it was constructed and validated at a particular time and in a particular place. To be of continuing value, the ATLG inevitably will require modification as public discourse about sexual orientation evolves. Items will be reworded or replaced. (It is noteworthy, nonetheless, that the original items remain usable after more than a decade.) In this process, ongoing assessments of the scale's reliability and validity will be necessary.

In short, the ATLG—like all scales in this area—represents a work in progress. To date, it has proved to be of considerable value in my own empirical research. I hope that this overview will encourage others to use it as well.[9]

Notes

1. Before publication of Weinberg's 1972 book, Churchill (1967) had used the term *homoerotophobia,* which he derived from the more general *erotophobia.* The latter term described a negative cultural orientation toward sexuality in which "sex is regarded not merely as somehow inherently evil, but also as somehow inherently dangerous" (p. 19).

2. This is not to suggest that no previous empirical research had considered heterosexuals' reactions to homosexuality (see Herek, 1984a, for examples). The principal difference between the older studies and the research from the 1970s and after is that the latter were more likely to reflect an explicit value orientation in which homosexuality was considered a legitimate and nonpathological alternative to heterosexuality.

3. The data described in this section were reported in detail in Herek (1988).

4. Because the topic of the focus groups and the national survey was attitudes about AIDS, and because of time constraints, the ATL-S items were not included in these studies.

5. In a follow-up study (Herek, 1987b), I devised an objectively scored method for assessing functions, the Attitude Functions Inventory (AFI). With the AFI, it proved possible to separate the self-expressive function into the value-expressive function (corresponding to the similarly named function described by Katz, 1960) and the social-expressive function (corresponding to the social adjustment function described by Smith, Bruner, & White, 1956); see also Herek and Glunt (1993a).

6. Researchers should be aware that the two-item sets appear to elicit somewhat different intensities of attitudes. In one study (Herek, 1988), the original ATG items (and alter-

nate-ATL items) elicited more negative responses than did the ATL (and alternate-ATG) items.

7. In a 1986 paper, I noted an inconsistency between survey data from national probability samples on the one hand, and laboratory and questionnaire studies with (usually) undergraduate student samples on the other (Herek, 1986b). Whereas heterosexual males typically manifest more hostile attitudes toward gay people on self-administered questionnaires than do heterosexual females, a similar gender difference has not been observed in national surveys. I suggested that the discrepancy resulted from the content of items used in the two types of studies—that the gender difference is associated with personal affective reactions (which are typically assessed in questionnaire studies) rather than with attitudes concerning moral beliefs or civil liberties (which are typically assessed in national surveys). I hypothesized that a gender difference would be observed in a national probability sample if items assessing heterosexuals' personal feelings were administered. As described above, when the ATLG items were administered to a national sample, the expected gender difference was observed.

8. In several of the original factor analytic studies that preceded development of the ATLG, a *beliefs* factor emerged that included assertions about the characteristics of gay men and lesbians. These items were intentionally excluded from the ATLG, which was conceived as a measure of attitudes rather than beliefs (see Herek, 1984b, for further discussion of this point).

9. I sometimes receive requests for written permission to use the ATLG scale in a research project or thesis. In my view, such permission is not necessary. Because the ATLG is a published scale—part of the scientific literature—I consider it to be a tool that is available to anyone who wishes to use it in responsible, valid, not-for-profit empirical research. Recognizing that some graduate and undergraduate programs—and some psychologists—do not share this approach to assessment instruments, I hereby grant permission for any qualified researcher to use the ATLG in not-for-profit research that is consistent with the *Ethical Principles of Psychologists* (American Psychological Association, 1992).

References

Allport, G. W. , & Ross, J. M. (1967). Personal religious orientation and prejudice. *Journal of Personality and Social Psychology, 5,* 432-443.

American Heritage Dictionary of the English Language (3rd ed.). (1992). Boston: Houghton Mifflin.

American Psychological Association. (1992). Ethical principles of psychologists and code of conduct. *American Psychologist, 47,* 1597-1611.

Bayer, R. (1987). *Homosexuality and American psychiatry: The politics of diagnosis* (2nd ed.). Princeton, NJ: Princeton University Press.

Black, K. N., & Stevenson, M. R. (1984). The relationship of self-reported sex-role characteristics and attitudes toward homosexuality. *Journal of Homosexuality, 10*(1-2), 83-93.

Churchill, W. (1967). *Homosexual behavior among males: A cross-cultural and cross-species investigation.* Englewood Cliffs, NJ: Prentice-Hall.

D'Emilio, J. (1983). *Sexual politics, sexual communities: The making of a homosexual minority in the United States, 1940-1970.* Chicago: University of Chicago Press.

Dunbar, J., Brown, M., & Amoroso, D. M. (1973). Some correlates of attitudes toward homosexuality. *Journal of Social Psychology, 89,* 271-279.

Gonsiorek, J. C. (1991). The empirical basis for the demise of the illness model of homosexuality. In J. Gonsiorek & J. Weinrich (Eds.), *Homosexuality: Research implications for public policy* (pp. 115-136). Newbury Park, CA: Sage.

Hansen, G. L. (1982). Measuring prejudice against homosexuality (homosexism) among college students: A new scale. *Journal of Social Psychology, 117*, 233-236.

Henley, N. M., & Pincus, F. (1978). Interrelationships of sexist, racist, and antihomosexual attitudes. *Psychological Reports, 42*, 83-90.

Herek, G. M. (1984a). Beyond "homophobia": A social psychological perspective on attitudes toward lesbians and gay men. *Journal of Homosexuality, 10*(1-2), 1-21.

Herek, G. M. (1984b). Attitudes toward lesbians and gay men: A factor analytic study. *Journal of Homosexuality, 10*(1-2), 39-51.

Herek, G. M. (1986a). The instrumentality of attitudes: Toward a neofunctional theory. *Journal of Social Issues, 42*(2), 99-114.

Herek, G. M. (1986b). On heterosexual masculinity: Some psychical consequences of the social construction of gender and sexuality. *American Behavioral Scientist, 29*(5), 563-577.

Herek, G. M. (1987a). Religion and prejudice: A comparison of racial and sexual attitudes. *Personality and Social Psychology Bulletin, 13*(1), 56-65.

Herek, G. M. (1987b). Can functions be measured? A new perspective on the functional approach to attitudes. *Social Psychology Quarterly, 50*, 285-303.

Herek, G. M. (1988). Heterosexuals' attitudes toward lesbians and gay men: Correlates and gender differences. *Journal of Sex Research, 25*, 451-477.

Herek, G. M. (1991). Stigma, prejudice, and violence against lesbians and gay men. In J. Gonsiorek & J. Weinrich (Eds.), *Homosexuality: Research implications for public policy* (pp. 60-80). Newbury Park, CA: Sage.

Herek, G. M., & Capitanio, J. P. (1993). Public reactions to AIDS in the United States: A second decade of stigma. *American Journal of Public Health, 83*, 574-577.

Herek, G. M., & Glunt, E. K. (1991). AIDS-related attitudes in the United States: A preliminary conceptualization. *Journal of Sex Research, 28*, 99-123.

Herek, G. M., & Glunt, E. K. (1993a). Public reactions to AIDS in the United States. In J. B. Pryor & G. D. Reeder (Eds.), *The social psychology of HIV infection* (pp. 229-261). Hillsdale, NJ: Erlbaum.

Herek, G. M., & Glunt, E. K. (1993b). Interpersonal contact and heterosexuals' attitudes toward gay men: Results from a national survey. *Journal of Sex Research, 30*, 239-244.

Hood, R. W., Jr. (1973). Dogmatism and opinions about mental illness. *Psychological Reports, 32*, 1283-1290.

Hudson, W. W., & Ricketts, W. A. (1980). A strategy for the measurement of homophobia. *Journal of Homosexuality, 5*(4), 357-372.

Hugick, L. (1992, June). Public opinion divided on gay rights. *Gallup Poll Monthly*, pp. 2-6.

Irwin, P., & Thompson, N. L. (1977). Acceptance of the rights of homosexuals: A social profile. *Journal of Homosexuality, 3*(2), 107-121.

Katz, D. (1960). The functional approach to the study of attitudes. *Public Opinion Quarterly, 24*(2), 163-204.

Kite, M. E. (1984). Sex differences in attitudes toward homosexuals: A meta-analytic review. *Journal of Homosexuality, 10*(1-2), 69-81.

Larsen, K. S., Reed, M., & Hoffman, S. (1980). Attitudes of heterosexuals toward homosexuality: A Likert-type scale and construct validity. *Journal of Sex Research, 16*(3), 245-257.

Levitt, E. E., & Klassen, A. D. (1974). Public attitudes toward homosexuality: Part of the 1970 national survey by the Institute for Sex Research. *Journal of Homosexuality, 1*(1), 29-43.

Lumby, M. H. (1976). Homophobia: The quest for a valid scale. *Journal of Homosexuality, 2*(1), 39-47.

MacDonald, A. P., Jr., & Games, R. G. (1974). Some characteristics of those who hold positive and negative attitudes toward homosexuals. *Journal of Homosexuality, 1*(1), 9-27.

Millham, J., San Miguel, C. L., & Kellogg, R. (1976). A factor-analytic conceptualization of attitudes toward male and female homosexuals. *Journal of Homosexuality, 2*(1), 3-10.

Nyberg, K. L., & Alston, J. P. (1976). Analysis of public attitudes toward homosexual behavior. *Journal of Homosexuality, 2*(2), 99-107.

Schneider, B. (1986). Coming out at work: Bridging the private/public gap. *Work and Occupations, 13*(4), 463-487.

Smith, K. T. (1971). Homophobia: A tentative personality profile. *Psychological Reports, 29,* 1091-1094.

Smith, M. B., Bruner, J. S., & White, R. W. (1956). *Opinions and personality.* New York: Wiley.

Weinberg, G. (1972). *Society and the healthy homosexual.* New York: St. Martin's.

Weinberg, T. S. (1983). *Gay men, gay selves: The social construction of homosexual identities.* New York: Irvington.

Wells, J. W., & Kline, W. B. (1987). Self-disclosure of homosexual orientation. *Journal of Social Psychology, 127*(2), 191-197.

Author Index

Subject Index

About the Editors

Beverly Greene is an Associate Professor of psychology at St. John's University in New York City, where she maintains a private clinical practice. She received her Ph.D. (1983) in clinical psychology from the Derner Institute of Advanced Psychological Studies of Adelphi University in New York. She has served as a Director of Inpatient Child and Adolescent Psychology Services and Clinical Assistant Professor of Psychiatry at Kings County Hospital, in Brooklyn, and Supervising Psychologist-Clinical Assistant Professor of Child Psychiatry at the Community Mental Health Center of the University of Medicine and Dentistry of New Jersey at Newark.

A fellow of the American Psychological Association, she is the first recipient of the Association for Women in Psychology's 1991 Women of Color Psychologies Publication Award. She is also the recipient of Division 44's 1992 Award for Distinguished Professional Contributions to Ethnic Minority Issues, recognizing her development of scholarship on lesbian affirmative theoretical perspectives and clinical applications with African-American women.

She is a member of the editorial boards of *Women & Therapy* and *Feminist Family Therapy,* guest consulting editor of professional journals, and an author and coeditor of a range of professional books and journals on psychotherapy with African-Americans; the interactive effects of race, gender, and sexual orientation in the psychologies of women of color; applications of feminist psychology with diverse populations; and the development of curriculums in clinical psychology on cultural diversity in psychological services delivery. She is coeditor of *Women of Color:*

Integrating Ethnic and Gender Identities in Treatment and coauthor of *Abnormal Psychology in a Changing World.*

Gregory M. Herek, an Associate Research Psychologist at the University of California at Davis, received his Ph.D. in social psychology from that institution in 1983. He was a postdoctoral fellow at Yale University and served as a faculty member at Yale and the Graduate Center of the City University of New York before returning to UCD to assume his current position.

A noted authority on prejudice against lesbians and gay men, antigay violence, and AIDS-related stigma, he has published numerous scholarly articles on these topics. In 1992, he coedited *Hate Crimes: Confronting Violence Against Lesbians and Gay Men* (Sage); he wrote or coauthored 6 of the book's 18 chapters. His current empirical research includes studies of the mental health consequences of violence against lesbians and gay men, community and identity among gay and bisexual men, and public attitudes concerning the AIDS epidemic.

He is a fellow of the American Psychological Association and the recipient of the 1992 Outstanding Achievement Award from the APA Committee on Lesbian and Gay Concerns. In 1989, he was the first recipient of APA Division 44's annual award for Distinguished Scientific Contributions to Lesbian and Gay Psychology. He is Past Chair of the APA Committee on Lesbian and Gay Concerns. His advocacy work has included testifying on behalf of the APA for congressional hearings on the U.S. military ban on gay male and lesbian personnel (1993) and antigay violence (1986), assisting the APA in preparing *amicus* briefs for state and federal court cases concerning gay and lesbian issues, and numerous appearances in national and local media.

About the Contributors

Anthony R. D'Augelli is Professor of Human Development in the Department of Human Development and Family Studies at The Pennsylvania State University. He received his Ph.D. (1972) in community/clinical psychology. He is coeditor of *Lesbian, Gay and Bisexual Identities Across the Lifespan.*

Nanette K. Gartrell is an Associate Clinical Professor of Psychiatry at the University of California, San Francisco, where she teaches ethics and feminist therapy theory; she also has a private psychotherapy practice in San Francisco. She received her B.A. from Stanford University and her M.D. from the University of California, Davis. For the past 11 years she has been documenting sexual exploitation of patients by mental health professionals and has published this research extensively. The *Western Journal of Medicine* published her most recent survey in August 1992 on sexual abuse by internists, obstetricians-gynecologists, surgeons, and family practitioners. She is also coprincipal investigator of a national longitudinal study of lesbians having children by alternative insemination.

Carla Golden has been teaching the psychology of women for 16 years, first at Smith College in Northampton, Massachusetts, and currently in New York at Ithaca College, where she is an Associate Professor of Psychology. She has lectured widely and written on a variety of topics within feminist psychology, and is best known for her work on the development of women's sexuality and feminist psychoanalytic theories of gender development.

Mary E. Kite is an Associate Professor of Psychological Science at Ball State University. She received her Ph.D. (1987) in social psychology from Purdue University. The author of numerous publications on stereotyping and prejudice, she is currently Chair of the Task Force for Minority Issues for Division 2 of the American Psychological Association. She was named Outstanding Junior Faculty at Ball State University for the 1991-1992 academic year.

Lawrence A. Kurdek is Professor of Psychology at Wright State University, Dayton, Ohio. He received his Ph.D. in developmental psychology from the University of Illinois at Chicago. His research interests include the development of relationship quality in gay/lesbian and heterosexual couples and the relation between child/adolescent adjustment and family structure/family process.

Charlotte J. Patterson is an Associate Professor of Psychology at the University of Virginia. She received her Ph.D. in psychology from Stanford University and actively conducts research in developmental psychology. She has published widely in the areas of social and personal development among children and adolescents, and has served on the editorial boards of *Child Development, Developmental Psychology,* and other prominent journals. She currently serves as guest editor for a special section of *Developmental Psychology* to focus on sexual orientation and human development. Her comprehensive review of the social sciences literature on children of lesbian and gay parents was published in *Child Development* in 1992. Her Bay Area Families Study is an ongoing study of psychosocial development among children who were born to or adopted by lesbian mothers.

Suzanna Rose is an Associate Professor of Psychology and Women's Studies at the University of Missouri at St. Louis. As Founder and Director of the St. Louis Lesbian and Gay Research Project, she has investigated lesbian and gay relationships, sexuality, and victimization. Her other research interests include heterosexual dating and friendships, women's career development, and the effect of women's studies courses on feminist activism. She is a Fellow of Divisions 35 and 44 of the American Psychological Association and received the 1992 Christine Ladd-Franklin Award from the Association for Women in Psychology for her contribution to feminist psychology.

Esther D. Rothblum is Professor in the Department of Psychology at the University of Vermont and Past Chair of the Women's Studies Program at that institution. She was the University Scholar at the University of Vermont for the 1992-1993 academic year. She received her Ph.D. in clinical psychology from Rutgers University. Her research and writing have focused on mental health issues in which women predominate, including depression, weight and stigma, procrastination and fear of failure, and lesbian issues. She is coeditor of 11 books, including *Loving Boldly: Issues Facing Lesbians* and *Overcoming Fear of Fat,* and is coeditor of the journal *Women and Therapy.* She was awarded a Kellogg Fellowship, which focused on travel to Africa to study women's mental health. She also has received a grant to travel to the Antarctic to focus on women's stress and coping and is the recipient of the Distinguished Scientific Contribution Award from Division 44 of the American Psychological Association.

Ariel Shidlo is a staff psychologist in the HIV/AIDS unit of Lutheran Medical Center, Brooklyn, New York, and has a private practice. He received his Ph.D. (1992) in clinical/community psychology from the State University of New York at Buffalo. He is the current Chair of the Task Force on AIDS of the New York State Psychological Association. His chief areas of interest are the role of internalized homophobia in lesbian and gay mental health and psychosocial factors associated with AIDS-related high-risk behavior.